Core Resource

EDUCATION BY
CHOICE

The best interests of the child shall be the guiding principle of those responsible for his education and guidance; that responsibility lies in the first place with his parents.

UNITED NATIONS DECLARATION OF THE RIGHTS OF THE CHILD

EDUCATION BY

CHOICE

The Case for

Family Control

by

John E. Coons

and

Stephen D. Sugarman

UNIVERSITY OF CALIFORNIA PRESS
Berkeley • Los Angeles • London

University of California Press
Berkeley and Los Angeles, California
University of California Press, Ltd.
London, England
Copyright © 1978 by
The Regents of the University of California
ISBN 0-520-03613-1
Library of Congress Catalog Card Number: 77-20318
Printed in the United States of America

1 2 3 4 5 6 7 8 9

*To the parents who controlled us,
the women who chose us, and the
daughters and sons who educate us.*

CONTENTS

FOREWORD

James S. Coleman

For a number of years, the possibility of an alternative to the present system of public education—an alternative in which the state is no longer the sole provider of publicly supported education, and in which children are no longer assigned to particular schools—has been discussed and debated. The plans for such an alternative have been referred to by a number of terms: vouchers, entitlements, education stamps. The plans, in all their variations, involve giving parents and children a choice of the school the child will attend, withdrawing that authority from the school officials who, acting as agents of the state, exercise it now. In most of the variations, this choice may extend beyond the public school, to private schools as well. The premise underlying all these plans is that better education would result if parents and children had a greater opportunity for educational choice than is now available to them.

The polarization of opinion about such plans reflects a division on very deeply held values, involving beliefs about the proper division of authority between the state and the family, beliefs about the dangers to social cohesion of deviant doctrines, beliefs about the relative abilities of professionals and their clients to decide what is best, and beliefs in the importance of maintaining the existing institutional order.

As a consequence, strange bedfellows appear, defying classification as liberals or conservatives, or egalitarians or elitists. Milton Friedman, Christopher Jencks, and Mario Fantini can be found among the advocates of some such plan; the American Civil Liberties Union and the American Federation of Teachers oppose it. It would be welcomed by the Black Muslims, the urban free schools, and the Catholic Church, and opposed by many Reagan Republicans and New Deal Democrats.

A thoughtful person might be led to ask why this alternative, the alternative of family choice, has arisen from so many quarters in recent years. I believe the answer lies in a fundamental clash between the locality-specific base on which education is built in this country, and increasing economic interdependence, including the increasing state and federal sources of educational funding. The organization of education around localities—neighborhoods, suburban towns, villages, rural areas, and sometimes counties—when coupled with the increasing separation of work from residence has meant that education has become increasingly differentiated by locality. More and more, families with sufficient income are able to group their children with others of like kind, by moving residence. Side by side, almost, will be two schools with very different levels of financing, very different curricula, very different quality of teachers, and very different student body mixtures. This disparity of finances, program, and personnel is far greater than that which existed when a school served an independent community, with all its economic levels. And what variation did exist had a reasonable justification when each school district raised its own funds from its own taxes, and when taxes raised in each district were principally a result of economic activity in that district as a self-contained economy. But now neither of these conditions holds. About half of school finances are now provided at state or federal level, and in all districts the taxable wealth depends on economic activity outside the district as well as within. Thus, the locality basis for education is increasingly undermined, and there is an increasing rationale for state or federal control of the education which is increasingly paid for at the state and federal levels.

As this occurs, as small residentially proximate groups which constitute a community become no longer able to make educational decisions collectively which affect their children, it becomes important to find an alternative to an increasing centralization of those decisions. One such alternative is to return that choice to the individual level, to the parents and children themselves. If that alternative was attractive and desirable when school districts were largely independent (and I believe it was even then), it becomes almost imperative now.

It is because of these social changes, I believe, that from diverse starting points and for diverse reasons more and more educators and persons interested in education are coming to see educational entitlements or vouchers as the correct way of organizing education in the future. But as the discussion of this alternative develops, extensive examination is necessary of the philosophical issues involved, the variations that are possible in a voucher plan, and the questions of implementation.

This book initiates exactly that kind of examination. Its authors have arrived at this voucher alternative from a different starting point than most, that of financial equity in education. Their earlier book (written with William Clune), *Private Wealth and Public Education*, has been probably the single most influential element in the court decisions, beginning with *Serrano*, that have led state legislatures to revise their school-aid formulae to bring about financial equity within the state. And it is their principle of "district power equalizing" which has served as the major conceptual tool behind the revision of these formulae.

But even in that earlier work, Coons and Sugarman noted that the ultimate (and one might say, proper) extension of the idea of power equalizing was not merely to the district level but to the family level, to give "family power equalizing." And this is precisely what a voucher system does—provides equal educational resources to children, regardless of their family's residential mobility or economic ability to afford private school. Indeed, as Coons and Sugarman have found, once the state undertakes to provide truly equal educational resources to the children of its residents, any solution other than a voucher system in which individual parents and children can exercise a wide range of choice involves serious complications that are difficult to resolve short of full state control of educational decisions.

In this book Coons and Sugarman examine most of the issues that must be resolved in instituting a system of family choice in education. They address head-on some of the strongest arguments against voucher plans, including the fear of indoctrinating children in ideological extremes, and the concern that a voucher system could lead to increased racial segregation. They argue convincingly that a voucher system could well reduce the ideological strains in society, rather than increase them, and they show ways that constraints can be imposed on, or incentives applied to, the schools (rather than the families) to protect against possible segregating effects. (I believe the segregating tendencies are somewhat stronger than they indicate, and consequently I feel that somewhat stronger constraints or incentives might be necessary than some of those they suggest.)

This book on family choice constitutes an important step in the developing conceptual base for systems of family choice in education. It is the product of a quest by Coons and Sugarman for equity in education, but the solution holds promise for far more than equity in the educational and social benefits it can bring.

INTRODUCTION

If . . . rebellion could found a philosophy,
it would be a philosophy of limits,
of calculated ignorance, and of risk.
He who does not know everything
cannot kill everything.

—ALBERT CAMUS, *The Rebel*

Imagine a people aspiring to live in harmony, to cooperate in production and defense, and to distribute society's rewards in a just manner. Suppose, however, that they are divided a dozen ways about the nature of the good life—some valuing personal striving and acquisition, others pleasure, others quiet and the life of the spirit. How would such a people design the education of their children?

The question is important, for the society described is this one. America is, to be sure, one nation—even a people of sorts—and we think it on the whole a generous people with a concern for social justice. Yet in its vision of individual human perfection, America is a virtual menagerie. Despite a superficial sameness born of an industrial economy, there is no American ethic or, if there is, it is passing. Dedicated work and dedicated consumption remain a central theme but no longer dominate the mass of personal aspirations; the work ethic competes with challenging cultural, religious, and artistic world views for the loyalty of individuals. This pluralism of individual views about what it is that makes for a fully human life has its impact on education. If there ever was a national understanding about adult society's responsibility for the young, there is no longer. There remains, nonetheless, a general conviction that a just society makes ample provision

1

for the formal portion of children's education and assures a measure of fairness and rationality in its distribution. But distribution of what? Given the diversity of values among American adults, in what should publicly supported education consist?

For us the answer lies in subsidizing a much wider range of private choice than is now the case. It is an approach freighted with personal values and, in particular, freedom. There will be much here about familiar libertarian institutions such as private schools, markets, and competition. Yet our theme is also egalitarian; it holds for one area of the child's life the socialist ideal of an equal portion—his full share of a particular good. Our objective for education is an equality of freedom. We believe the traditional conflict between liberty and equality may here be tempered. By moving away from the distribution of compulsory packaged education, government can begin to redistribute the means of self-determination in the formation of will and intellect.

Arranging the redistribution of educational choice is complicated. Simply granting choice to the child is unfeasible. Liberty is an awkward ideal to implement for persons who are dependent by reason of age, illness, insanity, or any other condition. When the person is a child, the problem is compounded; children lack personal sovereignty, but not in the straightforward manner of an adult suffering permanent mental disability. Children constantly accumulate the stuff of self-determination; from the outset they have a portion of human independence, and they will have the whole. As the child's own claim to liberty is not static, it may be protected only by an authority that is both ready to promote the child's interest and adaptable to the stages of individual maturation.

Are there criteria for identifying such an authority? We will argue that the interests of children are best served in a decentralized polity giving maximum scope to free, chosen, communal relationships that are generally organized on a small scale. Systematic domination of education by large enterprise (public or private) ought, therefore, to be disfavored. This suggests to us the strengthening of the family's role in education and the growth of a teaching fraternity which is related to the family as professional to client rather than as master to servant. Family choice for the nonrich could lead to an end of the American double standard: Among those who can afford private school, society leaves the goals and means of education to the family; for the rest of society, the

informing principles are politically determined and implemented through compulsory assignment to a particular public
school.

Our aspirations, however, are modest. There is here no
intention to justify the prompt dismantling of the educational
edifice. Our hope is only to show a new framework for debating
the question of a just educational order and to stimulate
tolerance for experimentation. We have not canvassed every
justifying argument for our conclusion. And the prediction
of every social consequence of family choice is plainly undesirable in a book designed only to support experimentation.
Therefore, for example, we have fully analyzed neither the
opportunities nor the risks for teachers under the regime we
propose. Nor have we imagined all the ways in which family
choice might affect the linkage between school and work.
Our objective demands not proof but only plausibility. Nor
does our argument need complex academic trapping. The
paraphernalia of scholarly debate has been reduced to a
minimum, and we address ourselves to the broad audience
of those concerned with educational policy.

Some personal history may help clarify the context in which
we write. Since the early 1960s, at Northwestern and at
Berkeley, we have been involved (mostly in collaboration)
in the analysis and practical reform of school policy. We have
been interested primarily in school finance and governance
and the pursuit of racial integration. In the mid-1960s, with
William Clune, we developed and later published a constitutional argument that could, where adopted, eliminate wealth
discrimination among public schools while enhancing the
traditional systems of local control and governance.[1] In books
and articles we have published statutory models for school
finance schemes based on either political units (the school
district) or primary social units (the family). Since 1968 we
have participated actively in the process of legislative reform
and in litigation, mostly as friends of the court.

The incubation of our views was assisted from 1972 by
the Childhood and Government Project. This five-year enterprise, generously funded by the Ford Foundation and the
Carnegie Corporation of New York, was a part of the Earl
Warren Legal Institute of the University of California, Berkeley. The faculty and staff of the project represented a broad
spectrum of disciplines and an even broader set of value
commitments. On issues as inflammatory as ours the project
tended to become an intellectual bear-pit, and we thank our

colleagues who always combined their intellectual assaults with personal affection—all to the enrichment of our work and our lives.

There are some deserving special thanks for special generosity. Dr. Gail Saliterman has been an enthusiastic critic with a keen nose for lurking absurdities. Professor Robert Mnookin of Berkeley at several points offered crucial substantive and organizing insights which we hope have received justice at our hands. Our sometime collaborator and permanent kibitzer Professor William Clune of Wisconsin has made his good judgment felt in a number of respects, and, as in our first book together, James Coleman has given us a head start with his generous and thoughtful foreword. Finally, while the typing could not have been much fun, we thank Judith Kahn, Eloise Schmidt, Laura Bergang, Barbara Lewis, Eva Scipio, and Pam Kolacy for their inspiring hypocrisy.

It is inevitable that certain of our criticisms of the existing order will be resented by some who have devoted their lives to the present scheme of public education. To them it may seem no expiation that elsewhere we continue to engage our energies in the improvement of that system in more traditional ways. Therefore it is important for our view of ourselves that we repudiate the demonology of the public school baiters. Although we would free the child from an unchosen education, our deepest hope is that the deliverance prove reciprocal. In the long run the public school itself could emerge the stronger for having surrendered its crutch.

I
SETTING THE STAGE
FOR EDUCATIONAL CHOICE

He may not, as unvalu'd persons do,
Carve for himself, for on his choice depends
The safety and health of the whole state.

—WILLIAM SHAKESPEARE, *Hamlet*

Chapter 1

HOBSON'S CHOICE: YOUR NEIGHBORHOOD PUBLIC SCHOOL, TAKE IT OR LEAVE IT

Ye have not chosen me, but I have chosen you.

JOHN 15:13

Choice has never been wholly erased from public education. Typically children are assigned to school not by lot or I.Q. but by residence. Families may move, and there are some differences in style and curriculum among the school districts and among schools. A number of school systems even permit families living in the district to select among local public schools, allowing students to travel out of their neighborhood to schools with vacant desks. Among the school districts of Vermont and New Hampshire, family choice systems of substantial size have been quietly operating for generations; in recent years a federally supported family choice program— termed "the voucher experiment"—has been carried out within a public school district in California. Finally, almost everywhere there is some choice among offerings within the modern high school, both as to academic track—college prep, general, vocational—and as to individual courses. Thus, there appears to be some potential for personal choice within the public school system.

Such choice, however, is exceptional and narrow in scope when compared to the range of interests held by the families that use public education. Satisfying the preferences of individuals has rarely been a major objective of the system. In general the family gets what it wants only if it is lucky enough to live in a district where the local school officials and the majority of families, operating within the constraints of politics and state law, agree with the family's own preferences. At least this is true for those families who cannot afford private schools or lack the resources, sophistication, or time to find the right public programs and then maneuver their children into them. And these are not only families with low incomes. Certainly most middle-income families with more than one child in school, high medical costs, a single working parent, or similar problems are also limited in their choice of education.

Consider the following case: Ann Orlov is eleven. She and her younger brother Larry live in the city with their parents Harry and Jean. Harry earns $14,000 as a policeman; Jean adds $3,000 as a part-time secretary. Ann attends Willis Elementary, the neighborhood public school. She is not unusually bright but has shown a strong interest in art and in the lives and work of artists. She dislikes Willis, in part because so little time is devoted to her special interest. She studies art in a community program on Saturdays, but otherwise—apart from a 45-minute once-a-week art class taught by a specialist—she regards her formal education as a waste of time. She would be delighted to spend her days following the art teacher around, but that is out of the question in view of all the other children to be served. Ann's regular teacher finds it inconsistent both with his own role and with Ann's needs for her to be allowed to sit alone in the back of the classroom all day and draw. The Orlovs have asked the principal at Willis, a sympathetic woman, for aid or advice. Unfortunately she sees no way to help Ann short of enrollment in another school.

Ann has begged to go to school elsewhere. She would prefer a school that emphasizes art, but would be happy even to be assigned to a teacher whose regular class routine responded to her interests. Her parents want to help, but there are problems. The Orlovs cannot afford Bellwood, the arty but expensive private school that Ann thinks she would like. The modestly priced local Catholic school might serve, but the Orlovs oppose this solution on religious grounds. They might discover a public school in the city with an attractive art program or teacher, one located within reasonable traveling distance; but the school authorities would have to approve Ann's transfer from Willis, and this is not likely. Of course, the Orlovs could move to the attendance area of the other school. They could even move to a different school district. A number of their former neighbors have done so, and some are pleased with the outcome.

For the Orlovs, however, there are limiting conditions. Policemen are supposed to live in the city, so a change of districts for Harry might mean finding a new job. And for very many reasons—the park, the neighbors, shopping, the church, the cost of moving—the Orlovs prefer their present neighborhood and would find it painful and expensive to move. Their gravest concern is for little Larry, who loves Willis's strong music program, including a boys' chorus in which he solos. Harry and Jean feel any move would be a serious gamble for him. Even for Ann a move would be risky. If the student body in the new school is separated into ability groups, the school might assign Ann to the wrong program. More important, the Orlovs are worried that, even if the family moves, subsequent shifts in teaching personnel or official policy might leave the whole family even worse off than before.

Armin Schroeder is a young art teacher in the public schools of a blue-collar suburb adjoining the city. He has developed a proposal for a comprehensive elementary curriculum in which the teaching of basic subjects would be built around the symbols and materials of the artist's world. Schroeder has tried to persuade his school authorities to give him an experimental school, but, though sympathetic to experimentation, they are already committed in other directions. In any event, Schroeder's success in his own district would probably be of little help to Ann Orlov; even if there were spaces available, she is not likely to be granted a special transfer outside her district.

Schroeder does not have the capital to start such a school on a private basis. Even if he could raise the money, he would probably have to charge more than $1,400 a year tuition; he might be able to attract a rich clientele and survive, but he prefers not to run an elitist school. Possibly enough families like the Orlovs would try his school to make it viable—if they could afford it. Most would feel they could not. The Orlovs' savings are insignificant and their responsibilities weighty; family resources are already diminished by $700 paid yearly in various taxes that support education, and the public school is "free." Under these circumstances even wealthier people often forego the private alternative they might prefer.

There is no easy way to tell if the needs and wants of most families are served by the local public school. The widespread criticism of American education in the 1960s and 1970s suggests they are not. Rather it seems likely that the preferences and phobias of many go undiscovered and unsatisfied. In place of compulsory assignment, many children and their families might prefer programs emphasizing science, the classics, McGuffey's reader, music, the Baltimore Catechism, or the sayings of Chairman Mao. Some might want an outdoor school, a school in a living room, a school that starts at 7:00 and ends at noon, a school with the long vacation in the fall, or a school whose teachers are artisans or otherwise employed part-time outside the school. Likewise, many teachers might wish they were free to enlist children in the enterprise of learning by offering the bait of their special abilities in dance, botany, French, Chinese culture, or the teachings of Muhammed. What we do know is that—even given a harmony of objectives among school, teacher, parent, and student— many families find it extremely difficult today to get the child and the preferred experience together except by happy accident.

These frustrations of the system tend to be taken for granted. Yet the lot of the Orlovs and Schroeders of our society is, in a major respect, abnormal. If what Ann and her parents want and what Schroeder has to offer were something other than education, the Orlovs could simply choose it and, if necessary and possible, buy it. Ann's other needs—even those of the greatest importance—are ordinarily met in this way. The family purchases the food she eats and the shoes on her feet. In each case, the choices are made by the parents or child alone, or, more likely, they are the result of a process of selection in which the child and parents decide together. Of course, those marketing the product influence choices, and the government regulates some purchases. But generally, the state is content to trust the Orlovs with sophisticated decisions regarding food, hours of rest, and other important matters affecting the child. Only when it comes to education has the state, deliberately or otherwise, virtually emasculated the family's options. In place of the family it has created an organizational structure which finds it difficult to provide for Ann—even where there are public school teachers who could and would provide it—the form of education that the Orlovs find most appropriate.

Why has the state adopted this policy? Is it the fear that

some parents will choose inadequate education or none at all? This is a prudent concern. On grounds of simple fairness children should be guaranteed reasonable access to education whatever their parents' views. There are also the social benefits that are supposed to flow from education. These individual and social considerations together suggest the state should strictly enforce the parent's legal duty to educate. Would that not suffice? The humane response is that the right to education should not be limited by parental resources; parental duty means nothing to the child if the family cannot afford to educate him. Therefore, additional collective action is necessary, and unless the child is to be taken from his parents, this requires a subsidy of the parents by the state. Only in that way can the child's hope for education be delivered from the economic limitations of his family.

Perhaps the poor could simply be given money. But in a cash grant plan, education would compete with other wants of the child and with wants of other family members—including adults. Were the legal duty to educate one's child easily enforced, this might not be a serious problem. However, earmarking the subvention for spending on education would far more easily assure that parents did not make alternate allocations, either to themselves or their children.

But these observations carry us only a short distance toward a justification of the status quo in which tuition-free public education is made available to all. They leave unanswered two substantial questions: Why is the education subvention provided to those who are not poor? And, more importantly, why is it provided in kind? We will address these questions in order.

Many families today can afford to pay for the education of their children without state assistance. Others could provide for the education of their children if the state had not already appropriated a substantial portion of the family's resources through education taxes. And the number that could finance their own children's schooling would increase dramatically were parents able to borrow the money through government-guaranteed loans which they could repay over a long period.[1] In short, ought not the state rest content with providing education grants to the children of the poor and loans to the middle class?

The answer is probably no. There are several plausible justifications for making tuition-free education available to children in all income groups. Eliminating income tests helps to avoid stigmatizing the poor in the manner they now experience in public hospital wards and in welfare. Alternatively, education subventions for all families could be seen as a benefit for large families, regardless of income—a fiscal cousin of the tax deduction for dependent children. Or maybe subventions to the middle and upper classes should be seen as a crude system of coercive loans for educational purposes; the school tax system in effect forces parents to borrow for their children's education and to repay over their lifetime. Finally, perhaps children themselves should be viewed as the borrowers who return the cost of their education through the taxes they pay as adults. Taken together or perhaps separately, these are reasonable justifications for the subsidy to nonpoor families, especially if the middle and upper classes bear a fair share of the taxes supporting the system (a matter outside our present concern). In no way, however, do they advance our understanding of the state's decision to provide the subsidy only in kind through publicly owned and administered schools. We now turn to that important question.

A family's poverty threatens more than its children's education; without money it cannot afford food, clothing, or shelter—for parents or children—any more than it can pay tuition. During this century, our society has increasingly taken collective responsibility to assure the poor, particularly those with children, their basic needs. In doing so, government has discovered several approaches in addition to in-kind distribution; outside of education, a variety of techniques has been tried. Housing exemplifies the full range of political instruments.[2] Sometimes housing for lower income families has been provided directly through the construction of government-owned apartments with subsidized or free rent; this is the nearest analogue to our public education system, and has been the least successful effort to improve housing through government. Under other programs, however, private landlords have been encouraged with a variety of tax benefits and subsidies to provide low-income housing that meets certain specifications. A third technique provides poor families with housing coupons to be used toward payment of their rent in a dwelling of their selection; experimentation with this approach is now going on. Finally, and today most frequently, the poor are simply given cash to help them bargain in the private rental market.

The bulk of our "welfare" programs now are of this last type.[3] Instead of government potatoes, poor families today are usually given money for the purchase of soup, soap, or stockings. In general this seems wise; not everybody likes potatoes or is nourished by them. Of course, some will decide to nourish themselves on booze, and this is a problem, especially where children suffer as a consequence. Thus the government sometimes earmarks the transfers to narrow the range of choice; for example, under the food stamp and Medicaid programs the government provides stamps or cards that can be used only to satisfy needs for food or for health care. Even with their restrictions, such programs are very different from those that simply give the recipients government soup and government doctors. Stamps and cards allow their holders to choose among foods and physicians.

Why not distribute school dollars in this way and permit the family to choose among educators? Just as some children may be allergic to the government's potato, some may be allergic to its schools or teachers. Yet the state has chosen not only to operate its own schools but, in practical economic effect, has required most children to attend them. The decision to leave the average family powerless regarding education, while permitting its choice of material goods, seems eccentric. Many families might be content with a relatively uniform and choiceless style of health maintenance or even an imposed diet, if it were adequate. Concerning the training of minds, a wider variety of opinions seems to obtain. One would suppose choice to be more, rather than less, significant to the family with respect to education than other human needs.

Of course, the stronger interest in choice might be seen as the very problem. Defenders of the status quo remind us that a certain level of education is essential in a democratic society, and that if families were given money to purchase education where they pleased, some would select the scholastic equivalent of booze. This fear is justified if the only alternative to herding the nonrich into public schools is outright parento-cracy. But such a policy dilemma is hard to credit, at least on its face. The public and private schools created under any politically viable system of family choice would be required by law to meet a fair minimum standard. The child of the wayward parent would not face the dubious exchange of one educational autocrat (the state) for another (the parent); instead, he would be party to a balanced regime. The state would mandate that all children receive whatever elements of education command a public consensus. This could proba-bly assure no more than exposure to the agreed minimum, but note that this is equally true of the existing scheme. Indeed, one argument for more voluntarism is that it will increase the rate at which children actually achieve the minimum. And beyond those politically determined essentials, families would be assured the economic capacity to pursue their educational preferences. This book considers the pros and cons of that kind of world.

The policy and legal issues posed by this idea are many and difficult. Giving nonrich families any substantial area of self-determination in education is outside the American experience of the last century. The prospect troubles many educators and other interest groups who are comfortable within the present structure and would be subject to unfamiliar jostling in a family-influenced regime. Their opposition is neither entirely partisan nor their arguments all self-serving; these critics can also have the interest of children at heart and view family choice as a retreat from a professional vision of excellence. Mention family choice in their hearing and the story of Ann Orlov will be transformed like *Rashomon.* It will become a saga of rescue by public educators from a history of parental poverty and neglect, private school venality, and pupil frustration. From the critic's perch, family choice is pictured as a system designed by a radical cabal (right or left), in which the schools are permitted to exclude the poor by controlling tuition, the parents are allowed to negotiate kickbacks from the school, and the principals are encouraged to abuse their charges and to admit and expel whom and as they choose. Nor is the regulation of such evils a complete answer to such criticism. Even if careful drafting could control parental and bureaucratic abuse, the possibility would remain that any particular taste in education is shared by so few in a given area as to be incapable of satisfaction. According to the critics, there is no way that Ann Orlov's story can be assured a happy ending no matter what educational polity is imagined.

But her story, as we have told it, has this important quality: It is not a romance but a report of present conditions. One has only to read Mario Fantini's *Public Schools of Choice* to appreciate how little educational liberty is discoverable even by one who defends the public system as a potential source of choice:

> [Public education] cannot, as presently structured, deal effectively with both diversity and the demand for compulsory education. It is attempting to force each member of our very

diverse student population to adjust to the *one* process offered
or be branded as a failure. . . .

The structure of public schools dictates that the energies
of all the professionals working inside be aimed at making
one rather monolithic educational process work for everybody. All efforts, whether by teachers, principals, counselors
or supervisors, are now aimed at trying to improve the one
uniform system.[4]

Where systems produce user dissatisfaction, the common
course for Americans is to experiment with alternatives. And
there are few areas of public activity in which user vexation
is more common than public education.

We hold no loftier objective than this: experimentation with
systems that increase family choice. Even opponents of choice
ought not to be too grimly opposed; presumably the experience
could vindicate their alarums and suggest that the state should
intervene in the parenting process not less but more—both
earlier and more decisively. Realistically, we know that the
opposition to experimentation with choice is strong; thus we
cannot merely assert the desirability of a fair trial but must
assess as objectively as we can the full range of the critic's
warnings. When he objects that the professional educator
makes the best choices for the child, we must take him
seriously; when he argues that the state must funnel the nonrich
into its own schools in pursuit of broader social goals such
as racial integration, we will respond respectfully and at length.
And when the critic raises concerns about the jobs of public
school teachers, we too will value their reasonable expectations. However, the test cannot be whether we have proved
a case for liberty in education. Our objective is simply to
convince an audience of fair-minded readers that regulated
family choice systems deserve a substantial trial including
support from federal, state, and local sources.

The grant to families that we propose would come in the
form of a scholarship that would be limited to something
defined as "school." What could qualify as school might be
very diverse, but it still would be limited to education. In
this respect some might accuse us of timidity. It is not that
we think spending on other things is unimportant to children.
We can imagine the provision to families of a "child's needs
voucher," allowing the family to prefer the child's clothing
to his education. Indeed, given present public spending levels,
it is plausible that both the benefit to the child and the societal
return would be greater if government shifted dollars from

investment in education to, say, the care of the child's health.

But subventions confined to education have a tactical rationale. Educational grants appear more politically credible than subsidies spendable on a long list of children's needs. In one respect they would even be politically preferable to grants limited to health or day care. Unlike those programs, the public investment for education is already both massive and broadly accepted; school subventions to families would merely change the authority controlling their expenditure. The restriction of choice to education may be justified by the need to keep change gradual. Indeed, even if one wanted eventually to divert public school spending to day care, child health care, or even to general income redistribution, providing education subsidies could be a strategically sensible first step. Families would gain experience in the disposition of a substantial resource, and critics would gain information about the habits and preferences of the nonrich. The behavioral response to the new opportunity could give a dash of realism to the debate concerning the relation of family income to the parental capacity to consider and represent the child's interest.

THE ROAD AHEAD

It is crucial to our argument to ascribe purposes to education. In the chapters ahead we do that and then ask how an increase in family authority might affect their achievement. Perhaps the most difficult problem in education is fixing its purposes. By comparison the hurdle of actually organizing and running a $70 billion national system of schooling are trivial. Even after such a system was assembled, those who fathered it often had conflicting notions of what it was expected to do. The issue of purpose is central because of the bond between the structure and effects of a system. If the purpose of school, for example, is to assist imperialism, presumably it ought to be organized in certain ways with particular sorts of persons in charge. These might not be the same persons or the same style or structure one would choose to promote quietism, classical studies, a tender regard for nature—or the interest of the child. In commissioning an educational regime, society willy-nilly makes decisions, implicit or explicit, concerning the desired product. If it chooses the family as educational agent, it will very likely promote some outcomes more efficiently than others.

Although we cannot canvass the relation of family choice to all imaginable educational objectives, we must consider its probable relation to those most commonly held in our society. As we will explain in detail, we have concluded that three themes are discoverable in American society which taken broadly embrace the primary objectives for the schools. These are the following: to serve the best interest of the individual child; to foster a consensus supporting the constitutional order; and to achieve racial integration. Part II is devoted to arguments concerning the best interest of the child. Part III takes up the themes of consensus and integration. We conclude that greater reliance on the family will improve the capacity of schools to serve the child. We also predict that well-designed voluntary systems will solidify societal commitments to ordered liberty and will contribute to the achievement of a society which is racially integrated in both the physical and moral dimensions.

In Part IV we describe the variety of administrative, fiscal, and pedagogical devices that might be employed to advance family choice in a manner consistent with the three policy objectives noted and with other important purposes. We realize that merely releasing families into the educational market with scholarship in hand may not automatically produce unfettered choice. For example, if in time a small segment of private enterprise came to control the supply of education and offered too narrow a choice of options or too effectively propagandized the family, we would have exchanged one monopoly for another. Thus, in Part IV we will concern ourselves with possible limits on market power and school advertising. Similarly, assuming that some families will wish to have their children learn from particular teachers who do not happen to have standard credentials, we will in Part IV discuss changing the teacher certification requirements that now apply to those in publicly financed education.

Although a sizable portion of this book is devoted to the description of *techniques* for increasing choice, at this early point the reader needs perspective more than detail. Hence we turn next to a brief history of the efforts to give the family a primary role in publicly financed education.

Chapter 2

THE INTELLECTUAL HISTORY
OF CHOICE IN EDUCATION

At all times sincere friends of freedom
have been rare, and its triumphs
have been due to minorities . . .
associating themselves with auxiliaries
whose objects often differed
from their own.

—SIR JOHN ACTON,
The History of Freedom in Antiquity

ROOTS

The view that the state should merely befriend and expedite education rather than determine and impose its forms is scarcely new. Over the course of two centuries a scattering of civil libertarians, economists, churchmen, and friends of the poor have consistently urged the distribution of public resources to the family to purchase its children's education. Thomas Paine seems to have been the first American to have suggested it (in 1792 in *The Rights of Man*),[1] but he was only the carrier of a foreign infection. Paine's earlier traffic with individualist philosophers in the mother country had coincided with the appearance of such ideas in Adam Smith's *Wealth of Nations* in 1776. In exposing the pathologies of protected monopoly, Smith had found a rich source of example in the schools and universities of his time. Insulated from competition by their endowments and responsible only to the faculties in charge of instruction, these institutions had become ingrown and stultifying: "The endowment of schools and colleges have [sic] . . . not only corrupted the diligence of public teachers, but have rendered it almost impossible to have any good private ones."[2]

Smith's principal interest was to put the creativity and energy of teachers to the test and stimulation of the market. A family stipend for schooling would arouse the industry of pedagogues,

18

and efficient teaching would be rewarded by prosperity. Smith never elaborated the details of any plan by which families would reward good instruction; he merely suggested that the choice of a school by parents would trigger a subsidy from the government to the school. It was left to Paine specifically to suggest giving lower class families the opportunity for schooling through what today might be called a negative income tax scaled progressively in favor of the poor, coupled with a parental duty to purchase adequate education.

Paine's suggestion reappeared several generations later in the work of J. S. Mill. In 1859, Mill developed the implications of his commitment to individualism in his celebrated essay *On Liberty.* [3] Where Paine had emphasized the family, Mill was more concerned with the child; yet their proposals were similar. Mill argued that promotion of family liberty through the subsidized but unfettered educational power of the parent would be anything but liberty for some children. If one's primary concern is for the individual, the child's own liberty and well-being must be sought. Mill did not, however, conclude that the child should be herded into a state institution for his liberation. To Mill, diversity in opinion and conduct was indispensable to the enjoyment of liberty. Thus, parents should be required to provide adequately for the child's education, and, where they could not meet all the tuition in the school chosen by the family, the state should make up the difference. Mill's plan included a great deal that has reappeared in the debates of the last decade.

In the United States the somewhat contrasting emphases of Paine on the parental right and Mill on the child's right were both swallowed up after 1875 in the enthusiasm for compulsory public education. The nativisms of the twentieth century jeopardized even the autonomy of the wealthy until the Supreme Court in 1925 pinched off legislative threats from the states with its decision in *Pierce* v. *Society of Sisters.* [4] In that case an Oregon referendum had sought to force all children into public schools, but the Court held that the Due Process clause of the Fourteenth Amendment protected private education and added that it gave the family a right to choose such education where it met reasonable state standards for quality.

RECENT REVIVALS

The idea of a substantial role for the family in formal education dies hard. For thirty years after its rescue by *Pierce* the hope was kept alive first by church-related interest groups and later by Southern segregationists. At the beginning of the 1960s, economist Milton Friedman gave it intellectual respectability with his brief treatment of educational policy in *Capitalism and Freedom.* [5] Friedman put Mill's analysis into modern economic dress. Like his classical predecessors, he rejected the wisdom of governmental provision of education through public schools. His plan was even more streamlined than Mill's or Paine's. Children in all economic circumstances would receive the same subvention in the form of vouchers spendable in state-approved schools. It would amount to an equal division of the total educational budget among the pupils of the state. Though simpler in design, the plan in one respect seems more ambitious than its forerunners; it takes more revenue to provide a voucher to all than merely to the needy. However, the extent to which the net economic effect of Friedman's proposal would differ from those of Paine and Mill would depend in large part on the incidence of the taxes used to fund the universal voucher plan.

In the decade after Friedman's influential vignette, three groups promoted the concept of family choice in various forms. Friedmanite economists and the parents' rights enthusiasts found themselves bedfellows with a group of radical philosophers of education such as John Holt, who saw choice both as an end to a sterile public monopoly and as an economic basis for the burgeoning "free" school movement. The published arguments of the three groups tended to be rather abstract. None presented a detailed legislative proposal or inquired into what the new relationship among parents, children, and the state would be. Little was said about the probable fate of children—especially children of the poor—under specific systems of choice. This was not because these groups were unconcerned about children or about the poor, but because their ideological commitments tended to overshadow what should have been central issues of principle and practice. This has been irksome to unaligned supporters of choice, because the manifest biases of these three groups gave opponents fair ground to dismiss the concept as an intellectual artifact largely of radical and sectarian design. [6] In fact, however, these earlier proponents provided valuable if isolated insights which have awaited synthesis and clarification; their distinct conceptual postures are worth understanding for their own sake and as a step toward clarification of the issues as they shifted in the 1970s.

The Economists. Friedman and his followers view education through the lens of the laissez-faire economist. They are eager to create an educational market in which consumer tastes will govern what is produced. They see consumer choice today strangled by the inefficiencies of requiring parents either to change family residence or to become school politicians in order to alter their own child's situation. Because they assume the market is the mechanism best able to match what is offered with what is desired; consumer sovereignty is for them the ultimate test. Friedman is fond of illustrating this by comparing the variety-rich modern supermarket with the uniformities he associates with public bureaucracies such as the post office.

To rely on standard theories of consumer sovereignty and the behavior of bureaucracies, however, finesses the question of whether family choice is good for children. Friedman focuses not on the child but the household, viewing it not so much as a collection of individuals with potentially competing interests, but as an impenetrable economic monad. This is not surprising; most economists have done the same. Wealth transfers within the family are difficult to observe empirically, and most economic indicators are based on the household as a unit. Analytical and policy literature seldom transcends the data.

This collective view of the household economy may be adequate for many purposes. Perhaps, for example, the average family's consumption of food and shelter can with few exceptions be safely viewed as communal, with the parent merely playing the role of purchasing agent for the community. But whether or not the collectivist model describes family consumption generally, as applied to education it can easily mislead. The reason is that the nurture of the mind may be a more individualistic affair than the nurture of the body; if so, individual interests within the family may be the appropriate unit of analysis. To the extent that the wants and needs of his mind diverge from those of the collective family or other members of it, the individual child must be viewed as the principal and separate consumer. It is a truism that, on the same diet of learning, one child can be getting his school needs satisfied while another is starving.

If the aim of education is the best interest of the child, and not of the collective family, the problem here is plain. One must justify giving the family choice by showing it to be a competent agent for the child. To plump for consumer sovereignty thus merely raises, and does nothing to answer, the crucial question of the child's own welfare under a family regime. It is pleasant irony, but fair, to tweak Friedman for the collectivist cast of his family economics. In Chapter 4 we will present the argument that the child is in fact well represented by his family.

The economists' emphasis on the family unit can mislead for a second reason. The purposes of education may be broader than the interest of the child, incorporating social goals of many kinds, goals that are established through political majorities. The economists seem to assume that in choosing education families will also seek and achieve these social goals. Plainly this can be wrong whenever significant numbers of families reject majoritarian goals. Suppose, for example, that a particular legislature decides that schools should foster a martial spirit in order to enhance national military power, but 40 percent of families want to indoctrinate children with pacifism. To endow families with choice in this case would frustrate, not advance, the public goal. Thus, unless there are reasons for family choice which somehow transcend majoritarian objectives, its proponents must argue and not simply assume that choice will serve those objectives. In Chapters 6 and 7 we will so argue with respect to the goals of civil harmony and racial integration.

The Parents' Rights Enthusiasts. The parents' rights view of family choice has grown up around the United States Supreme Court's holding in *Pierce* v. *Society of Sisters.* [7] Since that decision in 1925, parental choice of private schools has enjoyed federal protection, and private school interests have lobbied for tax money to support the exercise of this right. *Pierce* has become the political symbol of the authority of parents over their children's education.

Within reasonable limits, parental authority should be cherished in an open society. However, parents are not owners of their children, and the interests of the generations are not always identical. Thus, the emphasis of the parent groups on the rights of adults has sometimes appeared unbalanced. Parental interest in the child's education is everywhere accepted as legitimate, but it would be difficult to defend the taxation of nonparents if that interest alone were involved. In the triangle of interests represented by parents, the child, and the state, the parent cannot be first and may come third. Probably for most Americans the interest of individual children is the key justification for public support of education. This is certainly our own position. Thus, we view parents primarily as potential instruments of the child's welfare; the chief issue is whether family choice would be a blessing for children, not whether it is a right of the parents.

Indeed, the principle in *Pierce* may ultimately rest on the assumption of consistency between parental choice and the child's interest; if that choice were to be proved harmful to the child, *Pierce* itself would become insupportable. Other considerations, such as family integrity and the parents' religious preference, may reinforce the *Pierce* right, but only as long as these interests seem to promote the good of the child. Where that becomes problematic, our confidence in the right itself begins to erode. This explains our sense that there is something awkward and nearly irrelevant about the notion of the parents of a seventeen-year-old asserting *their* rights under *Pierce* to send their child to military school. We await with interest the first litigation in which such a child asserts *his* right to attend instead the local public high school.

The Radicals—Individualism Perplexed. Mill's emphasis on the child's own liberty resurfaced in the 1950s and 1960s. Paul Goodman, John Holt, and a handful of other radical critics painted a new image of school as jail;[8] Everett Reimer, Ivan Illich, and others added the argument that school was the opiate of the technocratic consumer society and ought to be abolished.[9] These critics shared the view that school was essentially stultifying and that public resources for learning should expand rather than contract the opportunities for human choice. They stood for human autonomy through new forms of learning. Ironically, with the possible exception of Goodman, this cluster of "kid-lib" philosophers may have unintentionally aggravated society's insensitivity to the child's own interest.

The problem has been the common tendency of these critics to apply plausible standards of adolescent autonomy to younger children. The frustrations of precocious teenagers are advanced to support broad demands for liberation from school without distinction of age. One can imagine that certain forms of deschooling might be desirable; it is difficult to see that escape from school implies educational liberation for little children. Under no system—conventional or radical, schooled or deschooled—will a six-year-old exercise control over his learning. His impotence is not the political or cultural artifact of a cruel society. It is the lack of strength and experience in the child. The notion of liberating small children is nonsense. One might as meaningfully speak of the liberation of the unwanted infants of Sparta by exposure. Their deliverance from one dominion merely subordinates them to another. Little children will not be liberated; they will be dominated. The only question is by whom and for what ends.

This iron law of infant subjugation is not altered by examples of "permissiveness" in education. The child may be exposed to an eclectic set of experiences and given options galore. In every case it is the parent or the school that is permissive, not the child. The child's experience in "open" or "closed" institutions may have a profound effect on whether he later becomes truly liberated, but that only reinforces the point. The choice of experience is but another form of adult intervention affecting the possibility of the child's ultimate autonomy.

We are not saying that children can never influence their own lives or that their self-direction is undesirable. Quite to the contrary, even very young children should have their opinions heard and considered and can be self-directing within a considerable and constantly enlarging range. That range should be viewed as broadly as possible, if only because children are fully human creatures who face moral choices like the rest of us and need room to make mistakes. But childhood liberty is possible only within a protective regime that is ready to act as a backstop when necessary to ensure that the child survives in good health and with a growing capacity to exercise his ultimate liberty.

The "liberation" thesis gains relevance as the child advances in age; we shall ourselves embrace much of it here. As a model for adolescents and adults it makes considerable sense; [10] but until that point (different for each observer and each child) at which the child sheds the last vestige of his natural subordination, important decisions must and will be made concerning the form and degree of his domination. In what ways, how long, by whom, and for what ultimate objectives shall the subordinate child be directed coercively in whole or in part? Shall the state make all the significant choices, or shall this power be shared with parents and the child? In what degree and in what form shall it be delegated, and with what guarantees to the child of minimal content and quality? Is the family capable of choice? Of conditional choice? These are practical issues obscured in the radiance of the freedom rhetoric.

The Beginning of Synthesis. Building on the work of economists, parents' rightists, and radical educators, new advocates
of educational choice began, in the late 1960s, to give the
debate broader dimensions.[11] First, they proposed that administrative guarantees be incorporated in any plan in order to
diminish the risk that experimentation with choice would
seriously injure the interests of children. Such advocates
regarded unrestricted parental power as insufficient protection
of those interests, and the first model proposals contained
regulatory structures designed to prevent neglect or abuse
by either parents or educators.

These advocates also sought to regulate schools in ways
that would advance what they viewed as desirable social
policy. For example, certain forms of choice were condemned
on the ground that they might further isolate ethnic and racial
minorities and the poor; likewise the protagonists addressed
the perennial constitutional problems—state and federal—
concerning the giving or refusing of aid to religious schools.
That constitutional and policy commitments be reconciled
with choice became an accepted objective of reformers. Later
we shall consider forms of regulation designed to achieve
simultaneously as many such goals as possible.

POVERTY AND CHOICE: WHO LACKS CHOICE?

The most recent wave of interest in experimentation with
family choice supported by public funds emerged principally
from the poverty programs of the last decade.[12] The new
outlook toward education was part of a broader hope to give
the poor more control over all aspects of their lives. A welter
of new schemes for increasing the economic options of
low-income families was proposed in both the Johnson and
Nixon administrations. Even many conservatives came to look
with favor on forms of guaranteed annual income for adults,
with additional allowances for those responsible for children.
It was natural that this support of financial autonomy for
the poor should extend to education. Following the nomencla-
ture employed by Friedman, the federal Office of Economic
Opportunity called proposals for this objective "voucher"
plans; we later discuss OEO's one voucher experiment.

However, the families left without options by the existing
schooling arrangements are not only the "poor," as policy
makers customarily use the term. While it is true that those
with choice are the "wealthy," an extension of that choice

to the rest of society would necessarily affect not only the poor but much of the middle class.

Conventionally defined, the poor are those with income below the "poverty line"—about $5,600 for a family of four in 1977. Such families have no choice in education because they are without access to the resources needed to purchase private schooling, and government has not seen fit to offer much in the way of options. But suppose a family surpasses the official government poverty level and has in addition an amount sufficient to pay the tuition at private institutions for each of its children (say, $1,000 each for elementary-school-age children). Does it now have a choice? By no means; nor would it if both the poverty level were raised to a more realistic figure (say, $9,000) and the family were refunded some or all of what it now pays through taxes to support public education. At any level of income short of genuine affluence, the middle-class family faces two realities strongly inhibiting the choice of a private school. The first is the availability of an assigned public school free of direct tuition. The second is the fact that a child's consumption of private education will typically take place during a small part of the parents' working lives and will have to be paid for in that brief span of years, since adequate educational loans are not available to spread those costs over a longer period. These factors induce most families with incomes well above the national average to forego any serious thought of private education for which they would have to pay full-cost tuition. Thus, the proposals considered here speak to substantially more than half the families of America.

While it is this broader class of nonrich who lack choice, the narrower official classification "poor" remains relevant for one important purpose—measuring the extent of injury. Lack of choice probably causes harm in relation to the degree of a family's poverty. This is so for three reasons: The poorer the family, the less its ability to furnish home remedies for educational ailments; the poorer the family, the more difficult it is to escape an underfinanced or mismanaged public school or school district by changing residence; and the poorer the family, the less its ability to induce the public system to provide the alternative classroom or program it prefers.

One must reckon with the theory that hard-core poverty represents a subculture most of whose members reject the planned and measured life with its gratifications deferred during periods of investment, including education.[13] This theory would make the character of education largely irrelevant for such families in traditional academic terms; school is to be valued only insofar as it serves the present functions of amusement and custody for the child. This perception of the poor is consistent with their academic performance. However, it remains but one of several competing theories of poverty; no one knows how the poor would react if empowered to ,make significant choices defining their own future—as in the case of education. Even conservative sociologists argue that there are many slum families that do not fit the saturnine model of poverty and who very much want out of their condition. With some frequency they or their children transcend their early circumstances. Certainly these families suffer from a choiceless environment; they at least might cherish and exploit new options for their children.

If which class suffers most is in doubt, it is nevertheless clear that society's general presumption that parents should speak on behalf of their children is simply abandoned with respect to education. The combination of compulsory school attendance, the public school administrative structure, and the taxing apparatus displace the normal parental-choice standard and substitute a presumption that only rich parents are the best judges of their child's educational interest. With respect to food, clothing, and shelter, all families are fit to choose; in matters respecting basic loyalties, intellect, and fundamental values—in short, where the child's humanity is implicated—the state must dominate the prime hours of the average child's day. Whether a distinction of this sort among economic classes is good public policy is the basic issue.

OTHER REFORMS DISTINGUISHED

To clarify our subject further and fix its boundaries, we will briefly distinguish family choice from other popular conceptions of changes needed in public education. Competing reform concepts include "accountability," curricular reform, community control, school-site budgeting, and the abolition of schools. The abolitionists (for example, Illich) need but the briefest of distinctions from those who would emphasize choice. The latter would abolish nothing; they seek not to narrow the range of educational options but to enlarge it. They hold that schools, even of the traditional sort, should be available so long as somebody prefers them.

Accountability requires a more complex distinction. This broad concept has taken several forms, but a common theme is perceptible. [14] Each version of accountability would approach reform in the manner of a prosecutor; the objective is to deter and punish educational wrongdoing through the operation of some public process. There is an assumption that in education, as in the criminal law, society through government can prescribe and enforce norms of behavior—in this case, for those who operate the public school systems and, in particular, the teachers. The norms can be objective in form, as, for example, standardized tests of student achievement; they can be subjective, taking the form of evaluations of teaching by specified persons. Or the norms can be a combination of objective and subjective standards.

The overall concept of accountability and its various possible procedures mirror other public processes for dealing with deviance. When the breach of a pedagogical norm has been alleged and proved (for example, "incompetence of the teacher" or "failure" of his students), the venial offender is given probation plus incentives for rehabilitation. Serious offenders and repeaters are put in academic jail, that is, excluded from the society of the school by dismissal. The offender, whether an individual or institution, may even suffer the professional equivalent of capital punishment by losing the indispensable license or credential. Some zealots would compel the offending person and his institution to make financial restitution to those injured by their misdemeanors. The administrators of the system of accountability norms and procedures could include superintendents, academic peers, parents, pupils, licensing agencies, and various combinations of all these. Even the judiciary may become involved, as, for example, when a former student seeks damages for the injury suffered by his teachers' failure to meet the minimum standard for reading instruction. [15]

Family choice resembles accountability in one respect. It too seeks a standard of responsibility and a process for enforcing it. However, accountability embodies its standards in legal norms and public process, both politically derived; by contrast, family choice would derive its controlling norm of behavior not from politics but from private preference. It would be left to each family to set its own standard for educational performance. And the standard would be enforced not by public process, but simply by the family's withdrawal of the child from the substandard school experience and its selection of an alternative provider of education. The process would be low-key, nonpublic, and nonaccusatory. The "accounting" would consist in the diminution of the offender's clientele. However, these distinctions have their limits; they do not hold for every aspect of education. Most advocates of choice would in fact accept some minimum public standards for teacher behavior and have them publicly enforced; for example, some would not rely solely on families to protect the child from corporal punishment at school or the employment of tranquilizing drugs.

The curriculum reformers take still another tack, which is also distinct from choice. They perceive the fault of education to consist in its content. Schools teach the wrong things and fail to teach the right things. There is too much (or not enough) "basics," "career education," or "affective learning." They would employ government at various levels to ensure that the content of education is altered as they perceive it should be. The family choice fraternity by comparison has little interest in any specific content. Granted, one must be able to recognize the experience as education, and a minimum content should be publicly enforced. Beyond this bare minimum the content would be whatever individual schools and teachers offer that satisfies families.

The relation of family choice to the community control movement is more subtle and is important to understand. The rise of the communitarians in the 1960s was as much a social as an educational phenomenon.[16] In general it was an effort of minority groups, especially urban blacks, to gain political control of their neighborhood schools. Without seceding from the larger school district (their primary fiscal support), subsections of various cities hoped to become—and in some cases did become—relatively autonomous in the style and governance of their schools. Community elections created community school boards which in turn selected local administrators and influenced educational policy. The concept made a great deal of sense as the logical extension of the existing policy of "local control." It was also promoted as a way of humanizing the public system by creating smaller educational communities. Some also expected to improve pupil performance by linking the school more intimately to the child's early family and cultural experience. Some of these purposes may actually have been advanced, though there is little evidence that academic achievement of the traditional sort has improved.

The difference of this movement from the concept of family

choice could be stated in several ways, but essentially it lies
in its concept of community. The ideal community perceived
by those seeking minidistricts is the population of a physical
territory; the concept is initially geographic. This population
becomes a community through a political mechanism; it votes
and discloses majorities who thereby become entitled to
determine what is in the interest of the whole. There are
winners and there are losers. Because the school system
remains compulsory, the losers get the kind of school the
winners prefer.

The community in the choice model is not geographic-
political. It is a community of shared educational interest—the
would-be "losers" have the option to join with others in schools
that represent their tastes and objectives. When schools are
freely chosen, they may include families from many neighborhoods. Thus, to the extent that neighborhoods are socially
or racially segregated, the school of choice—unlike the community control school—constitutes a medium of integration.
This description is, of course, the ideal; what the reality might
be is a matter reserved for detailed discussion in Chapters
7 and 8.

Finally we should distinguish family choice from the burgeoning movement for "school-site budgeting."[17] Stripped of
its complexities, this is essentially a decentralized fiscal model
in which each *school* receives its per pupil share of the district
pie plus the widest possible autonomy in its expenditure.
The school-site model often incorporates elements of user
influence into its structure, including parent and pupil coun-
cils with varying degrees of power. Thus, assignment to the
school may still be compulsory, and there are winners and
losers, but there is greater chance for individual parent pressures to have impact. Of course, as in any political-geographic
model, those in the minority may sometimes get very little
of what they seek without moving their residence. Only a
family choice model has the capacity to build communities
of interest. This is not to say that the school-site model could
not be modified in the direction of choice, as, for example,
by giving every family its selection among all the schools
in the district.

Note that family choice differs from all these other reforms
in its focus on a single element, namely, the process by which
students are linked to a particular school. All its impacts are
a consequence of shifting the responsibility for this linkage
from the political process alone to a combination of public

and family authority in which the primary public activity is to support, inform, regulate, and facilitate the judgment of the family.

CHOICE SYSTEMS DISTINGUISHED

A word of caution: it is crucial to distinguish among choice plans. For example, the definition of eligible schools is critical. Mario Fantini would limit the family's choice to programs within public schools;[18] Stephen Aarons would allow in addition only private schools run by nonprofit membership organizations;[19] Milton Friedman envisions the participation of profit-making schools as well.[20] Along another dimension, Christopher Jencks would provide grants of greater dollar value to the poor;[21] Theodore Sizer and Phillip Whitten would limit the subsidy to the poor;[22] elsewhere, we proposed a plan in which the amount of a family's subsidy depended on both its wealth and its willingness to spend a portion of that wealth for education.[23]

There are many other specific issues of law, economics, and justice which can be and have been differently addressed: Judith Areen has worried about whether religious schools could constitutionally participate;[24] David Sonnenfeld has focused on what sort of voice parents and students should be guaranteed in the operation of the schools they have chosen;[25] Hugh Calkins and Jeffrey Gordon have thought about providing public funding of private school attendance only for minority-group children;[26] Steven Klees has explored the information dissemination aspects of an educational choice plan;[27] and the Center for the Study of Public Policy has labored over the public management of family choice.[28] Any decision-maker ready to embark on an experiment needs to resolve all such issues, as we attempted to in an earlier, more technical volume.[29] We will assess the more crucial of these issues in an informal way in Part IV.

For now it seems preferable to avoid these technical concerns and deal broadly with the basic connection between family choice and the purposes of education. We do so by limiting our assumptions concerning apparatus and administration. Later these assumptions will be relaxed and modified to suit the discussion. Therefore, in evaluating our analysis of purpose in Parts II and III, we invite the reader to assume the following: that each year there is to be provided to each school-age child in the experimental area(s) a scholarship certificate entitling the child to education in the public or private school of his family's choice; that the child himself, as he gains maturity, will be given increased formal power over the choice made; that families will not face significant schooling costs above the value of the scholarship (for example, no added tuition); that participating schools will be approved by government, but requirements for approval will be limited largely to concerns about safety, fraud, and minimum educational inputs; that an effective information and counseling service will be provided to assist the family in making an informed choice; that, subject to space availability, children will be admitted to schools of their choice, with admission by a state-conducted lottery when there is excess demand for a particular school; that adequate transport will be provided free; and that the present population of teachers will be given substantial job protection in the transition years. The reader whose curiosity concerning other aspects of regulation needs immediate satisfaction is invited to begin with Part IV.

The degree of true freedom that families will have depends in significant part on forces external to the educational system that will influence what families choose. In many respects this influence seems appropriate; it is sensible that families respond to the knowledge that certain educational experiences contribute to effective political participation. On the other hand, some of these pressures may, for a variety of reasons, be seen as undesirable, depending on one's values and beliefs. For example, many think that the increased use by employers and colleges of standardized tests for the selection of applicants is not a good thing; yet driven by that reality, families may be enticed into selecting a traditional educational program for their child that they believe is not truly best for his personal development. This example illustrates that the introduction of family choice requires sensitivity to the world outside of schools that may or may not be changing; we address this problem too in Chapter 10. However, we should make clear now that we do not agree with those who think there is little point to making changes in American schooling until fundamental changes have been made in the rest of our society.[30] Indeed, among those who hold such a view we perceive considerable conflict as to just which direction change should take.

II
THE BEST INTEREST
OF THE CHILD

The good of subjects is the end of kings.

—DANIEL DEFOE,
"The True-Born Englishman"

Chapter 3

THE ELUSIVENESS OF THE CHILD'S INTEREST

"Do you suppose," the Walrus said,
"That they could get it clear?"
"I doubt it," said the Carpenter,
And shed a bitter tear.

—LEWIS CARROLL,
"The Walrus and the Carpenter"

Let us suppose that our society's sole objective in education is the best interest of the individual child and, accordingly, that in no case will government deliberately use a child as the instrument of a social policy inconsistent with his well-being. Though somewhat unrealistic, this limiting assumption will help us in the next three chapters to speculate about the impact on children's welfare of a sensibly regulated family choice system. The best-interest-of-the-child formula is a primary theme of the national dialogue about education. Most Americans believe that schools can be "good for" children if ordered in particular ways; although children are excluded from the politics which shape education, their welfare is a common justification for the system. Many—including ourselves—consider it the only acceptable justification for the compulsory aspects of school. If family choice were inconsistent with the child's educational welfare, there would be little to say even for experimentation.

If our society seeks to further the best interests of each child, what educational system should it adopt? For reasons given in Chapter 2, educational self-determination by the child is excluded as a policy alternative; except perhaps for older children, nature offers society only an option among various forms of paternalism. The question must be whether the present regime of paternalism is the best response or whether another is more promising.

We begin our answer by examining what is believed and known about what education should and can do for children. This may help turn us toward one regime or another. At the threshold of this inquiry we find this general picture: Among the many who claim to speak for children, there is fundamental conflict concerning both the ends and means of education. In this society, aside from agreement about the child's need for elementary skills, there is dissensus about the values that should inform his training. Some of the dissensus we will describe consists of conflict among persons with strong, clear views; some of it represents simple puzzlement—the incapacity of individuals to reach any view at all on a particular issue of values, such as religious training. Furthermore, even where there is a consensus concerning goals—for example, the three R's—often there is disagreement about means. And there is typically no empirical basis for what consensus does exist regarding the means; that is, in view of how little we know about causation in education, assertions that x and y will yield z too often lack foundation. Let us now examine this general picture more carefully.

CONFLICT AND PUZZLEMENT: THE EVIDENCE

Many claim to know the child's interest in education. With regularity blue-ribbon commissions describe its essence, and the bolder ones tell us how to achieve it. It seems the final revelation of every savant since Socrates, and our libraries groan with the weight of their opinion. At budget time each year school superintendents and union spokesmen describe the child's interest in excruciating (if conflicting) detail. Child psychologists make handsome livings giving advice on the subject. We have not read all these books or heard all the experts, but what we have read and heard makes us skeptical. Beyond the broad generalization that it is good for children to be educated, we see a vast ocean of conflicting ideological and professional currents, a genuine and entertaining Babel.

To be sure, there are themes that reappear in any discussion of educational policy. One is the distinction between consumption and investment; commentators agree that, in economic terms, education represents both. By consumption they generally mean the present enjoyment the child draws from school life; by investment they denote education's effect on the child's future ability to secure a good job, to participate effectively in the political process, and to lead a rewarding private life. A second theme is that individual children widely differ both in their potential for learning and in the ease and manner with which they can realize that potential through formal education. A third theme is that no one has the capacity to learn everything in a lifetime, let alone by age eighteen; therefore, choices must be made regarding how much emphasis is to be placed on physical coordination, information retention, techniques of human interaction, thinking processes, skills such as reading, and all the other things that can be called education.

But the wide acceptance of these three themes does not tell us how the trade-off between consumption and investment is to be made, or whether a child will enjoy one experience more than another, or what constitutes a good job, effective political participation, or a fulfilling life. The themes do not help us discern a particular child's potential or how to teach in order to develop it. Nor do they guide our selection of the skills and content that individual children, or all children, are to master from among everything that is called education. And, again, while there is perhaps consensus about basic learning objectives that nearly all children should attain— roughly the three R's—as to the means of their achievement there is both puzzlement and conflict.

Surveying the specific recommendations of the experts, one finds that some would teach children to work, others to loaf. Many exalt education for "life," others for the after-life; some for responsibility or self-control, others for fun. Some hope to abolish schools altogether; others would eliminate only private or only public schools. Some would loose the children; some would bind. Some propose career education, others classical. If one seeks "the answer," the picture is discouraging. No wonder many social scientists and educational leaders are truly puzzled.

It is not that children are wholly mysterious. Certain physical abuses are clearly *not* in the child's interest, and some positive needs of children can be identified. Few doubt the advantage of mastering minimal physical coordination, fundamental academic skills, basic information about society, and those elementary forms of behavior necessary to deal with other people. On this clutch of objectives, there is an effective consensus. The problem is that there is no consensus on the means to achieve these objectives; even if there were, the depressing failure of social science to uncover the components of producing basic educational achievement should make such agreement suspect.[1]

But this is only the beginning. Beyond the boundary of

these minimum standards of personal development both value dissensus and dispute over method dominate the landscape. In this terra incognita, if pedagogical science has discovered the best interest of the child, that information is but the recondite property of one of the warring elites—and which one?

Yet these are only the experts. Perhaps a different pattern might emerge if one examined the structure of education itself; it is imaginable that a consistent philosophy of what is best for children is discoverable in our public institutions. If so, however, this is not evident once the inquiry passes beyond the provision of the basics. Value conflict and uncertainty pervade the structure of governance and support from top to bottom.

The national government has understandably been slow to assert any clear educational objective for children; this restraint is consistent with our federal structure and tradition. Although Congress has singled out for financial assistance some children who in particular respects have been neglected by the states, national policy has generally gone no further than to seek greater equality for children in the opportunity to pursue whatever educational goals the states have set for them.[2] Most states, however, have so decentralized decision making as to suggest an incapacity to discover an optimal policy. Their school districts take noisy pride in their independence, and to a degree they are truly different from one another. It would be hard to show that the schools of prosperous, white Tenafly seek the same educational good for their pupils as do the black schools of nearby Newark. It is simply not the same experience to be a public school pupil in a San Clemente or a Grosse Pointe as it is in the ghetto or—for that matter—in a rural school or even a blue-collar suburb.

Differences in style and purpose are not attributable solely to differences in social class of the students; the curriculum and programs of school districts serving similar pupils can manifest a variety which is officially and deliberately chosen. Europeans frequently comment on this phenomenon, since such seeming variety is so different from the standardization of schooling characteristic of such nations as France and Austria.

The fiscal structures supporting public education seem to confirm the society's uncertainty about the child's educational need.[3] Nearly all states mandate a basic curriculum and environment and set a floor for school district spending, a floor which is guaranteed by the state. Local districts, however, are permitted to add to this minimum from their own tax resources, and most do so. How much they add depends on local tastes and local wealth.

As a result, school districts in most states vary greatly in the amount they spend above the guaranteed minimum. Such fiscal policy—which U.S. Supreme Court Justice Potter Stewart has called "chaotic and unjust"[4]—suggests that beyond what little (if anything) may be implied by their minimal guarantees and curriculum mandates, most American states have no substantive consensus concerning the best interests of the child. They are content to leave everything above the minimum to the accident of district wealth and the preference of local voters, whether the local units happen to be a small village or a city of more than a million people, whether the population is uniform or richly varied.

As with fiscal and governance structures, the substance of education varies from place to place. Scholars of educational law and politics have in this decade once more begun the task of reviewing the history and character of state legislative and regulatory control of educational style and content.[5] The raw material is enormous and summarization risky, but one conclusion about the motivation of government in education seems fair: Where central government imposes more than the mildest constraint on the school's content or method, the regulation has generally been adopted for reasons other than the interest of children.

The ideological fluff regularly enacted into legislation is no exception. Value prescriptions involving the teaching of patriotism, kindness to animals, "moral guidelines," evolutionary theory, and the like are essentially politically riskless gestures of the legislature that give symbolic satisfaction to activist groups, give offense to very few, and seldom affect teacher behavior.[6] Most important for our argument, these legislated maxims have only the most tenuous connection with any perceived advantage to the pupil.

Where regulation does bite hard—as with a requirement of teacher certification—the supporting rhetoric may be cast in terms of the interest of the child, but the real objective is often job security and the interest of those who control the training of new teachers and their entry into the market. One of the most striking examples of this is the increasing popularity of regulations limiting class size. In many states no class may exceed thirty pupils. Yet there is evidence that, within wide ranges, class size has little or no effect on pupil achievement; moreover, insistence on uniformity absorbs precious resources and interferes with experimentation and curriculum modification. [7] Advocates of limits on class size harbor no ill will toward children; yet there is little to suggest that they have seriously considered how enforcement of these rules will benefit pupils or even how such a benefit might be defined.

Finally, public behavior respecting racial and social integration of schools further reflects value conflict with respect to the child's interest. Proclamations aside, the behavior of government at all levels indicates that society is riven by discord on the wisdom of pursuing racial integration. Some school districts achieve integration; others try and fail; still others shrink from the task. Because of residential patterns and school district lines, most white students continue to attend school with fewer than 10 percent minority-group students; many schools enroll no minority students whatsoever. [8] While our national law forbids and sometimes prevents official segregation, it does not appear likely that affirmative integration will soon become either a constitutional norm or a social habit.

Even where society specifically pursues racial integration, the reason for doing so is seldom a consensus concerning the child's interest or how to achieve it. Liberal social scientists have struggled to prove that integration improves academic skills, but the evidence remains disputed and, in any case, not very strong. [9] At most, integration improves the skills of only some children, but just who these are is not always apparent. Some even argue that involuntary integration can actually hurt both the academic performance and self-esteem of certain children. [10] The verdict of the families whose primary objective presumably is their own child's welfare is similarly divided. In some areas, families appear to flee integrated schools; elsewhere they make economic and social sacrifices to create them. Even if all these conflicting collective and individual actions were taken in the name of the child's interest, they would only demonstrate once more that there is social division over the nature of that interest. The same appears true for integration by economic class. In some districts all ranges of families use the same schools. In others the patterns of residence in conjunction with neighborhood school assignments effect separations that are economic, ethnic, or both.

Consider further the manner in which most states control private education. The Supreme Court's 1925 decision in *Pierce* v. *Society of Sisters* clearly recognized the power of the states to impose reasonable regulations on private schools in the interest of both the child and society. In reality, however, state regulation is usually so minimal as to accomplish little, at least in educational terms. [11] In California, for example, the basic law fixing minimum standards for private school faculty requires only that they be "persons capable of teaching." [12] In fact, little effort is made to enforce even this or other petty constraints in the educational code. This is typically true even though "free schools" have become sufficiently numerous and influential to challenge traditional attitudes. In short, the state is apparently neither informed nor concerned about the practices of Catholic, Panther, Seventh-Day Adventist, free, and other private schools that educate 400,000 California pupils; California is content to let the family decide whether the private education now provided is in the interest of the child.

In this bewildering variety of official and private behavior it is difficult to identify any common societal perception of the child's interest, beyond the acquisition of a few basics. Moreover, *even if we limit our concern to these basics,* a parallel conclusion seems unavoidable: Though society has to this extent agreed on what is good for children, there is no agreement on the means to achieve it. Each generation of American experts produces nostrums galore for the teaching of elementary skills and basic social behavior. [13] But most quickly fall on evil days, and none has ever generated a true consensus even among educators.

The educational problems of non-English-speaking children in American public schools illustrate this dispute over means. Their mastery of the national language is an objective embraced by all, [14] but few agree on the method. A common solution currently employed is to offer English-as-a-second-language classes as a daily supplement to the regular school offering. Some, however, argue that the proper solution is to establish special language centers for pre-school-age children or newly arrived immigrants. Others claim that children should be taught "subjects" in their native tongue until they learn to speak English through exposure to other English-speaking people. Still others think that the children will learn English informally from their classmates, so long as they attend school where English is the dominant language outside of class.

Finally, some even hold that the main effort should be to teach the parents English. Many who have studied the alternatives admit that it is not yet possible to prove one route is best. Values only loosely related to the child's interest influence one's approach to the problem of linguistic minorities. Bilingual programs for non-English-speaking children from a specific linguistic group—say, the Chinese—often emphasize the minority culture. Some see such programs as beneficial because they preserve ethnic differences; others, however, view them as reinforcing undesired racial segregation, and still others simply cannot decide where they stand. Moreover, this dispute over assimilation exists within as well as outside ethnic communities.

A CERTAIN SAMENESS

Does all this demonstrate a state of societal indeterminacy respecting the child's interest above the educational minimum? Certainly this is the appearance, and the kind of evidence examined briefly here could be multiplied. Yet perhaps this confusion is all surface; the reality of education could be one of greater consistency than we have discovered. Perhaps a rough uniformity of actual practice has rendered state interference largely unnecessary because the educational system has been self-regulating. The examples we presented to suggest the state's great tolerance of variety may be the exceptions. Perhaps the state can afford to ignore them because of its confidence that the bulk of the system is in uniform harmony with an unwritten law.

There is much to support such a view. Among the majority of school districts there are important likenesses. Indeed, these *similarities* in style or curriculum are the more common complaint; schools are said to be too much the same and seek too uniform a product. Despite all we have said about the society's confusion over the child's interest, it is nonetheless true that in operation the public systems have achieved a certain sameness—one that goes beyond the provision of minimums related to basic skills.

Briefly, this is the uniformity we perceive. Explicitly the schools emphasize technology, uncontroversial information, and skills, an approach officially deemed to be "neutral." On its surface the intended message appears to have little philosophical content; by and large the schools shun explicit treatment of controversial moral or political issues. Implicitly, however, they endorse majoritarian social and political norms. Historically and currently they have striven with enthusiasm to produce "true Americans" by conditioning the children to the mind-set accepted in the larger—or at least local—society. This "hidden curriculum" relies principally on the social ambience of the teaching personnel, who are generally middle class and trained in similar institutions.

The similarities in the school's message are matched by the standardization of the setting in which it is delivered. Indeed, the most striking regularity is that of two dozen children sequestered five hours a day in the same room in the same building from September to June. It is not crucial that our particular interpretation of the sameness of the schools convince the reader. The important point is the reality of some such uniformity. If it exists, the question for our purpose is whether this sameness amounts to a collective effort to advance the interest of the individual child, or whether it can be explained in some other way. Perhaps the parallel behavior of schools represents a conscious strategy adopted on the child's behalf. Perhaps a subtle confederacy of influential pedagogues representing a unified theory of the child's interest has quietly persuaded society to impose this form on the educational order.

Experience suggests this is not the case. As we see it, the particular samenesses which characterize public education are chosen less often for their perceived educational advantage to the child than for other reasons—particularly for their unobtrusive harmony with majoritarian social and political standards. Their point is to forestall any political rocking of the school boat; smooth sailing is not a strategy adopted by the schools in the interest of the child but in the interest of the system and of the people who man it. This does not mean that public schools promote practices thought by professionals to be flagrantly harmful to children simply because they are acceptable to the community. Happily what the majority of adults find agreeable in content and style is seldom patently dangerous for children and may be comfortably accommodated by the politician or educator without professional embarrassment.

These samenesses, then, are less a child's salvation than the convenience of monopoly management. They are essentially the effort to maintain stability in school and perhaps, in turn, society through a safe political-social education for the children. Such policy is well intentioned, plausibly wise, and, in any case, to be expected. But its *raison d'être* is not the child. Our assumption at the start of this chapter, was, of course, naive; the instrumental use of children is common. Public schools are accustomed to seek objectives distinct from, if ordinarily consistent with, pupil welfare. Increased emphasis on math and science after Sputnik is an historic example. While this change in curriculum emphasis may not have harmed most children, and must have benefited many, the policy rested on other objectives.

Yet there is one sense in which American educational sameness could be rationalized as serving a child-centered philosophy: One need simply agree that a child's education is good for him to the extent that it keeps him in step with his ruling elders. Phrased this way, however, any experience which turns him toward a role that the existing society rewards—soldier, producer, informer—may be said to be best for the child. We are reminded of a photo in Bronfenbrenner's book on Soviet schools[15] showing a primary school poster lionizing a heroic child who has reported the ideological deviations of his parents. No doubt such behavior was, at some level, in that child's interest. But if anything the society does to make the child "fit in" is on that basis defensible as his advantage, our understanding of his interest as a distinct value is confounded, and policy pursued in its name is either fatuous, hypocritical, or both.

Finally—and perhaps most important in view of the manifest differences among children—there is something basically eccentric about using the sameness of schools to prove their devotion to the child's interest. One could more plausibly argue such a conclusion from the menagerie of state and federal funding and administrative policies described earlier. Unfortunately, that structural variety has never been intended for or tailored to individual children. It is simply the detritus of an educational politics in which to hold an intelligible position on the child's interest would be an imprudence.

Chapter 4

AMID PERPLEXITY, WHO SHOULD DECIDE?

When omniscience was denied us, we
were endowed with versatility.

—GEORGE SANTAYANA,
"The Sense of Beauty"

THE REAL QUESTION: WHO DECIDES?

At the social level we find conflict and puzzlement over values
and means; at the level of the child we find differing needs.
We are forced to conclude that society at large often cannot
know the best interest of the child. What then is the state
to do? How can the best interest of the child be pursued
by society when there is no collective perception of that
interest?

The beginning of wisdom here is getting the question
straight. We think the question for the state is whom it shall
empower to decide what is best. Societal benevolence should
move the state to locate power in those who seem most likely
to serve the individual child. What the state needs is a theory
of delegation whose object is the child's interest. It needs
relevant criteria for deciding which unit or units smaller than
society will best exercise the authority to decide for the
individual child when society itself is blind to his interest.
We will present and argue for particular criteria and a way
of approaching this issue that emphasizes decentralized authorities.

We pause at the outset, however, to acknowledge that society
is not literally compelled to adopt a decentralized system.
For example, a substantial faction concerned about children

and representing a single educational philosophy might successfully trade votes with groups such as farmers, unions,
or feminists to produce the political majority necessary to
make its solution the law for all; or advocates of two or more
conflicting educational programs might make mutual conces-
sions with the same effect. But this would be an outcome
difficult to justify for those cases in which society is in a
state of ignorance and conflict on the very issue of the child's
interest. All the more so if one agrees that different children
need different things. A substantive and uniform handling
of children mandated by legislation preferred by a faction
and procured by log-rolling and compromise (or for that matter
by executive fiat) seems prima facie inappropriate if our aim
is the best interest of the individual child. Any such solution
must inevitably ill-serve large numbers of children. It might
be tolerable if no alternative could be imagined. But society
has available decentralized decision-making arrangements
that, in varying degrees, can be relied on to pursue the interest
of the individual child. Indeed, there is already in place in
this country a "decentralized" educational regime. The important question is whether this regime is optimally designed
to benefit the individual child.

We do not claim that the state can discover one most
competent decider or group for every child. But we do suggest
grounds on which the state might identify a regime that will
be best for *most* individual cases—one whose responsibility
and authority to make decisions for each child's education
the state may recognize in at least a presumptive or preliminary
way. There are many plausible candidates for this role or
a share in it: a parent, the parents, the family, an educational
ombudsman, the city council, a school board, a teacher, a
group of professional educators, the state department of
education, the state or federal judiciary.

If the issue were the best interest of individual *adults*, there
would be little question about the standard for locating
authority. Even when society largely agrees on what is good
for adults, its commitment to personal freedom ordinarily
tolerates their "mistakes"; and where there is no agreement,
the commitment is all the stronger. There is a strong presumption that adults know their own interest, and this certainly
applies to their educational choices. It would be unthinkable
for our society to tell an eighteen-year-old where he must
receive his postsecondary education—to parcel out students
administratively and by compulsion among colleges and voca-

tional schools. To be sure, society may provide some influential incentives, but the final choice remains in private hands.

By contrast, society still assigns that same eighteen-year-old to his high school. Granted this practice is an extreme instance of indifference to individual freedom, it reminds us nonetheless of the difficulty of designing a dominion appropriate for children whose ability to exercise free choice in education is more and more problematic the younger they are. To repeat, the question is not whether six-year-olds will be independent in the manner of adults. That was decided by nature. What nature has left to society is the design of the paternalism most likely to advance the interest of the individual child.

Viewed as a system of decision location, the present educational structure can be described largely as a regime of local government employees and elected officials who have been empowered to decide what form of education is in the best interest of the children resident within their district. These agents—school board members, administrators, and teachers —are moderately constrained by higher government authorities and by the attitudes of local residents, which together set political limits on the range of tolerable educational practices. Children themselves rarely have anything to say about their school assignment except as it may influence the location of family residence. Once residence is decided, individual public school families have little formal voice in determining the education their child receives, though the sophisticated parent with spare time may employ harassment and persuasion to secure a preferred assignment.

If we were to attribute to this present "decentralized" scheme a primary concern for the best interest of individual children, its rationale would have to be that—apart from those families able to pay for private schools or a change of residence—local government agents make better school assignments for individual children they have never met than would the family, even were the family to be supported by professional counseling. The underlying argument would be that, by imposing on individual children the decisions made for them by professional and elected local decision makers, the public system gives them advantages unattainable by any other form of assignment. He receives the benefits of educational expertise while eluding the risks of mistakes, negligence, and exploitation by those amateurs who are his family. Power is placed in the hands of disinterested elders and experts who are outside the family yet are subject to public scrutiny.

By what standard would one favor or oppose concession of the power of school assignment to such persons if the interest of children is our object? Why, for example, should we favor this arrangement over one giving individual teachers more power? There is nothing in nature that dictates deference to public school authorities constrained as they must be by majoritarian norms that may not fit the particular child. To pursue this question one must first settle on criteria by which to locate authority over children. We will now suggest criteria which we think appropriate and defend them; from these criteria we will draw conclusions concerning the optimal dispersal of authority.

DECISION-LOCATING CONSIDERATIONS

Deciding who gets to decide for a child should be approached with the queasy discomfort appropriate to all paternalisms. Its justifying principle must be that, although the decision sometimes conflicts with that preferred by the individual affected, *the process should always incorporate the child's own voice expressed within a decision-making community that is knowledgeable and caring about him.* While this principle is essentially one integrated concept, we can clarify it by distinguishing three constituent elements—voice, knowledge, and caring.

Merely because the young child is by nature excluded from plenary control over his educational experience does not mean that his wishes and opinions should count for nothing. To the contrary, his voice in the matter should be important, though not determinative. By voice we mean simply the assurance that the child will be heard in his own behalf. This is a commonplace idea with parallels wherever decisions must be made for, and in the interest of, individuals by corporate action; the processes of cooperatives, churches, labor unions, and other human enterprises, private and public, provide abundant examples. Unless the individual is to be utterly preempted by the collective that serves him, voice is a crucial factor. To be sure, the importance of voice may vary depending on the reasons for yielding individual decision to the collective in a particular case. Hospitals, for example, should not hesitate to treat an unconscious and thus voiceless patient. Ordinarily, however, the affected individual should be "heard" whether he is a squalling infant, a dissident union member, or a senile elder.

If the child's opinion were all that mattered, he could decide for himself, but when the child's lack of maturity prevents his reliably deciding for himself, there must be other considerations besides voice. The person or community that decides for (and with) him must meet criteria in addition to its willingness to listen. Two other crucial factors to be considered are the character of the community's knowledge about the child and the degree of its concern for his interest. Whenever the child's preference is rejected, these qualities of knowledge and caring in the deciding authority help assure that the decision nevertheless is made in the child's interest.

Adult knowledge about a child can be of two kinds. One is the direct knowledge of a particular child, derived from personal observation and interaction. Through intimate and continued contact the adult comes to share in some degree the child's reality, what he perceives and what he is. This affective insight of the adult stands in contrast to knowledge gained through experience, study, and professional practice with children as a class of humans. Each of these two types of knowledge, personal and professional, has an important role to play in the decision-making process.

By caring we mean the appetite of the deciding community for exercising its power in the child's interest. This caring or concern can stem from personal affection; it can also be based on mutual self-interest. The conjunction of the two is ordinarily the ideal.

SUBSIDIARITY: THE PRESUMPTION FOR THE SMALL

These three criteria for locating authority do not automatically nominate the proper decisional unit. But the importance of voice, knowledge, and caring taken together does imply a distinctive and recognized approach to the question: the principle known to European political philosophers as *subsidiarity*,[1] a term uncommon to American politics but rich in potential application to any political order concerned with maximizing personalistic values. This principle holds that responsibility for dependent individuals should belong to the smaller and more intimate rather than the larger and more anonymous communities to which the individual belongs. Which unit is appropriate for any case will depend on many factors. Furthermore, the principle is flexible regarding the constitution of the group. It may be purely private and voluntary in the manner of a political club or it may be public and involuntary, as with a municipality. It may fall somewhere in between, as with the labor union or the family.

Although the idea of subsidiarity deserves full-dress philosophical analysis, here we must be content to justify it provisionally as the grist of common sense, tradition, and experience. These suggest that, in the run of cases, a small community is more likely to listen to and respect constituent voices, to know individual interests, and to be motivated to serve them—particularly when it is so structured that all members are affected by its decision about any member. Subsidiarity represents the impulse to preserve individualistic values within a collective.

But this preference for the small and personal is only a presumption; it yields to the necessity for employing the resources of the larger community. The lone laborer cannot effectively oppose the economic power of the corporate entrepreneur; he must, therefore, be encouraged by law to bargain collectively in the name of his own liberty. Many possible points for the location of authority lie between the individual and the society as a whole. Communities can deserve to be called decentralized though they are large in absolute terms. Such substantial collectives as bar associations, labor unions, clubs, churches, school districts, and the Red Cross are examples of units which, at least in comparison to central government, qualify as examples of subsidiarity. These units reflect a compromise; it is hoped that in each case aggregation has not eliminated more of voice, knowledge, and caring than is necessary for the discharge of the collective function.

Whether the trade-off has been made at the optimal point is a matter of judgment; the organizations just noted as examples may have too much collective decision making—or too little. Even if assignment by computer has become a symbol of all that is odious in large enterprises, there are times when neutral and anonymous decision making may be best. Alternatives closer to the natural or voluntary intimacies central to most lives may sometimes be unfeasible, but that question ought not be answered solely by application of a presumption. Thus, there may be collectives, such as school districts controlled by professional bureaucracies, which—after balancing strengths and weaknesses—appear superior to smaller units as selectors of educational experience for younger nonautonomous children. However, such a decision could be reached only after a complex process of inference.

Where the education of young children is the issue, on

principle one ought to *start* with the premise that the smaller community will decide, although this presumption must be challenged and tested against the claims of larger competing communities. The policy maker must evaluate the extent to which alternative communities provide the qualities of voice, knowledge, and caring and whatever else bears on their desirability as a location of authority over the lives of children in their own best interest.

THE SCOPE OF THE FAMILY/PROFESSIONAL DISPUTE

We believe that a shift of responsibility toward the *family* is desirable within specified limits and conditions. Before explaining that belief, however, we must clearly identify the decision makers with whom the family is to be compared. The existing educational regime with its professional garrison is the family's primary competitor for power over the child's school experience and is likely to remain so. Therefore, our case for the family will be presented primarily as a comparison of its promise with that of today's structure. We do not, however, ignore the possibility that small decision units other than the family could replace the present authority structure. One can envision, for example, the very small community comprised of one student and one teacher in which that twosome would decide authoritatively what educational experience the child would have. We discuss such alternatives later in the chapter.

In comparing the family with the present school community as deciders about the education of children it is important from the beginning to avoid the either-or fallacy which sometimes poisons discussion about choice. The question is not whether the judgment of the isolated and unassisted family is superior to the professional cadre of a school or a district. It is rather, when all available knowledge, personal and professional, about the particular child is assembled, to whom shall society commit the final choice?

Even if families were to acquire this power, the professional's role would remain central in several senses. First, the educational experiences actually offered by providers as well as any educational minimums required by law would be strongly influenced by those who have made teaching their vocation. Indeed, by shedding the official and bureaucratic constraints now limiting their discretion, teachers and groups of teachers could achieve a net increase in influence. The present capacity of a teacher to dominate a few families would be exchanged for the greater opportunity, individually and collectively, to design new schools and new teaching systems. Teachers would experience a growth in personal power by release from a regime whose rewards are seldom based on creativity.

Nor need the professional's new influence be confined to structure and system. His connection to the child himself would be not eroded, but enhanced; the child would benefit from both the family's special insight and his own. Families with choice need not, just as today's private school families ordinarily do not, make decisions without the benefit of counseling. The availability of professional help would be an important component of any family choice plan, and one would expect families to use it. Indeed, if regarded as part of the indispensable minimum, professional consultation could be made a condition of transferring the child from one experience to another.

In this context of collaboration the family with choice might function principally to secure the child from two dangers. One is misassignment: The family would hold the power where necessary to overrule the expert's preference. The other danger is the risk of institutional desertion: The family would operate as insurance against the classic risk of bureaucratic oversight, the danger not of bad decision, but of no decision. Not that the child is in danger of being simply unassigned; in a neighborhood system that is a function that could be handled by a clever ten-year-old or—as it often is—by computer. The justification for professional monopoly, however, would not be its map-making skills, but its expertise with individual children. Hence, in order to evaluate the existing system as a decider for children, a necessary premise must be that these experts are in fact addressing themselves to the question of the best experience for the particular child, and then trying to provide it. We are nagged, however, by the concern that because of the scale and anonymity of schools at present, no professional speaks—or is even capable of speaking—for many individual children.

THE CASE FOR THE FAMILY AS DECIDER

We come, then, to an evaluation of the family as decider. We will argue that, above the societally agreed minimum, as long as it has ready access to information and professional counseling, the family's claim to special competence is strong; that in its unique opportunity to listen and to know and in its special personal concern for the child, the family is his most promising champion and a fit senior partner of the decision-making team. The family's capacities for voice, knowledge, and caring are inextricable one from the other; indeed, to separate their description here would be excessively analytical. Each is a complementary aspect of the intimate and continuing domestic environment; each is a facet of the family members' relation to one another and particularly to the younger child. And that relation holds even for families whose members are not particularly fond of one another but who gladly or grudgingly accept responsibility. Note that by the family we consistently mean simply a community composed of a child and one or more adults in a close affective and physical relation which is expected to endure at least through childhood. Obviously this definition comprises much more than the nuclear family as it has been juridically defined. We are concerned with the intimacy and durability of the relation. Legal responsibility is ordinarily useful to confirm and support such a relation but is not indispensable for most purposes.

At the outset we concede that school professionals know more than families about how certain types of education have been found to affect broadly defined types or classes of children. Such knowledge is useful for many purposes; however, it does not translate into the kind of understanding about particular children that comes from prolonged domestic intimacy. Not that family knowledge is the only form of direct personal knowledge. The relevant insights of some families could be impoverished compared with those of the psychiatrist—at least one who has been given full opportunity to study a child over time. But here the useful comparison to the family is not the intensive professional relation of psychiatry available to the few; it is the shallow professional relation of education imposed on the many.

What can be said of the knowledge of school professionals about particular children? Educators deal with children principally in large groups. The basic system of matching the child to his school experience—neighborhood assignment—is almost wholly abstract; school selection for the child is made by government in total ignorance of the child's wishes or special qualities (unless he is so incapacitated as to be outside the regular system). At the school level, students and teachers are generally assigned to one another in an impersonal process. The individualization that occasionally does occur in teacher-student pairing is necessarily limited—there are only so many third-grade or geometry teachers, and below high school the child's voice is rarely involved in the assignment. Clever educators understand how to create a degree of warmth and community among the twenty-five children that have been assembled and assigned to them for the purpose of mastering a prescribed curriculum. But these pupils have varied capacities and special needs. The system does not and could not ask the teacher to understand each of his pupils in any deep sense. That task would require an intimate and continuing relation to the child over the full range of his experiences, scholastic and otherwise.

Had they the time, teachers have little of the training necessary to employ even the cruder diagnostics of children's problems. A teacher has not seen the child before September and will not likely see him again after June. The school commands but a small portion of the child's total hours, even during the school year. And there are so many children. The teacher can concentrate on the slow and confused and perhaps learn more about them, but then the successful pupils are left to be known only by their objective skills. Some children get fleeting additional attention from special counselors with more training, but the potential for real insight from that process is also marginal. And not every teacher or counselor is insightful and experienced—or even free from prejudice.[2]

Meanwhile, the child's family—untrained, sometimes less intelligent than teachers, and with its own prejudices—commands the lion's share of his time. For the first five years it has him largely to itself. It sees and shares his environment. It knows not only the raw details of the child's personal history, but may penetrate the child's own synthesis of that experience to a depth no school professional can even approximate. The family has that ineffable knowledge peculiar to a human relation that comes as close to being unconditional as any we know.

Commonly the family also has the advantage of being the child's ultimate confidant, the repository of his hopes, fears, and disappointments, including those about school. Ordinarily this is because the child wishes the family to share them. Sometimes, however, the message may be only implicit and unintended; even when a young child has chosen to withhold his emotions from all others, family members are likely to sense them. If nothing else, in the family as compared with the classroom, there are typically far fewer children and twice as many adults. Thus, if a child is faced with a barrier to learning that he himself can recognize, it will often be communicated first at home, particularly where the source of the problem at school is some human relationship.

The family's role as the child's confidant would be accentuated by providing the family with choice. The school grapevine and the child's own parents would quickly make him vividly aware that parents now hold—hence, he holds—influence over his education. His incentive to communicate within the family would be enhanced along with his capacity for intra-familial politics. Whatever the family's difficulties in our culture, it generally embodies the fullest opportunity—indeed, the inescapable parental fate—to hear the child and to understand his needs. By comparison that is a quality wanting in the professional.

Assuming that the family's understanding of the child is generally superior, how much does it really care? Does our family mythology obscure more indifference and even hostility than we care to face? Obviously adult family members may be selfish with regard to the children; their educational choices, like those of strangers, may be careless or based on parental convenience.

The relation of parent and child is no longer one of mutual economic advantage. The industrial revolution reversed the economic incentive to child-bearing characteristic of an agrarian economy and introduced a new potential for intra-familial conflict. Today the financial irrationality of parenthood is coupled with the general denigration of procreation sometimes associated with sexual politics and population control. These economic and social conflicts threaten to make parenthood a form of social deviance. Some argue that the contraceptive revolution adds yet another ingredient to a general recipe for parental abuse of children. They assert that a child whose birth is planned may tend to be regarded as merely an extension of the parental personality and thus available for exploitation like any other piece of property.

Perhaps. But from the same evidence we would draw the contrary conclusion. If parenthood has become both voluntary and a net economic burden, children should in fact be well treated. Adults choosing to be parents will be fewer, but those who do so will have accepted the role fully recognizing that in economic terms it will mean more give than take. Their motivation for parenthood must lie elsewhere, perhaps in the quest for a proxy immortality, perhaps in subtle biological promptings, perhaps in the hope to share and perpetuate what they have experienced as good in their own lives.[3]

Whatever their reasons, modern parents are likely to accord their children the full measure of attention lavished on the other values and valuables for which they have been prepared to sacrifice. The analogy to property, intended as insult by fastidious critics, unwittingly identifies a virtue of parenthood. Characteristically, property commands the personal attention of its owner; such luxury items as children would surely not be left wanting wax and polish, especially when they will be thought to reflect their parents. There is infinitely more to parenthood than maintaining its chattels, but this proprietary sense deserves respect and is flouted at risk to the child and society, unless some substitute regime of unmixed altruism can assume the same function. In the meantime, to the extent parents, by law or otherwise, lose their power to influence the lives of their minor children, so may they lose interest in the children themselves.

A more widely recognized source of the parent's commitment is his perception that the formation of his children's character is a political act of profound significance. He is consistently reminded by the presidents of General Mills and the United States that children are "all our future." The parent cannot be unaware that he is considered responsible for a piece of that future. This sense of responsible political power may be especially effective among adults lacking other authority roles. The prototypes are the conventional housewife and the assembly-line drudge. The sculpting of an ideal human provides a worthy aspiration for the majority who will never be responsible for another enterprise of comparable import. Even if it is utterly fatuous, this aspiration supports the staunch commitment of the parent to the formation of the child as his personal contribution to the future of society.

But caring about the child is more than a bloodless affair of politics and property. It is the outcome of the endless human interaction, blunt and subtle, that forms the substance of family environment. There is no reason to treat as mere sentiment the human perception that children by and large are loved more by their parents than by crossing guards, scoutmasters, welfare workers, and teachers. Parental love is the historic archetype of altruism and deserves that reputation. If we are correct in believing that caring is important to reaching appropriate decisions, the issue is not whether parents care, but whether anybody else cares. As Bertrand Russell put it, "In addressing parents one may assume a sincere desire for the welfare of their offspring, and this alone in conjunction with modern knowledge suffices to decide a very large number of educational problems."[4]

Altruism is not the most obvious characteristic of the school system. The individual professional is usually a person of sympathetic and even unselfish nature, but the regime he serves is institutionally constrained in ways that often make disinterested judgment about the child difficult. And whether he cares about this individual child can even become irrelevant. It is hard to forget the way Ann Orlov's school district placed her in a school preferred neither by herself, nor her parents, nor the professionals. It did not matter whether or not persons interested in her well-being accepted the wisdom of the change she requested. They had no workable way of getting Ann the experience she and her parents sought. All their good will could not effect the desired connection, because the system was not structured to respond to such individual goals.

Moreover, even if the system provided a set of varied offerings, experience suggests that the process by which pupils are assigned to these alternatives might not reflect a caring decision about the child's best interest. It is often, for example, inconvenient or, worse, convenient to label a child "special" and thus qualify him for a program for retarded or otherwise handicapped children. Such labeling decisions involve time, money, and the equanimity of personnel. The teacher who wants a difficult child out of his hair has an incentive to have him relabeled; the administrator who wants the frantic teacher out of his hair has an incentive to agree. In California, recent litigation disclosed that large numbers of Chicano children with language difficulties were misclassified as mentally retarded.[5] These assignments were in some degree measures of convenience; each one represented a subsidy gained for the school district and a problem removed from the mainstream. No doubt the local system considered this a reasonable expedient under the circumstances, but that it could think so is itself a problem.

Even if one assumes that teachers are a uniquely altruistic and caring class of humans, a problem remains. Their caring by its nature must remain relatively cool and abstract. The teacher who becomes very deeply involved with even one child is properly regarded more as neurotic than professional.

To the extent this occurs he is plainly substituting for the parent. In our judgment, this is not a model role for a teacher.

The question "who really cares for the child?" can be put in a different way by asking who will bear the responsibility for mistakes made in judging the interest of the child. Those most threatened with the consequences of bad decisions are likely to see to it that better ones are made for no other reason than self-interest. This thought is akin to the point about children as property. Wise policy seeks to link the authority for decisions with the personal responsibility for their consequences. While most professional deciders do not have to suffer the social consequences of bad decisions made for children, families—because of their permanent bond with the child—generally do. Being rendered simultaneously powerless and responsible in relation to their child's education is sensed by the family both as an injustice to itself and a loss for the child.

Let us elaborate. When a child's education is faulty today, who is hurt? In contemporary jargon, who is accountable? Is it the professional? To be a teacher, a board member, or a superintendent doubtless entails responsibility of a sort for educational outcomes. If too many of their pupils fall too far below those in comparable school districts on some standard measure, the educators may be professionally embarrassed. However, in no case need they remember the names and faces of the victims. No teacher will be forced to share his home and table with the failures who spent a thousand hours in his class before mercifully passing from his professional life and personal consciousness. Personal accountability of this sort is reserved for families.

For better or worse, the family lives cheek by jowl with those alumni who can find neither jobs nor themselves. The family spends a lifetime rationalizing the scion's failings to relatives and friends. For good measure of insult, society and the school professional blame the family for producing the educationally defective product; this is a curious indictment considering the nonrich family's subordinate role in the schooling process. Here is accountability with a vengeance. One great virtue of family choice would be to resolve this irony by linking responsibility to authority.

It is possible, of course, to reject the whole argument; far from improving decisions, perhaps responsibility and affection merely create anxieties and destroy the good judgment of the decider. To some that may be a plausible excuse for the status quo; the family bears the stigma of the child's failures in order that the professional can retain his sheltered objectivity. The argument seems to us plainly spurious. No doubt responsibility could in some families interfere with good judgment; parents could care too much to be rational. But there is no evidence that such debilitation is widespread among families now choosing their children's doctor, or among the clientele of private schools. We would be surprised if the nonrich were peculiarly susceptible to this form of neurosis when selecting schools.

Moreover, giving the family the option of exit and transfer may serve as therapy for the school system itself. The professional would no longer be in a position to impose but only to persuade. His role would be to explain to the parent and child the reasons that the child's interests require the path he prescribes. The relationship would approach the classic model of physician-patient or attorney-client. Though initially irksome to some, the relocation of the final choice in the family might in the long run elevate the performance, morale, and status of what has been a never-quite profession. Even if an expert's opinion were based on technical information unintelligible to the family, there is no reason to assume that the family would either ignore the advice or blindly accept it. Most likely its decision would depend on the degree of trust generated by the professional in the totality of his relation to the family.

There is yet another reason for educational institutions and competent individual educators to embrace the classic model of professionalism. A record of client satisfaction significantly affects the doctor's or lawyer's capacity to control his practice and to maintain professional standards. Under family choice, educational institutions and educators ought to feel this same pressure toward professional responsibility; their performance would affect the quality of their career.

In short, giving the family an opportunity to choose its desired educational experience could render the strengths of school and family coordinate where historically they have competed. Of course, we do not argue that every public school professional will find these changes to his liking or advantage. Given the choice, those families who strongly prefer religious education or a political indoctrination different from that presently imposed in public school might leave the system no matter how much professional attention is lavished on them. If so, a certain number of professional positions would necessarily shift to the private sector, and some of those now in public education would have to follow the jobs. Perhaps nothing could console some of them for the loss of their captive clients, and some may have an undying attachment to public employment. Professionals in private schools have shown no need of either. In any case, the advantages to the children involved seem worth the adult discomfort entailed.

The continuity of the average family suggests yet a final reason why it can be counted on to act in the child's interest if given the authority. Every unemancipated child who is not a ward of the state holds a position in a family which will endure at least until the termination of childhood. Paradoxically, a principal virtue of this long relationship is the ability of the family to change its mind. Precisely because it endures, the family is in the best position to observe the outcome of an educational decision, to learn by the experience, and to experiment with a new solution.

By comparison, the fleeting relation of a teacher or counselor to the student can produce an unhealthy immutability in treatment. School-watchers over the last generation have become aware that professional decisions—right, wrong, or random—normally are not reversed. School tracking patterns exposed by prolonged litigation in the District of Columbia exemplify this risk. Children there were classified according to results on the crudest of test instruments; those assigned to lower tracks rarely rose higher or experienced any other significant shift in classification despite the fragility of the original judgments.[6] Studies suggest that this pattern is anything but unusual.[7] Moreover, assignment at random or by neighborhood is no guarantee of an appropriate school or teacher.

The best protection against permanent misassignment is to give the power of reconsideration to those who must bear the consequences of error over an extended period. The family is not likely to ignore for long its child's annoying complaint before taking steps to understand and, together with the child and his counselors, to seek to correct the problem. The family is not likely to tolerate for long the assignment of the child to a special program that yields nothing but frustration and stigma. Its intervention on occasion may make matters temporarily worse, but at least that intervention can initiate an intelligible search for alternative solutions; and the family will be around to seek them long after the child's teacher and counselor have moved on to new children, new problems, and new schools.

OTHER SMALL DECISION UNITS CONSIDERED

One should not, of course, assume that the only solution to a dispute between family and the public school bureaucracy is to bestow the final power to decide on one or the other of them. One alternative approach would place responsibility to decide for particular children on a neutral third party. This would not mean an education court or ombudsman. Such institutions are not suitable to make the many decisions required concerning the child's education. Decision-making about what learning experience the child should pursue from month to month, even from year to year, requires ongoing monitoring and is quite different from the one-time decisions that courts or ombudsmen are typically equipped to make. Determining whether a child should be ordered to undergo doctor-recommended emergency surgery despite parental objections is an obvious contrast to the monitoring of a continuing process of education. The same may be said about child custody disputes between divorcing parents. Even though a final divorce decree and child custody award can be reopened and in that sense are continuing, a strong presumption must favor both the initial custody decision and the decisions made by the custodial spouse. Imagine what it would be like if every dispute over whether the child should watch certain television programs or go to a particular summer camp—or where the child should attend school—could be litigated on an ongoing basis. No doubt some grossly eccentric child-rearing decisions threatening harm to the child can be properly litigated; but we could have little confidence that a court or ombudsman, having to decide great numbers of claims, could do a sound job ferreting out which educational proposals were optimal for the particular child.

A more promising possibility is the appointment for every child of a personal educational guardian who is to take an ongoing interest in his education. The guardian might be someone trained as a teacher. Such a person would become the child's educational parent. Yet if a guardian is to be close to the child in the way that model parents are, the call for guardians is really a call for better parents. And without a huge expenditure of money to hire a multitude of trained guardians each responsible for but a few children, why would

we expect guardians to be better parents for educational
purposes than most parents themselves are? Indeed, how
would we ever assure the crucial attribute of caring without
actually making the guardian the parent? Finally, the caring
and responsibility provided by parents comes free of charge;
one suspects the more efficient solution would employ whatever funds are available to help parents become more effective.

It might be argued that the child's public school classroom
teacher should be seen as the child's educational guardian,
and that this intimate pair could serve as the optimal decision
unit for selecting the child's educational experience. Ordinarily, however, the teacher's only choice for his ward is whatever
the teacher happens to be doing in the course of his duties;
in any case, he is hardly in a position to select whatever
he deems best for the child. The teacher usually has no choice
as to which children will be his responsibility; and if there
is one thing candid teachers agree about, it is that what they
do is not best for many of their students. To be sure, teachers
can often arrange the transfer of students who do not fit their
method. But here the teacher's lack of neutrality is particularly
troublesome. How many teachers would seek to transfer out
of their classes the eager, sweet, smart, and likable child?
Finally, at least under the current regime, the individual
teacher is simply in no position to prescribe and carry out
the program he sees as the child's best interest either within
or outside his classroom. To achieve that would seem to require
separating the teacher-guardian from the public structure and
giving him authority and a range of options. But that puts
us right back into the dilemma posed by the model of the
independent educational guardian. Short of huge increases
in spending it does, indeed, seem necessary to give ultimate
power either to the family or to the public school bureaucracy,
at least over a fair range of important educational decisions.

Favoring the family would not be without risk. Each
decision would become a complex blend of the family's
subjective calculus of the child's interest and the more objective advice of the professional. Flesh-and-blood parents would
make mistakes. Some children would be hurt. Having encountered no proposals realistically promising a casualty-free system, we are not afraid to experiment with altering the present
one so manifestly rich in potential error. The family is a
natural alarm system to signal the grossest mistakes. We think
it sensible to risk individual correctible mistakes made by

friends, if only to ensure against systematic and often permanent mistakes by strangers.

CHILD CHOICE

We have referred to the child's own role in the decision process primarily in terms of his capacity to be heard within the family. We have assumed that, in cases of intrafamily disagreement, the choice belongs juridically to the parents. We have preferred to call it family choice instead of parent choice because of our conviction that the child's role in the process of selection will be very important in most families. Few parents would choose simply to ignore the wishes or obvious needs of the child. This model of choice is appropriate for the younger child.

In the maturing child, however, there is both a growing capacity and need for independent choice. The eighteen-year-old whom society recognizes as the best judge of his own interest did not become so overnight. Rules of the game which recognize the child's increasing insight seem needed. What rules can best guarantee this transition to individual choice is a difficult administrative question; under a choice scheme, experimentation with a number of techniques for gradually expanding the child's power would be possible. One is the staged redistribution of legal authority, recognizing rights consistent with the developmental pattern of the normal child. For example, at age twelve the child could enjoy a veto over the family's choice; at fourteen he could have choice, hence the initiative, but subject to parental veto; at fifteen or sixteen he could be free to choose among all options recognized by the society as meeting his minimal needs.

Such a multilevel regime of choice would have two broad structural effects. First, it would maintain throughout the elementary school years more of the family influence that now recedes with the initiation of formal education. Second, it would lower the age at which children begin formally to determine their own educational experience. Put differently, parental power that now obtains during the preschool period would last longer, while child power that now exists as to college would arise sooner. In each case the role of the state would tend to become less arbitrary and coercive, and more supportive of individual liberty.

It is, of course, problematic how much such legal recognition of the child's own option would by itself add to his influence, at least if one assumes his continuing membership in the family. Obdurate parents still could choose to bargain with other privileges at their command—bicycles, cars, money, hours. Most children in making their choices would continue to be influenced by the counseling of parents, professionals, and other adults; in fact, the label *family* choice continues to describe such a regime. But whatever its practical limits, legal recognition of the child's own right could give parents of elementary pupils an additional incentive to make the process of decision from the earliest years a shared activity with the aspiration that such sharing among generations would become a lifetime habit.

TREATING EDUCATION LIKE CHILD-REARING GENERALLY

Outside the boundaries of formal education, this society is strongly committed to the family as the appropriate locus of decision on behalf of the child. It is a commitment that has persisted despite a century of "child welfare" legislation. Today, with the blessing of the law, families permit or require children to do manual labor at home, attend radical rallies, read the Bible, compete in Little League, meditate, do four hours of homework, climb dangerous mountains, or do nothing whatsoever. To say whether these experiences are beneficial or baneful requires in each case a calculus more subtle than anyone knows. Hence, society imposes few specific requirements in the way of parenting. Beyond the basics it would not know where to begin—so it does not.

There is no reason to view this policy favoring family choice as an abdication of responsibility by the state. It is, rather, a principled application of subsidiarity. Absent a consensus to the contrary, society accepts the superiority of the family judgment with regard to the child's rest, nourishment, recreation, and other crucial decisions. Policy for each child remains the prerogative of the appropriate small community that hears, knows, and cares.

Still, society has not deferred entirely to the family. Parents have certain legal obligations to the child. If he is seriously neglected or abused, the parent may be punished and the state may take over the parenting function; the child has a right that it do so. Children who are swatted, sweated, and starved trigger the minimum guarantee of state protection they obviously require. The presumption in favor of the family yields to the manifest needs of the individual child.

By shifting to family choice in education we mean to bring that field more in line with society's treatment of child-rearing generally. Family power would by no means be unbridled, but the daily supervision of the child by public authority in public schools would be replaced by other legal mechanisms for his protection. Some of these devices would be of the sort now employed to protect the child from parental misfeasance in areas outside education. Hence, we will briefly identify the general types of controls society imposes on the family's handling of its children.

Apart from schooling, *affirmative* obligations of the family are usually put in the most general terms—families must feed, clothe, shelter, and provide medical care—and these obligations are put in the form of minimums. Moreover, families largely satisfy these obligations through the private market. Even the rare, specific, affirmative legal mandate, such as smallpox vaccination, is generally complied with by having a private doctor perform the inoculation. And, as we observed in Chapter 1, where families are thought too poor to comply on their own, the state tends to provide financial subsidies such as welfare, food stamps, and Medicaid rather than apartments, hot meals, and state physicians. That is, the family is given the choice among available goods and services and those who provide them.

Legal prohibitions—*negative* regulation—also shape the family's role. Some are quite general in form, such as the restraints on child abuse. On the other hand, some are very specific, such as age restrictions on employment, curfew hours, and the use of alcohol; in some of these cases, however, the prohibitions may not apply when the parent consents or participates.

Apart from particular affirmative and negative directions, parents themselves must meet a minimal general standard in order to preserve their status as legal guardians. Legal intervention to remove the child is available for extreme cases in which the family utterly lacks the capacity or will to protect its child members. Apart from any specific violation, parents who are grossly incompetent through illness or otherwise may lose custody irrespective of their good intentions toward the child.[8] Considering the vast population at risk and the informal (and sometimes formal) screening given children in school and in other governmental and private programs, a striking aspect of all such regulation of the family is the minimal number of violators brought into the legal system. No doubt, a few would-be offenders are deterred by potential legal sanction; also there are some unreported violations. But the primary explanation for the low number of cases is that the legal norms reflect a broad social understanding to which most families automatically conform.

The specific legal sanctions which are imposed on transgressing parents vary considerably depending on the rule violated, the likelihood of repetition, the needs of the individual child, the availability of substitute homes, and other factors. Although often available in theory, fines and jail for the parent, being little help to the child, are generally avoided. More often, the state provides social services in the home to remedy a short-term problem or to teach basic skills to the parent whose failures are unintended or, in any case, can be corrected without separation from the child.

In more extreme cases, the state may provide the child a substitute for the parental home through institutional or foster-care placement or through termination of parental rights and adoption. This can take place with parental consent or by compulsion. In either case, the state strives to safeguard the child in those isolated cases in which there is strong evidence that the normal presumption of family competence is inappropriate. Occasionally these serious cases combine the use of the criminal sanction against the parent with the institutionalization of the children, but the state's main effort is to establish conditions under which the normal presumption of family dominion may be restored.

It is difficult to find an analogy to the state's present treatment of the education of the nonrich. Charity hospitals, public housing, and distribution of surplus commodities are similar to education when used to assist families to comply with what are legal obligations to their children. Yet in substantial respects these programs differ from state policy toward education. The number of families eligible for charity hospitals, commodities, and public housing is and has been tiny compared with the number to whom public schooling is offered. Perhaps most important, the degree of interference with private choice in these areas is far different from the detailed prescriptions of the pupils' life in public education; no regulations mandate the schedule or frequency of the child's visit to the state's doctor, and families are not constrained in the manner in which they prepare food provided by the government. Finally, even these few analogies to education are widely viewed as failures; they are being phased out and replaced by programs such as food stamps and Medicaid that emphasize choice.

If education were provided in this more typical mode, would this signify the state's total withdrawal from the field of education? By no means. A general prescription in favor of family choice would anticipate state intervention when the evidence justified it. Thus, as emphasized in Chapter 1, the state, first, would continue its fiscal support because of the limited economic capacity of nonrich families; but the education would be chosen by the family in the way that a food stamp family decides what it eats. Second, the state would enforce the societal consensus concerning educational minimums and guarantee their provision in a variety of ways. It could, for example, insist on the child's attendance at a program that meets minimum requirements of the type now applied to private schools. This is the most likely approach; we will have much to say about it in Chapter 10.

Alternatively (or perhaps additionally), the state might intervene as it does through the system of family courts that deal with child neglect, that is, by taking up the cases of those relatively few children whose education has been seriously neglected. The initial mechanism for this approach, however, should not be a court; an administrative inspectorate might better be commissioned to challenge the educational assignments. The powers of the inspectorate could be flexible, like those of the family court. It could be given authority to order educational counseling for families found to have violated their responsibility. For more serious cases it could hold a veto power over particular choices, forcing the family to make another choice. Under certain circumstances it could even be empowered to substitute for the family in selecting the child's educational experience; if necessary, foster parents could be assigned the authority to make the choice. Intervention by such an inspectorate might be triggered by evidence of either substantially below-minimum achievement by the child, or choices plainly inappropriate to his needs, or both.

A variety of administrative, legal, and policy questions must be faced in considering any such mechanism for adjudicating the failures of specific families. The existing system of providing foster care for allegedly neglected and abused children is under attack because of the chronic incapacity of social workers and courts to define the child's "best interest."[9] Such vague standards invite subjective and arbitrary judgments.

They also invite middle-class social workers and judges to substitute their values for those of poor families. A system of this sort for regulating education might find it equally difficult to articulate standards. Nevertheless, an objection about vagueness is whimsical if offered as a justification for maintaining the status quo. No standards of child welfare could be more vague than those offered to justify our existing educational regime. If vagueness concerning the child's interest is inevitable, it seems appropriate for all the reasons we have named to give the family first choice and to place the burden on the state to demonstrate the educational failures.

THE FAMILY AND THE MINIMUM

Societal indeterminacy as to the child's interest has permitted us to argue for decentralizing much authority to the family level. Yet we have agreed that there is a societal consensus as to a desirable "minimum" of education, one composed of certain skills in language, mathematics, physical coordination, and social convention plus some basic information about society. Therefore, even if family choice serves the child's best interest on the whole, we must ask whether it is an appropriate means to achieve the minimum. Should society monopolize education until the child has managed to acquire the minimum, allowing family choice thereafter? There is no prima facie reason for thinking so; there is no consensus about the way to achieve the minimum—only agreement that particular children have "failed." So long as the technique for avoiding failure remains problematic, we think the capacity of a regulated family regime to achieve the minimum is greater than that of the existing structure. Under family choice, children might well achieve the minimum—avoid "failure"— in numbers greater than under the present dispensation.

A story sad but true illustrates why this might prove the case. In 1973 Peter Doe was a man of eighteen, of average intelligence and a graduate of a public high school in San Francisco. He is distinguished for our purposes by the fact that he could not read; for example, it was apparently difficult for him to understand an employment application form. Peter's mother engaged a poverty lawyer to sue the school system on Peter's behalf. The mother was upset at the system's failure to educate Peter and doubly annoyed because, she claimed, when he was in school the system had always pushed her aside. Year after year it had sent home report cards showing

Peter making normal progress and had parried all her objections and inquiries with a soothing brush-off. Having no other choice, she continued to hope that the school was doing the right thing.

Peter did not achieve the minimum (nor did his lawsuit make any headway).[10] Might he have done better if other school choices were fully open to the family? There is no way to give a confident answer, nor will there ever be—without a fair trial of voluntary systems. Is this an isolated case? The degree of national public interest manifested in the Peter Doe litigation suggests it is not. The incidence of the failure of pupils to achieve the minimum is significant; this is certainly true among dropouts and truants, and there is wide agreement that it holds even among faithful school attenders. Social science research and our experience support the fear that a substantial number of children who lack minimal skills sail through the system as did Peter Doe—without being identified to their families as nonperformers. Even if such school failure touches only a small percentage of students, this can amount to hundreds of thousands each year.

What effect would the liberty to attend a school chosen by themselves and their family have on children who are potential academic failures? In our opinion a significant proportion among the dropout and truant cadres would today be engaged in some organized pursuit of the minimum had they not been effectively expelled from that pursuit by compulsory assignment to a school experience they plainly despised. They might not have given up on school if they could have selected their own educational experience. Of course, even in a choice system, some students may conclude that it is the very pursuit of formal education they despise; and for some dropouts even a willing return to that pursuit would prove to be a waste of time. But the incidence of these inevitable "failures" is worth testing. The risk is zero; choice could not make achievement of the minimum any more remote for these young persons than it is now.

For those still in school on a regular basis—certainly including all the younger children—the family's ability to choose the school might also prove effective in reducing the incidence of failure. Peter Doe is an example; he played the game to the end and lost. It is hard to imagine that, given the choice, Peter Doe and his mother would have left him year after year to the mercies of a school so marginally concerned with his performance. The family's authority would

seem especially helpful when the child's problem is a performance block arising out of his personal aversion to a
particular school. It is understandably difficult for a principal
or a superintendent to initiate change; it is not easy for him
to concede that his school is wholly unfit for a normal child
with reasonably good behavior. The family suffers no such
inhibition.

Society could augment the family's ability to spot and correct
such problems by providing it with the means to purchase
periodic and independent evaluations of the child's progress.
This objective review could be financed, for example, through
"stamps" redeemable for recognized professional service.
Would family insight combined with disinterested expertise
result in performance from children now failing? We do not
know, but we think it sufficiently plausible to warrant the
attempt. The risk created by family choice is that some who
now succeed would fail because they and their families would
make injurious choices. But there is no basis for such an
expectation. No one suggests that those who today choose
private schools are so plagued.

Some argue that experimentation with choice is dangerous
for psychological reasons; since parents could no longer blame
the failures that do occur on the system, they would have
only themselves to blame. Worse, society might then conclude
that failures get what they deserve and that nothing more
should be done for them. We find this argument unpersuasive.
Applied consistently, it would exclude most efforts at assisting
individuals and families and favor maintaining the worst side
of government. It is cousin to the strategy of nourishing
injustice until sufficient pressure accumulates to effect massive
change in one step. We are not so cynical, so revolutionary,
or so ready to sacrifice current generations while awaiting
the revolution. Moreover, we believe that if existing rates
of failure persisted under a family choice plan, it would force
us to assess the responsibility of a just society to produce
minimum education for all. Perhaps at that point it would
be sensible to experiment with a scheme working in quite
the opposite direction—one where collective child-rearing is
the legal norm. But one cannot responsibly consider such
authoritarian solutions until the voluntary alternative has been
tried.

Chapter 5

AUTONOMY AS THE GOAL:
A PERSONAL VIEW

The world is full of wickedness and misery
precisely because it is based on freedom—
yet that freedom constitutes the whole
dignity of man and his world. Doubtless
at the price of its repudiation evil and
suffering could be abolished, and the world
forced to be "good" and "happy."

—NICHOLAS BERDYAEV,
The Meaning of History

In Chapter 3 we concluded that, beyond shared objectives concerning minimal attainment, no societal consensus exists concerning the educational interest of children or the best way to achieve it. Then in Chapter 4 we drew the policy conclusion that such a premise implies for the state. However, we are not the state, and indeterminacy at the level of the state need not impede our holding a personal view of the child's interest. This chapter presents that personal view. Here we ask how family choice might advance or obstruct our own primary objective for the child, which is his attainment of autonomy as we will define it.

In the early part of this chapter we describe what we mean by autonomy and what sorts of educational ingredients might promote it. We then ask what authority structure is likely to ensure that children receive such education. We explore whether public monopoly serves the growth of the child's autonomy and decide that it probably does not and could not, even if autonomy were its goal. Thereafter, we examine whether enlarging family and pupil choice might advance the child's autonomy.

AUTONOMY DISSECTED

There are two useful archetypes of the successfully educated human; these may fairly bear the labels "conditioned man" and "autonomous man." The first denotes the individual infused with a particularistic knowledge, committed without question to specific values, and loyal to an ordained pattern of behavior. The adult with an effective and unquestioning belief in the tenets of a particular faith—religious or secular— is the exemplar. By contrast, "autonomous man" is distinguished by an intellectual and moral independence. Allegiance to particular values and behavior is consistent with autonomy, but that allegiance must be the fruit of continually examined assent.

Note that these are models of desired *outcomes,* and not of the means to achieve them. There may be a natural assumption that each model implies something about the appropriate means to its own achievement, but this could deceive. Conditioned man may not be the inevitable outcome of a heavy indoctrination; conversely, leaving the child to his own devices does not guarantee autonomy. When dealing with humans the issue of efficient means is always difficult. In this chapter we will seek to discover the most promising road to autonomy. As a first step, however, we need a clearer idea of the contrast between the two archetypes; in reality there is considerable overlap, and the definitions are anything but crisp.

Autonomous Man. For us "autonomy" is the full development of the child's latent capacities for independent reflection and for judgment on issues of personal morality and social justice; it is the link between intellect and responsible action. The perception of moral possibility is humanity's principal distinction among the company of Earth.

Autonomy as we mean it does not assure that the child will make the maximum contribution to the GNP; indeed, it could jeopardize this end. It is likely neither to make him happier nor to increase his hedonistic capacities. Autonomy will simply promote his personal and probably painful exploration of himself, the world, and his responsibility to that world. We know no worthier objective. Of course, no thoroughly independent mind exists; and no education, however effective, repeals the relative servitude of each of us to his particular genetic and external circumstances. The concept of autonomy nevertheless suggests an indispensable intellectual and ethical ideal—to achieve the highest degree of mental and moral self-determination and sensitivity which circumstance permits.

Defining autonomy once for all is beyond our scope. As we proceed we will accumulate helpful perspectives, but to the very end it remains an abstraction. However, we can eliminate three possible misconceptions. First, autonomy does not imply a lack of assent to propositions (if that were possible); it merely denotes the manner in which propositions are held. Conditioned and autonomous minds alike may hold strong and sometimes identical views. What is peculiar to autonomy is the willingness and capacity to seek and evaluate information relevant to those views and to revise or abandon an assent already given. This difference from the intelligent, informed, but strongly conditioned mind is no doubt one of degree. Perhaps it is best thought of as a procedural distinction; the autonomous mind automatically accords intellectual due process even to its ideological enemies. Is this merely ethnocentric? So far autonomous man looks suspiciously like a good law student with a conscience. But autonomy does not exclude concern for the capacity to enjoy, produce, or—especially—to love. Autonomy is wholly compatible with—often indispensable to—these other qualities.

Indeed, the second misconception about autonomy is to view it as a lonely separation of the individual from collective values, human support, and charity. Autonomy can, of course, involve a rejection of family ways, ethnicity, childhood religion, and even the clusterings of our adult lives, especially marriage and children; but it need not. Granted that some adults who remain closely linked to the ancestral family are crippled and diminished by that connection; others are strengthened and enlarged in their independent lives by the enduring synergies of the family bond. Autonomy is not rescue from mother and father. Indeed, the ability to keep intact one's early associations and experience and to integrate them into adult life seems often—though not inevitably—associated with autonomy. The orthodox Jew who has shed not a jot of his tribal culture may be more autonomous than a misanthropic hermit—in a cave or an urban apartment; the question for either is not whether the symbols of his life are communal but whether they are a crutch. The habits of hermits can become a compulsive and enslaving ritual; the shared ritual of the religious Jew can amount to a liberating esthetic.

A third misconception of autonomy is to perceive it as a threshold of personal power—as the capacity to get, learn, achieve, and create by the efficient use of one's brains, muscles, or money. For us autonomy is not a quantum of activity, either potential or actual. It is a state of personal being approachable by even the most wretched and objectively dependent of humans and often unobtainable by the wealthy and admired. Financial independence and political power can raise as many barriers to autonomy as they eliminate. What we mean by "autonomous man" can be further clarified by contrasting him to his counterpart as conceived by the educators who have made him their object.

Conditioned Man. Within the educational tradition that seeks to produce the conditioned man there are several mansions. All share the practical goal of teaching children implicitly to believe in and to do their teacher's view of the good, but there the similarity ends. The conditioners disagree about the substance of the truth and virtue they would ask their clients to accept. There is a distinct substantive difference between a Muslim and a Marxist school. More basically, however, there is a primary schism over the reality and role of human freedom. Curiously, the attempt to produce alumni with a strongly conditioned belief structure and behavior can proceed from the most polarized positions regarding free will and human responsibility.

Most such schools operate on an assumption that humans possess substantial free will. Certainly this is an explicit feature of most religious schools of this sort and is more or less explicit in the bulk of their secular counterparts. This assumption (which we share) is quite compatible with the aspiration to produce conditioned man (which we do not share). Indeed, in such schools this very freedom is regarded as a wild and dangerous thing; it is the educational problem. Freedom is viewed as notoriously subject to corruption and debility through original sin or its secular equivalents; man is grossly defectible and never more than barely self-controlled. In that view it is the task of education to infuse clear ethical conventions, erecting sheltering ramparts around man's flickering capacity to resist temptation. School should emphasize limits more fervently than it preaches a positive morality of aspiration.

The other tradition among those seeking conditioned man is distinctly more deterministic. It puts little stock in human volition, believing that, at least for the ordinary individual, environment fixes attitudes and actions. But this is for the conditioner a hopeful premise. If environment can be effectively controlled, individual belief and behavior may be

transformed and our society improved. Schools should systematically apply stimuli designed to reorder the ailing American psyche. Through education children can be induced to
share the civilized outlook of the conditioners, if only the
latter can themselves come to agreement. Further, one need
not suppose that this manipulation is to be accomplished
through instruments of pain ("aversive stimuli");[1] on the
contrary, the canny behavioralist will rely primarily on friendly
persuasion.

Insofar as it approaches a thoroughgoing determinism, such
a position suffers the classic difficulty of explaining the liberty
of the conditioner himself to judge what is health and what
is therapeutic policy. Is he an elite exception to the norm
of environmental determination? If he is himself determined,
what is the point of his message? We do not share the hope
of fixing for the child his own ultimate beliefs. To the extent
schools of this sort achieve their object, autonomy is the loser.

Granted, our model autonomous man could himself be
regarded as conditioned. He is "conditioned" to gather and
evaluate conflicting evidence and to judge and act on his
own. He represents what may be dubbed the "procedurally
conditioned man." Of course such an outcome could be made
to appear deterministic—the pupil is "programmed" to think
for himself—but so can any outcome. We think autonomous
man and conditioned man do represent distinct ideas, and
we are content to speak to those who consider the qualities
of autonomy as we have described them worth pursuing.

EDUCATION FOR AUTONOMY

Certain respected educators would make autonomy not only
the end but the means. They argue that in order to develop
properly the child must first be liberated from adult imposition.
As Herbert Spencer, a radical of another century, put it,
"Coercion in all its forms—educational or other—is essentially
vicious." He envisioned an age in which "the young human
. . . will spontaneously unfold itself into that ideal manhood,
whose very impulse coincides with the moral law."[2] This
view is part of an intellectual tradition that stretches from
Rousseau to Illich: The child comes trailing clouds of glory;
withhold adult hands lest he be corrupted. He will learn and
choose the good merely by exposure to life.

We disagree. A particular child of eight, "liberated" entirely
from constraints based on age, may indeed become an autono-

mous adult with the assistance of fortune, or perhaps in spite of it. But there is no evidence that such a strategy for autonomy could be generalized. We are convinced that the hope of autonomy for most children lies not in the elimination of coercion—at best a romantic sentiment—but in a guarantee that society will provide whatever temporary and diminishing subordination is most likely to yield autonomy as its ultimate product. Dietrich Bonhoeffer put the idea crisply: "It is of the essence of teaching that it seeks to render itself superfluous."[3]

Education in short must be a domination, albeit a transient domination, and is justified as the precondition of whatever degree of freedom man achieves. Obviously, it is impossible to describe any one ideal regime with this consequence. The form, the length, and the content of the adult-dominated education necessarily must differ from child to child. And we can offer no hard empirical proof for what we are about to assert. Yet we plunge on, hopeful that there are at least some common elements of a formal education that can be identified as conducive to autonomy.

In good part, these common elements are obvious and traditional. Every child should have command of an adequate verbal and mathematical language. He also needs to know something of history, philosophy, culture, and science. Such elements are not grossly different from the minimums about which there is societal consensus described in Chapter 4—nor are they intended to be. But autonomy requires more than minimums; we believe it demands the child's exposure to and dialogue with issues of justice and personal morality. His education should draw him into that human exchange about the nature of the good life which in large measure is the central subject of the permanent debate among a democratic people. We will call this experience simply *engagement.*

It is unclear at what age engagement should begin. Nor can anyone be certain how explicit should be the method at the earlier stages, nor whether the child's first formal engagement with moral learning should be an exposure to a consistent set of values or to a range of conflicting viewpoints.[4] Structured analysis of ethical problems may be rather pointless for younger children; yet organized forms of direct experience involving responsibility for the welfare of others might turn out to be very fruitful preparation for the dialogue to come.

Efforts to provide the child with "engagement" often appear among the so-called "free" schools. In spite of their label, these schools do not typically share the laissez-faire outlook of a Herbert Spencer. In practice, if not always in rhetoric, they are seldom free in the sense of being indifferent to the way the flower in their charge unfolds. Children are not permitted to act on spontaneous desires to administer torture; nor do their teachers wait idly for them to experience an irresistible impulse for geometry. The school is active and intrusive, albeit in its own subtle way. Herbert Kohl, for example, views their pedagogy as a conscious instrument for revolution.[5] Their approach may be one road to autonomy, though so far there is no reason to conclude that their particular form of adult-child interaction is unusually effective in this respect.

We do not argue that formal engagement with social responsibility and the basic minimums are absolute conditions of basic autonomy. Just as education fails, unaided nature or informal processes often seem to succeed. A person who has never been outside his home state or inside a high school may be just as serious in his concern about ethical issues and as considerate of other humans as is the person who has been drawn to his autonomy through formal education. Yet the intellectual side of education is worth pursuing, because ignorance limits the capacity of humans to see moral questions in full context. Indeed, ignorance puts some issues of distributive justice quite beyond the effective reach of persons who would consider them seriously and contribute to their solution if it were intellectually feasible for them to do so.

Those promoting autonomy should seek an arrangement which will foster the child's personal engagement with good and evil and with the issue of his own role in the pursuit of a just order. That arrangement may be family choice, a reformed public system, or simply the status quo. The remainder of the chapter is devoted to this issue.

PURSUING AUTONOMY THROUGH THE PUBLIC MONOPOLY

Perhaps the existing regime serves the child's interest in achieving autonomy. The principal arguments for this are based on conceptions of neutrality in teaching. Some say that *value neutrality* in education is the optimal milieu for children to engage the issues of justice, and that compulsory public

schools best represent that neutral milieu. We will consider
two conceptions of value neutrality, each claiming to promote
the process of moral encounter we have called engagement.

The Institutional Neutrality Argument. Neutrality is commonly
thought of as a commitment of the institution, the curriculum,
and the teacher to accord all ideas an equal respect and to
avoid indoctrinating children with the values of *any* adult
authority, professional or parent. This image of the pan-tolerant
teacher engaged in an open-ended exchange on all issues of
humane concern is a traditional ideal; here is Mark Hopkins
on one end of the log, the student on the other. In this country
the mantle of neutrality has been the working costume of
the public educator.

For the moment we will concede that a true value neutrality
would support pupil autonomy and challenge only the factual
basis of this interpretation of the public school. Although
in tolerant times and places our public schools may have
become eclectic to a degree, value neutrality has not been
a dominant characteristic. To the contrary, even though the
aims of public education have been mixed, often contradictory,
and have varied a good deal by time and place, our educational
history discloses intense commitments of the public school.

On the whole, a basic goal in most American public schools
has been the creation of one version of conditioned man.
The system has hoped to produce what the State of Oregon's
brief in the *Pierce* case called the "true American." This
chimerical fellow is not easy to describe, perhaps because
his nature is to avoid distinctions of either person or outlook.

> Mix the children of the foreign born with the native born,
> and the rich with the poor. Mix those with prejudices in
> the public schools melting pot for a few years while their
> minds are plastic, and finally bring out the finished product,
> a true American.
> The permanency of this nation rests in the education of
> its youth in the public schools, where they will be correctly
> instructed in the history of our country and the aims of our
> government, and in those fundamental principles of freedom
> and democracy, reverence and righteousness, where all shall
> stand upon one common level.[6]

This is the argot of 1925, and no educator would employ
this particular flummery today. Nevertheless, the core is the
familiar and largely unquestioning commitment to national-

ism, the aims of government, and the existing social and economic system. This resolve to produce "true Americans" has persisted from the crusades against Prussianism, Romanism, and Marx to the phobias of our own time. As they enter school, children may reflect ideologically diverse backgrounds, but once there such human variety is seen as a problem, not an opportunity. Private eccentricity may be tolerated but never cultivated by the common school. Incipient differences among children are the rough edges of society which are to be eliminated; they are not distinctions to be cherished.

The proper product is a fundamentalist rectitude embodied in personal models of the American Gothic—industrious, flinty, intelligent, and narrow. Such persons may be "independent"—indeed, the word is an American institution—but this must be understood largely in economic and technological terms, and not as personal autonomy. The rhetoric encourages competition for status, but the resulting meritocracy makes little room for aberrant moral pilgrims. Rugged individualism and diversity may be valued in the market or the laboratory, but similar creativity in other areas— religion, politics, life style, social behavior—is not. Ask the Amish.[7]

The pervasiveness of ideology in the schools has not been much diminished by First Amendment strictures. The Constitution has frustrated only the cruder forms of pious edification, and the vacuum has been filled by subtler persuasions wisely preferred by more sophisticated purveyors of gospel. The work of apostles can be seen in the books, pictures, teachers, silences, and ambience of our public schools. The civil religion includes the virtues of hard work, accumulation (high consumption in pre-ecology days), marriage, small families (today), thin girls, aggressive boys, reverence for applied sciences, health through professional medicine, denial of death, and (above all) "belonging"—with additions and variations according to time and place. Some states specifically legislate the teaching of virtue, including such elements as the social contributions of industry and labor and kindness to animals. California recently adopted an official set of "Moral Guidelines" for classroom use.[8] The National Education Association's response to Watergate has been a new program for teaching morality; according to an NEA director, the proposed lessons "show that the system is fine, but some of the people that

are in it have caused some very serious problems."⁹ Insofar
as the neutrality argument is based on the empirical state
of public education, it is wrong.

The state's effort to produce true Americans is consistent
with our conclusion in Chapter 3 that there is no societal
consensus as to the best interest of the child. The programs
just described are designed primarily for the interest of the
larger society, not the child. To conclude otherwise would
concede, as we explained earlier, that anything the society
does to the child to make him "fit in" is ipso facto in his
best interest.

The Neutrality-through-Opposites Argument. Public schools,
.it could be argued, promote an alternative form of neutrality
to the extent that they are staffed by teachers with conflicting
values. Children receive one message, candidly delivered, one
year (or hour) and another the next. Thus, even if systematic
institutional neutrality is a mirage, perhaps a kind of un-
planned but functional neutrality operates through the recip-
rocally offsetting views of the teachers. Such an institutional
clustering of opposites might embody the very neutral and
healthy moral dialogue essential for autonomy.

We do not believe, however, that children receive a wide
enough spectrum of teacher views to support the idea of an
equipoise of influences. Teachers generally—and particularly
in the same geographical area—tend to differ relatively little
in social class and outlook. Moreover, what differences do
exist tend to exclude important species of strong value commitment. Nor is this surprising. Teachers are public servants
who must qualify and be selected for a licensed official role
by acquiring a prescribed set of educational experiences.
Bureaucratic and union pressures reinforce their sameness.
They are frequently hired by a principal who has risen from
the ranks of teaching. The last thing one would expect is
a colorful band of individualists. We conclude that any
argument for the current model of public education as an
architect of personal autonomy will have to be based on some
feature other than its neutrality.

Of course, public schools have not succeeded in making
"true Americans" of us all. Not only have the means employed
often failed, but in fact many public schools do unobtrusively
support various and creative forms of engagement with fundamental issues of justice and morality. Prominent among these
is the tenacious if battered tradition of the liberal arts; where

it remains alive, it is an important influence. The liberal arts tradition compels its clients, in a holistic way, to confront the mystery of being human. Its principal object remains the adult who is prepared to decide responsibly for himself and act on what he believes is the good, the true, and the beautiful. Such persons are properly described as autonomous, and they seem to be with us still. In addition, many individual teachers have sufficient independence in outlook and life style to provide a sense of alternatives to the individual child. Indeed, considering its burdens as a political institution, one can give American public education decent marks overall for its performance as an incubator of human autonomy. Nevertheless, if society wished to develop the child as an independent moral agent, it would almost certainly employ a different strategy.

A New Public Strategy? Though public schools are not "neutral" today, they may reform themselves or be reformed. A consensus may arise for a redesigned public monopoly which would be neutral in its ideology and committed to the promotion of human autonomy. We find such a prospect uninviting.

The problem is not that the institution is political, that it is public, or even that it is a monopoly. The problem is that it is education, and the idea that education can be neutral is a fantasy. The most ardent apostle of neutrality, teaching in a private school which is dedicated to neutral instruction, is driven to basic value choices. Books must be chosen, time allocated, and certain subjects and viewpoints presented instead of others. Like radio frequencies, not everyone can be heard; and listeners have limited time and attention. G. K. Chesterton exaggerates only slightly: "It is quaint that people talk of separating dogma from education. Dogma is actually the only thing that cannot be separated from education. It *is* education. A teacher who is not dogmatic is simply a teacher who is not teaching."[10]

The process of teaching values is often scarcely conscious. It concerns what the teacher excludes as much as what he emphasizes. It is implicated in dress, manner, and tone. Norman Williams puts it succinctly: "We are all moral educators whether we like it or not."[11] By and large, this seems correct. The Mark Hopkins ideal would be difficult to find in human form.

Moreover, the very pursuit of neutrality can be its own undoing, if, as we suspect, the average teacher's impartiality would frequently appear to the student as dogmatic indifference. In practice, the primary value transmitted by the teacher may be the emptiness of all values. Within this moral vacuum the pupil attitude effectively encouraged is one of riskless noncommitment. Possibly the average teacher can be trained to maintain an equilibrium of competing values, but our own experience suggests that unless one deals with a sophisticated, and usually adult, audience, neutrality too commonly comes across as a flaccid legitimation of ethical detachment.

Nor in imagining this would-be neutral regime can we fail to reckon with the bureaucracy. Even if our society decides that state schools are to pursue autonomy through neutrality, the schools may not faithfully implement that policy. Reform would require more than overcoming the habits and largely middle-class background of its teaching force, perhaps abolishing credential requirements, or even dislodging many of the teachers (an even more formidable task). The institutional priorities of organizations also raise barriers. Bureaucracies have their own agendas. In sum, it is not easy to imagine how one would proceed to force a functioning monopoly faithfully to pursue the autonomy of its captive audience.

Perhaps the state could uncover some technique more reliable than neutrality for creating autonomous children; we would welcome experimentation along any reasonable lines, but at present we are unsure what such an experiment might be. This leads us to the conclusion that, whatever its theoretical appeal, autonomy through neutrality is an impractical goal; therefore, justifications of public schools, current or reformed, on the grounds of neutrality simply fail to convince.

AUTONOMY UNDER A FAMILY CHOICE SYSTEM

Optimism about choice as a regime for achieving autonomous adults rests on the proposition that a curriculum and milieu sympathetic to the particular values preferred by the family may be especially conducive to that goal. This proposition is a more radical challenge to the existing system than is the denial of the practical possibility of neutrality. It rejects the assumption that neutrality is useful.

The child's need to establish for himself a stable and self-respecting position in relation to the extended world is a commonplace of modern psychology. It suggests the efficacy of binding the younger child's home values to his formal education as a means of promoting emotional security and appreciation for the role of personal values. In short, there may be a fruitful linkage between tribal ways and the path to independent moral judgment. Kohlberg suggests that the family culture may represent a developmental stage necessary in acquiring a fully autonomous morality. For many, that need may continue after reaching the statutory age for beginning formal education. Hence the plausibility of "an appeal to the implementation of already existing social and moral values held by these children."[12] One need not share the Amish code to imagine that the capacity of a child of Amish parents to make moral judgments could prosper in an Amish school; the same might be said of any sectarian pedagogy whether religious or secular.

The most important experience within schools of choice may be the child's observation of trusted adults gripped by a moral concern which is shared and endorsed by his own family. The content of that concern may be less important than its central position in the life of the institution. Even where particular values seem narrow and one-sided, a child's engagement with them at a crucial stage of his development might secure his allegiance to that ideal of human reciprocity which is indispensable to our view of autonomy. The very simplicity of the school's message may arouse in particular children or age groups a greater appreciation of the need for commitment than could be expected from a neutral approach. A parochial style could be the most effective to stimulate the child's capacity to "identify" with others—the trait Robert Heilbroner has described as "the soil in which are rooted all possibilities of morality."[13] In the light of modern psychological research (the work of Kohlberg and others), this hypothesis seems as plausible as the traditional notion of professionals that compulsory and early severance of the child from his home culture is an act of merciful liberation.

In a family choice scheme many kinds of homes would in effect be represented by the various schools; it should be possible in a practical way to forge recognizable links between the particular child's home experience and the style of his school. Given such social and psychic linkage, children might feel "at home" with the school and more receptive to the school's message. When children in a Black Muslim school learn that a black hero suffered a particular injustice, the process of identification and empathy with that hero is relatively easy; and the process of moral engagement has begun. When they hear that the black race has been victim of injustice, the children are invited to carry their identification and empathy with heroes to a level of abstraction embracing persons whose names they will never hear. Some children will then go the final mile; with help or on their own they will sense what is implicit—that injustice is not a black but a human problem. The most partisan of moralities in the end rest on universals; indeed, that universality is often at its plainest in the rhetoric of minority sects and peoples. Reading *Elijah Speaks* one would have supposed that traditional virtue and the golden rule were his invention.

Empathy and moral engagement might be greatly assisted by the tendency of a choice system to assemble children whose outlooks are at least compatible. An important part of the school experience fostering the younger child's engagement with ethical matters is the rubbing of elbows and ideas with fellow students. That they would share a faith or social outlook does not trouble us. Indeed, it may be an advantage to our purpose. While conflict under some conditions can stimulate growth, the quality of the moral dialogue, particularly in the early years, may rest on a relative compatibility of view among the children. Interchange employing a common and familiar set of values may be the most complex kind of moral engagement possible for younger children. Because of its greater potential for home-school linkage, family choice may produce that minimal degree of commonality among students which invites easy participation in such dialogue. This is not meant to justify separation by income. Experience with parochial and other private schools suggests that reliance on family values often assembles pupil peers of widely varying incomes.[14] Gloomy predictions concerning the role of class and income in school choices are premature, at least in a system which assures true equality of access.

The idea of protecting children from their parents' inadequate values comes easily to an educated elite, but early severance from familial roots may be bad medicine for some children. A curriculum and style that look ideal to the sophisticated adult may simply perplex and terrorize the younger child who has yet to achieve a stable self-image; this may be particularly true of children from minority homes. That this risk is widely if vaguely perceived appears from the arguments supporting community control of schools. The hypothesis that closer connection to the home will promote the child's autonomy percolates through the rhetoric of community control. Let the *local* adults wield the power, it is said, so that the children may prosper in a familiar and amiable milieu.

The argument, unfortunately, is quite misleading in this context. A major weakness of the community control movement is that, while it relies on linkage to the home, for many families it lacks the capacity to deliver. Community control cannot serve the objectives of those families who do not share the community ethic as it is defined by majoritarian politics. An inner-city community school or a Navaho school is attractive only insofar as it is affectively linked to its clientele, and it is linked only insofar as the family wishes the child to be there. If 30 percent of the Navaho families are offended by the school and want six different secular and religious styles for their children, a solution imposed on them by their "community" oppresses these local minorities by ignoring their differences. On the other hand, a solution which tries to recognize all local minorities within one system would be enormously cumbersome.

The problem is common to direct political solutions for the variety of individual needs. In theory, to promote autonomy the state could simply order its schools to link *every* child's home and school environments, but in practice any workable system with that objective would have to resort to family choice in its administration. In theory, the state could even order all families to promote automony in their own choice of schools; a more futile gesture would be difficult to imagine. If the linkage rationale is plausible, there is clearly no justification for pursuing it by political mandate. The prudent approach is to let families and their educational counselors determine together which children will be served best by the homelike atmosphere and which will profit from some form of severance from home values. Many families might wisely conclude that their child's best interest is served by a school that operates as a marketplace of ideas, exploring widely divergent values, many of which would be strongly contrary to the family's home values.

Finally, direct political solutions generally involve a good deal of compulsion. In the absence of consensus we see no reason to impose on minorities even the preference for autonomy. In fact, under any circumstances there is something manifestly contradictory about ordering the pursuit of autonomy.

Linkage and the Maturing Child. Although we suspect that younger pupils are typically too fragile to benefit from ideological challenge, clearly challenge becomes manageable, hence fruitful, with advancing years. Having achieved a degree of ego strength, the maturing child can feel comfortable testing new and conflicting ideas; after all, it is the child, not the parent, who is to feel "at home." For older children, the invitation to explore variations in teacher values, competing moralities, new classmates, and their own ideas should ordinarily contribute to autonomy. The average child of twelve should be ready to cope with and profit from the challenge of increasing ideological and cutural dissonance.

This view of the child's need and capacity is compatible with the structure of family choice we have assumed. It supports the earlier suggestion to limit the parental right of choice to the elementary level. Once in junior high, students should be given increasing control over their own education. Properly designed, the system would promote the joint scrutiny by parent and child of the range of school choices. By his participation in this process the child, supported by family solidarity, can effectively advance his own autonomy. Choice for the older child also responds to the critic's proper concern that unduly prolonged linkage of the school to the home would threaten the desired confrontation of the child with conflicting views and represent a kind of unintended school for producing the conditioned man. Increasing the child's own choice with age facilitates his engagement with a mix of views—but it does so within self-regulated frontiers of interpupil dissonance. If conflict reaches the threshold beyond which fruitful communication diminishes, the child controls the exit. The adolescent can surround himself with a value environment in which he, with a little help from his friends, has some years to probe, reject, modify, or embrace what is offered.

An interesting question about autonomy is raised by the mutual influence of adolescent peers within a system of choice. Teenagers are often described as the most clannish of humankind. It could be argued that the diminution of adult influence—parental and professional—would deliver the adolescent to herd instincts and in this sense be less a liberation than a constraint. Perhaps teenagers stand in the greatest need of coerced variety in curriculum and association. On the other hand, their very clannishness, if it exists, may be in part an artifact of the modern high school; it may represent the half-conscious repudiation of an imposed morality by a captive audience. Juvenile freemasonry might diminish once society gives youth responsibility for shaping its own education. Moreover, if we credit the common belief that children learn well from their peers, we should be exploring ways to exploit this resource.

Some who share our objective may reach the opposite conclusion respecting the appropriate means. In their view, family values already dominate the child and inhibit instead of promote autonomy. Reinforcement of parental views during the period of elementary school merely exacerbates the problem; they foresee twelve-year-olds so conditioned in family values as to be unable to take an independent step toward autonomy even if the choice of schools becomes formally theirs. These critics would rather rely on the present public school system, even with its limited possibility of exit. They hope that the very conflict between family values and public school values will constitute a healthy neutrality and that neutrality will assist the child's optimal development. If children are not made to feel at home, in itself this is no loss. Indeed, such a linkage is a threat to the child's profitable introduction to the mainstream ideology pervading public education. Besides, it is impractical to rely on home-school linkage as an aid to autonomy in the case of families with minority values. Television, they may remind us, will in any event confound the hopes of the family with minority views; it will undercut its values more effectively than any public school. For the family already in the mainstream, it makes little difference whether its values are reinforced within a system of choice or compulsion.

We recognize the force of this kind of speculation; it is not unlike our own, for both are heavily influenced by personal values. We are simply more inclined to take a few chances in the hope of a substantial payoff. As we view the present lot of children of nonrich families, there is little that they risk and much they might gain in autonomy by the employment of choice. The most serious threat to the autonomy of humans is not in the vagaries of individual judgments by families but in the calculated political commitments of whole peoples.

III
CHOICE AND THE AMERICAN COVENANT

Chapter 6

THE ISSUE OF
IDEOLOGICAL PLURALISM

And grateful for the wit to see
Prospects through doors we cannot enter,
Ah! Let us praise Diversity
Which holds the world upon its center.

—PHYLLIS MCGINLEY, "In Praise of Diversity"

The welfare of children is not the only concern of the schools. Educational policies are often designed to benefit either organized groups or the total society and may or may not be consistent with the welfare of the individual child. Two of education's collective goals have special importance to our theme. One is the maintenance of a consensus supporting order and liberty; the other is the achievement of racial integration. How would consensus and integration be affected by a regime of family choice?

Some critics see choice as a threat to the consensus that underlies an ordered liberty. To them individual decisions about schooling made by common people are inconsistent with the health of our basic institutions. They warn that the taste for variety could become a divisive Frankenstein destroying the very order within which it is to be enjoyed. Emphasizing that the American people are culturally and racially diverse, they view the present constraints of public schooling as forging among the young the common bond necessary to contain the stresses absent from more homogeneous cultures; by demanding that everyone both speak English and respect a similar set of values, America has sought properly, they say, to tame ideological and ethnic differences and to instill the right social attitudes. To these supporters of the status quo, any encouragement of individuals by government to cluster according to their own values is a step in the wrong direction, a dangerous extension of cultural pluralism that threatens to fuel intolerance and to undermine social cooperation.

Similarly, family choice is said to endanger the American aspiration for racial assimilation. Since the racial exception to the "melting pot" was eliminated in 1954, the American governments have more or less consistently endeavored to reduce segregation, and the schools have felt the brunt of the law's intervention. Where racial separation in schools has been traceable to public officials, the judiciary has generally been ready to desegregate by force, including compulsory busing. In some instances, political pressures to integrate have brought about new assignment schemes without litigation. But in choosing the remedy, one element has been almost constant: The child has been assigned to an integrated school selected by the government, not by the family. Is this because of some natural inconsistency between racial integration and family choice?

Part 3—this chapter and the next—will reflect on the probable effects of choice on consensus and racial integration. Our conclusions in this chapter about the relation of choice to consensus may be summarized as follows:

1. What matters is the consensus supporting the political conditions of order and personal liberty.
2. There is no reason to prefer compulsory public education over choice as the instrument of such a consensus.

Our conclusions in Chapter 7 about the effect of choice on racial separation in education may be summarized as follows:

1. A system of integration must be evaluated both by its capacity to produce a physical mix of white and minority children now and by its capacity to maintain that mix over time.
2. Systems of school integration containing substantial elements of choice would exceed systems of pure compulsion in their capacity to integrate education both at present and over time.
3. Neither pure compulsion nor systems of regulated choice would eliminate the all-minority school, nor is this to be deplored if enrollment is truly voluntary.

IDEOLOGICAL PLURALISM AND NATIONAL CONSENSUS

Critics of choice justify compulsion of the nonrich as necessary to promote common values and to resist ideological clustering. If educational grants became generally available, various groups would in their schooling separate physically and intellectually from their fellow Americans; critics fear that this would enervate or even impede the national enterprise as they define it. Note that the objection of these critics is not to the herding or propagandizing of children; they approve of schools that make children of nonwealthy families the captive audience of an ideology. They would, however, reserve this use of force to the state; they hold that consensus is enhanced more by public compulsion than by private choice. Whether that is so is the issue.

For this inquiry we need some factual premise about the kinds of schools that would become available under choice. However, just who would be the successful organizers of schools under a system of choice is difficult to predict without experimentation. It is conceivable that the taste for ideological variety would prove very narrow and the new schools would be much like the old; it seems just as likely that the unprecedented subsidy to their potential clients would stimulate distinctive schools founded not only by churches, political groups, and business, but by women's organizations, the elderly, the French, transcendental meditators, and a miscellany whose variety confounds prediction. There is clearly a multiplicity of self-conscious groups in modern America; some are ethnic, some religious, some social, and all are ideological. Many are puny; a few are potent. Some would start schools if their potential clientele could afford it.

Ethnic culture, alone or combined with religion, would surely produce some new schools. Pluralism of the ethnic sort seems to be enjoying a minor renaissance and has received establishment recognition among writers and intellectuals reawakening to the enduring and even endearing qualities of national/religious groups.[1] The Amish, who have carved their own niche in our Constitution, are no longer the only heroes. Such previously unromanticized specimens as Poles, Italians, Greeks, and Slavs have been rediscovered intact in their communities, and their surviving particularities recorded and admired. Their stubborn cultural survival, along with that of Indians, blacks, Old Believers, Mexicans, Puerto Ricans, Anabaptists, and Chinese, is today less often seen as a failure of democracy than as an achievement.

The persistence of such communities, especially when coincident with group poverty, poses difficult issues, and racial communities are to a considerable extent a special and troublesome case. Yet we would find it hard to regret the survival of any community if we could be sure that membership were

truly voluntary and that the state vigorously protected equality
of opportunity in society at large irrespective of an individual's
chosen life style, beliefs, or race. Choice in education would
support that equality but would at the same time permit the
maintenance of cultural integrity; we would be surprised if
this opportunity to cement group identities were to go unused.
In any event, to sharpen the divisiveness issue, we will assume
that it would be used.

At this early point we should also identify the place of
religion in the debate. Critics and friends of choice often
assume that the primary question about consensus concerns
religious education and that the answer lies in the two religion
clauses of the First Amendment. It is true that the debate
would be simplified if grants to families choosing religious
schools were judicially barred as an "establishment of religion"; it is also true that Supreme Court decisions have
rendered such an outcome plausible. Our views of the tangled
constitutional problems can be summarized as follows:[2] A
general scholarship plan intended to assist the purposes of
families and individuals and not the interests of institutions—
sectarian or other—might well survive constitutional challenge, even if families were permitted to choose religious
schools. If it would not satisfy the present Court, it might
another. Indeed, the specific exclusion of the use of such
grants at religious schools would be problematic under the
free exercise clause of the First Amendment.

However correct this view of the law, to state the issue
in constitutional terms falsely narrows the inquiry. There is
much more to ideology than religion; more to the point, there
are many secular theologies that would exceed the grasp of
the First Amendment, because in the contemplation of the
law they are not "religions." Divisiveness is a question
addressed not only to religions but to all versions of the good
life—whether pacifist, Presbyterian, hedonist, humanist, New
Yorkist, or Beverly Hillsian; thus, even in a system of choice
which excluded specifically religious schools, the issue would
be diminished only in range and not in principle. Still, for
many observers, the inclusion of religious schools seems to
sharpen the issue; hence, we will continue to assume that
sectarian education would be an option in any experimental
system.

What then, is the consensus that opponents of educational
choice believe jeopardized? The critics seldom specify, and

we will not try to force the matter into a false clarity. We do, however, assert that the only legitimate concern is for the consensus supporting our political institutions and not for the survival of some unitary conception regarding the proper ends of human striving. The issue is the probable effect of choice on that civic agreement, partly explicit (in the guarantees of the Constitution), partly implicit (in the individual will to protect the rights of others), that maintains the structure of ordered liberty.

To the extent that the critics' concern is this basic compact, the issue is substantial. They argue that variety should not be permitted to forge its own antithesis. In providing education we must be tolerant of minority ideas, but need we be so tolerant as the First Amendment? The question, after all, is not one of permitting free expression, but of supporting it with tax money. The burden of proof lies with reform. No clear and present danger from choice need be shown to justify the status quo; threats more subtle and remote are quite adequate. It is enough, for example, that aiding the choice of Birchite schools by blue-collar parents might stimulate fascism and threaten the very liberality that gave it scope. This is a traditional view with some appeal. It may be valid to a degree, though we doubt it. In truth no one has a clear idea whether its factual premise is valid or not. The opposite seems more likely to us; family choice should diminish the threat from violent and totalitarian ideologies and should support rather than erode consensus.

One would feel more sympathy with the critics of choice if they were less strident, less self-interested, and much more specific. We do not, however, pretend that the threat is wholly a canard of the teachers' unions. Often it is a sincere concern, the natural fruit of America's long effort to assimilate ethnic and other groups into the larger society. The man who fears divisiveness is the man stirring the melting pot. He senses danger in any policy which would encourage a child to suppose that he is not like all other Americans.

The assimilationist instinct is a decent one, but it suffers a natural weakness; its representative tends to confuse the indispensable consensus with those views peculiar to the dominant class, to which he often belongs. Subtly, the issue of whether there is a threat to the basic compact concerning order and liberty passes over into an inquiry into whether differences not cherished by the majority are to be encouraged. The nourishing of ethnic culture can thus appear a political

extravagance weakening the central gospel; the opportunity
to form a Muslim school sets the teeth on edge; the permissiveness of free schools seems to verge on indecency; and the
expansion of religious schools evokes visions of Ulster. Encourage such things by law? The assimilationist politely
declines. He concedes that the present dispensation is imperfect; but it is sane, it is improving—and it is his.

Perhaps the source of the assimilationist's anxiety lies
beyond the reach of objective analysis; yet the content of
his concerns about divisiveness is not wholly vague. It
includes three kinds of schoolroom phenomena: dissenting
ideology, emphasis on minority culture, and unorthodox setting or teaching style. In the end these three tend to converge,
for the objections to unconventional culture and style are
not truly disputes about method but a conclusion that the
offbeat medium is truly a substantive message, and that those
who employ it hold heretical commitments. This is realistic;
the values of a Summerhill or a Navajo school are unlikely
to be those promoted by All-American High. Thus, the critics'
concerns about culture and style are but variations on the
single substantive theme—ideological pluralism in education.

Various defenses of a pluralistic educational model can be
raised against the charges of divisiveness. One is, simply,
that choice would have little impact on the national consensus;
it would be ineffectual for good or ill. Alternatively one can
argue that, even if a detrimental impact on consensus is likely,
it should be tolerated for its offsetting benefits to children,
just as society tolerates a degree of air pollution. Our own
defense is different and more positive. We believe that cultural
and ideological diversity is a potential strength of our society
and consider it perverse to apologize for its encouragement
by government; we predict that such a policy would be a
healing experience for the nation.

We offer three supporting arguments. The first is that
consensus is fostered when those wishing to express minority
views through the schools are encouraged rather than alienated.
This argument is related to the familiar view that when a
government outlaws extremist political parties it often merely
forces them underground, thereby increasing hostility and
the risk of disorder. We believe that what is true of politics
is true of children and families. Official rejection of family
values is likely to generate dissensus; educational liberty is
likely to cement a stronger political bond among our diverse
peoples.

The second argument is that in order to remain not merely harmonious but vital, our society must cease to discourage and begin to encourage the challenge to majority values that is central to our traditions of free expression; otherwise it courts stagnation, much as the government that oppresses offbeat painting risks an unchanging and irrelevant art.

Third, variety among the schools has esthetic and, in turn, important social consequences. It stimulates positive individual and collective responses to beauty in the public order. Society needs variety in its institutions as a composer needs variety in the tones of his music. We consider these three arguments in order.

EDUCATIONAL PLURALISM IN AID OF CONSENSUS

The view that family choice would be a destabilizing societal influence is understandable. It is grounded in the historic American view that the civil order is promoted by systematic discouragement of the beliefs and customs of immigrant, black, and dissident minorities. That policy, imposed through public schools and other mechanisms, has often represented the discharge of a perceived responsibility to elevate the disadvantaged. But benign intentions do not make compulsion a sound basis for consensus. We do not know what America would be like with a different educational history. It is, however, possible that she would have evoked a more stabilizing allegiance had minorities been invited to enjoy the differences that gave them identity instead of submitting to reformation in the image of Horace Mann. We wonder by what criterion the experiment could be deemed successful.

But leave the verdict to history and assume that aggressive assimilation was in fact a master-stroke of American domestic policy, that compulsory public schooling of the nonrich generated a net increase in minority commitment to the national consensus. The crucial question remains: Does this policy still work? Presumably its alleged historic success stemmed from the belief of minority families that they would gain social and economic advantages by accepting this version of the good life. Such a belief can no longer be assumed.

The image of the immigrant and freedman mentality with its tolerance for effacement as the price of social mobility cannot be maintained. If that mentality ever really existed, it passed with the sixties. A convincing replacement of this picture of minority aspirations and attitude has yet to be drawn by social critics. That task is impossible at the moment, because minority attitudes toward the civil order seem truly in suspension. Their redefinition awaits resolution by a hesitant and shifting majority of what the individual citizen must hereafter be and think to qualify as a "true American." The ultimate answer to that question may seriously affect the contribution to consensus that may be expected from today's minorities. How would they respond to a society which so profoundly respected them as to support their unconventionality with majority cash?

Far from threatening an existing consensus, such an end to official culture could strengthen the social bond. The reasons for this are straightforward. In actively encouraging families to express their cultural and ideological diversity, the nation would substitute mutual respect as the ground of a social accord that has been based too long in the acceptance by minorities of an elite model. The bestowal of choice implies trust, and trust can beget trust, even among those of strongly different persuasions. This effect is reinforced when the matter at stake is as important to the affected individual as is education. The message that society respects the values and tastes of the nonrich in the formal training of their children could be a stride toward a more stable civil order.

The sociology of conflict supports this proposition. Social cleavages, so long as they are not expressed by violence, may represent strengths rather than defects of a social order.[3] Indeed, in evolutionary theory variety is accepted as a principal guarantee of survival, Nature rewarding the species that maintains genetic diversity. Easy application to human culture has its risks, but our reading of history is that when a society pursues social uniformity it risks stagnation.

The discussion has so far emphasized adult response to choice. Obviously the impact of a system of choice on the future attitudes of the children themselves is at least as important. It is commonly argued that even if the present system alienates minority and dissenting parents, society pays that cost in order to coopt their children. In spite of the parents, society wins the child's allegiance to the larger order through his immersion in a mainstream, publicly determined education. Empirically and as a matter of normal human response, this interpretation of the system may be incorrect for two closely related reasons. First, children are not so different from adults in their reaction to ideological compulsion. Indeed, they are likely to identify with their parents in their resentment and alienation, just as they are likely to share their parents' fidelity to a system which respects the family values. Second, if we were correct in Chapter 5 about the impact of family-chosen schools on the self-regard of children, these schools may be the most promising institutions to promote social cohesion. The emotionally secure individual is likely not only to be more tolerant, but also to be concerned with maintaining the social order which has respected him.

Finally, our use of "pluralism" should be distinguished from a phenomenon to which the same name is sometimes applied. Some social commentators use the word to describe systems of policy decision that are substantially influenced by organized and conflicting interest groups. This practice is said to characterize American policy making.[4] Critics of this system see organized groups—unions, business associations, ecologists, the A.M.A.—as usurpers of legislative authority.[5] The complaint is not that any one view dominates; indeed almost by definition there is insufficient power in any one group. The objection rather is that the mutually countervailing influences of interest groups on the political process invite the legislature to avoid resolution of important policy questions by irresponsible and standardless delegation to public or even to private agencies. The conflicts are then bargained out in an administrative arena where bureaucrats strike a balance among those represented, thereby ignoring the "public interest." Various versions of the pluralist process are observable in agencies, state and federal, and at all levels of educational policy formation. Not all observers regard this form of pluralism as undesirable. Many interpret it as a healthy and open system of compromise that expresses the complexity of the issues and of the different interests of the affected groups.[6]

Good or bad, this pluralism is a thing apart from the educational variety to be expected from choice. Indeed, choice represents a form of decision making that is almost polar to that of compromise among interest groups. Dispersal of authority to the family level would in fact restore the democratic element lost to education in the adoption of an interest group political model. Choice at the family level is both the antithesis of oligopoly and the source of that richer pluralism embodied in freely chosen institutions organically linked to individual humans.

Of course, the possibility of monopolistic tendencies in an educational "free market" should not be ignored; critics warn us that chain schools, like hamburger dynasties, could arise to dominate the market and dispense uniform, prepackaged, junk learning. Because of the low entry costs of new schools and because human values are difficult to "package," such danger seems remote; and the simplest antitrust rules would avoid the problem, as we will show in Chapter 9.

EDUCATIONAL PLURALISM AS A BRAKE ON UNIFORMITY

Any society needs a continuing reexamination of majoritarian values if it seeks more than physical survival. The American commitment to a robust freedom of speech is a wholehearted affirmation of that principle. More than a philosophy of individualism expressed in constitutional and statutory form, it is a social policy which views unconstrained intellect as a national resource; it exacts its costs in exasperation and outrage, but the investment is expected to pay dividends in creativity and in the quality of life. It is also a free society's primary defense against totalitarianism from within or without. This outlook was common coin for the founding fathers. In opposing official ideologies Jefferson argued that their only object is "to produce uniformity. But is uniformity of opinion desirable? No more than of face and stature."[7] Similarly, Madison's specific hope was that American society "itself will be broken into so many parts, interests, and classes of citizens, that the rights of individuals, or of the minority, will be in little danger from interested combinations of the majority."[8] The same may be heard on any Fourth of July. We believe it.

The imposition of value-laden public education on the nonrich stands in starkest contrast to this principle. Here our society appears prepared to run all the risks of official uniformity. For those viewing public ideologies as a threat, such policy can be justified only by the supposed exigencies of consensus. We have already argued that consensus is promoted more by choice than compulsion. Even if we were wrong— even if educational compulsion could buy consensus—it would be purchased at too high a price.

When the official line is officially compelled, it both preempts the expression of competing ideologies and, by implication, labels them deviant. Thus, those who challenge the majoritarian values of the public school fight a discouraging and unfair battle. While financially supporting the public establishment they must assemble additional private resources

to pay for their own conflicting message. Being addressed
to children, that message must catch them after the public
has consumed their primary energies in formal instruction;
it must then offset a conflicting message that has been delivered
with all the sacerdotal pomp of a large institution; and it
must convince the child that his holding values different from
other children is not socially deviant. Can there be doubt
that one effect of public education as presently structured
is to chill the expression of minority views?

Were a workable system of choice installed, the family
without wealth could make its nonmajoritarian views heard
without resort to the picket line and the street—forums closed
by culture to many dissenters. In having a school that represents their views, these families for the first time in this century
would acquire access to one of the major forums in which
our national identity is delineated. For school is media, and
its clients' ideologies would now enter the marketplace. Common men, with all their superstitions, prejudice, and candor,
would now enjoy spokesmen in one form of town hall that
is still imaginable in the modern state. The experience could
be immensely enriching for the society. As Whitehead observed, "[T]he clash of doctrines is not a disaster—it is an
opportunity."[9]

The role of the school in the intellectual life of this society
has been radically altered by social and technological change;
its continued coercive employment by the state as a means
of reproducing mainstream values has become an anachronism.
In the nineteenth century, the architects of compulsory public
education perceived that, for many children, school represented the only encounter with the world at large.[10] In the ghettoes
of the new cities and in sparsely settled rural areas, the school
became a rescue from oppressive isolation within the family;
it was indispensable to acquaint the child with those things
the larger society wished him to know and to believe about
America and the world. McGuffey's *Reader* and its equivalents
opened the student's eyes to the interdependence and commonalities of society; the compulsory common school tempered the pioneer's temptation to isolation and hostility and
helped fractious Americans recognize and accept their political
inseparability. At any rate, so goes the theory; we will assume
it sound as a piece of history.

Today the danger is not that the child will learn nothing
of the world and its normalities; it is that he will learn nothing
else. Before kindergarten the process is far advanced. He has

already encountered every human commonality discoverable
by purveyors of soap. He is steeped in the media's tribute
to the average consumer's taste for vicarious humor, news,
art, lust, music, and violence. Television is the strongest of
the many influences, but the message is ubiquitous; no child
escapes it in any area of his life. The result, as in 1875,
is isolation, but of a new and curious sort. In a certain shallow
and diffused way the child knows the abstract public world
that is created by others. What escapes him is the concrete
private world that he can create. The media can never convey
the ultimate supremacy of the individual life with its flesh-
and-blood relationships that do not switch with the channel
and that entail personal risks and responsibilities. Perception
of that reality depends on direct experience with others. The
child understands that movie stars are important. That the
ugly old woman next door—or that he himself—is important
may elude him.

Surely the role of schools in our time is not the reinforcement
of the common morality of the mass media. Society will neither
be glued together nor its creativity stimulated by ensuring
through every available mechanism that everyone enters
adulthood knowing the same things, using the same soap,
and valuing the same goals. If society is glued and inspired
at all, it will be because children have experienced directly
and in different ways the meaning and value of personal
commitment and have had the opportunity to see commitment
expressed as an ordered set of ideas vigorously promoted by
persons whose authority the children accept. Here is a role
for school, not to "broaden" the experience of the already
worldly child, but progressively to narrow and focus that
experience until at last the school has brought his education
to a point. Schools of choice are far more likely to provide
that honing than is a compulsory majoritarian system committed by its nature to noncommitment.

Critics of choice might agree with much of this and continue
to oppose. They would concede that uniformity is risky; they
would agree that, for the sake of our future, education should
become a marketplace of ideas. Where they part company
is at the definition of that marketplace. We have described
an educational system comprising a wide variety of schools
each promoting an idea. The critic, however, would define
the marketplace as a plurality of ideologies inside the same
schoolroom and all experienced by the individual child; each
school would have to satisfy the marketplace metaphor within

its own walls. From this perspective family choice systems could be thought pernicious on the ground that they tend to promote not schools which are marketplaces but merely a marketplace of schools, each of which is to its own students an isolated ideological enclave.

This important criticism deserves respect. It rests, however, on the assumption that compelled public education is now or could become an ideological marketplace for each student. But the public school by its own political nature must tend strongly in the direction of centrist uniformity; indeed, if it were truly to become a marketplace, it would be irreconcilable with the aims and methods of those who historically have used it to promote consensus. Thus, by the critic's own standard, the public school today is twice dangerous to intellectual liberty, for its monopoly position eliminates both models of the market, extinguishing variety among as well as within the schools.

The irony is that the political character of the education may itself be the primary obstacle to an intraschool marketplace; all our experience confirms this. By contrast, one of the likeliest products of choice would be at least some new schools devoted to that ideal. Certainly it is most closely approximated today by the elite private schools. We doubt that any school ever becomes a truly disinterested and unbiased forum for the debate of irreconcilable ideals, but the effort to become so—and whatever progress is made in that direction—should be attractive to many families. A system of grants to families would make such marketplace schools feasible.

CHOICE AND BEAUTY

Given the homogenizing pressures of an industrial culture, an educational policy favoring ideological variety could be interpreted as an esthetic imperative. The premise here is simply that beauty and ugliness are relevant in human institutions. Policy is properly judged by the form and harmony of its structure, because primal sensibilities affect the evaluation of public enterprise by those who experience it. Would the esthetic sense respond amiably and with acquiescence to the interplay of forms to be anticipated within a system of educational choice? We think so. The free multiplication of human response to the elemental task of education resembles the wild unity of high gothic—"the charm of uniformity in multiplicity."[11]

The sum of this prediction might be put simply—that variety is the spice of life and its encouragement by society will be respected by its most creative members. This appreciation must be distinguished from mere tolerance, an altogether separate prop for diversity; tolerance is perfectly comfortable with uniformity so long as it is freely chosen. The spice-of-life apologist, whether or not he holds strong views on the good life, takes positive pleasure in the pantheon of American gods and regards exhortations to unity with vague distrust. Faction, whether in the Republican party or the radical underground, is regarded as a sign of vitality. He is no anarchist but he suffers anarchists gladly, drawing the line at violence. Santayana ascribes the feeling to self-confidence: "If we were sure of our ground, we should be willing to acquiesce in the naturally different feeling and ways of others, as a man who is conscious of speaking his language with the accent of the capital confesses its arbitrariness with gayety, and is pleased and interested in the variations of it he observes in provincials." [12]

In the eyes of the liberal philosophers of the nineteenth and twentieth centuries, these sentiments enjoyed a utilitarian basis. Mill's celebrated chapter on "Individuality, as One of the Elements of Well Being" pinned the welfare of society to the public appreciation of private differences. The entire text of that work carries a strongly esthetic tone:

> It is . . . by cultivating [individuality] and calling it forth, within the limits imposed by the rights and interests of others, that human beings become a noble and beautiful object of contemplation; and as the works partake the character of those who do them, by the same process human life also becomes rich, diversified, and animating, furnishing more abundant aliment to high thoughts and elevating feelings, and strengthening the tie which binds every individual to the race, by making the race infinitely better worth belonging to. [13]

Some modern admirers of Mill seem curiously insensitive to the repellent sameness that characterizes much of education. The relish of the civil liberties establishment for variety in the arts seems boundless and genuine, yet this passion somehow coexists with a determination to preserve uniformity in education. [14] So far the ironies of their opposition to choice seem lost on the libertarians. Possibly, putting the case in esthetic terms will awaken these unconscious auxiliaries of the censor to contradictions long plain to others.

RACIST IDEOLOGY: A SPECIAL CASE?

Schools of choice should be healthy for the society, but they must demonstrate their case, and any general policy shifts must await experiments that reduce the uncertainty. In their most desirable form as experiments, schools would be free to promote whatever ideological orientation they prefer, with restrictions on curriculum limited to the incitement of criminal conduct. Such a permissive rule, however, would tolerate the teaching of racism. Even for many supporters of choice, the chance that public monies would assist racist schools is hard to swallow. For the traditional civil libertarian, it presents a problem similar to the protection of free expression for the Nazi party; it is tempting to make exceptions to principle, and some who would leave all other ideologies to the censorship of the family would here draw the line. For this reason we will give racist pedagogy separate consideration, although in most respects it appears logically indistinguishable from such other ideological conflicts as the optimal economic order, the number of persons in God, and sexual equality.

By racism we shall here mean simply the message of racial inferiority. That message may be implicit or explicit, and the difference we assign to these two terms will be important for our discussion. *Explicit racism* will denote a message of inferiority that is (1) subject to control of the school *and* (2) capable of proof in a judicial proceeding. This definition would include such phenomena as declarations in texts or by teachers and systematic exclusion from the curriculum of positive roles of the denigrated racial group.

The term *implicit racism* will here denote a message of inferiority that is *either* (1) beyond the control of the school *or* (2) conveyed by behavior incapable of judicial proof. An example of a racist message beyond the school's control is the peaceful, reciprocal manifestation by student peers of negative attitudes—fear, scorn, hate, or paternalism. An example of racism ordinarily incapable of proof is the difference in a teacher's attitude toward children of different races, whether conscious or unconscious; while such an attitude may be rich in racial implication and effectively communicated, its manifestation is generally so subtle as to be secure from demonstration in any public proceeding hostile to the school or teacher.

Explicit racism is not a wholly academic consideration. It should not be lightly assumed that existing law would preclude an avowedly racist curriculum in all government-financed schools of choice. Surprisingly, the law relating to the teaching of explicit racism in American schools is unclear; indeed, there is a constitutional tangle of the most interesting and difficult sort, and we will do no more than suggest some of the issues. As far as the public schools are concerned, American state and federal governments probably have considerable power to legislate against the teaching of racism. Some have not only adopted prohibitions, but have additionally demanded that their public schools teach positively about the contributions of minorities to American society.[15] We assume such laws are valid, but it is not clear that even the proscriptive form of law is constitutionally demanded. If tomorrow Alabama public high schools were to assign the reading of scholarly—or even polemic—works suggesting important genetic differences among races, and if its teachers were instructed to endorse these works, the legal consequence would be problematic. Assuming the state activity is confined to preaching and avoids the practice of discrimination, a firm constitutional prohibition is difficult to find. The state and its spokesmen preach about nearly everything else; why not this?

Of course, various legal theories can be imagined for challenging such behavior. One could argue that, as with the First Amendment's restraint on religious teaching, the state is implicitly forbidden by the equal protection guarantee of the Fourteenth Amendment to take *any* stand on racial issues. This theory seems unlikely, however, as it would logically exclude the teaching of racial equality as well. A rationale more consistent with the history of the Fourteenth Amendment is that while the Constitution does not forbid mere preaching, teaching about race in certain ways and contexts may amount to a *practice* of discrimination against minorities and in that event is prohibited.[16]

This theory, however, raises more questions than it answers. In the context of public school with its captive audience, is teaching itself not always practice? If it is, will all consideration of significant racial differences be forbidden? Or may the fault be mended by the schools' presentation of a range of contrasting evidence presented in a "balanced" manner? If "mere" teaching is not practice, when does it become so? What additional elements will amount to intimidation or disadvantage to minority children? And, where this occurs, would the defect be cured by excusing these children from the course, or would this exception itself be a form of forbidden discrimination? If the course is made elective for all students, is the problem avoided? Is the issue different if raised in a Northern school district with no history of *de jure* segregation? There are no clear answers to be drawn; indeed, few cases are close enough to constitute analogies.

Even if explicit racist teaching were constitutionally forbidden in today's public schools, there is a question as to whether the Constitution would have the same implication for private schools participating in a choice plan. To remove any doubt, a state could proscribe explicit racist teaching in such schools. While the state could not ordinarily ban constitutionally protected speech, and while in general the waiver of constitutional rights as a condition of qualifying for a government benefit is disfavored, [17] we predict that such a law would withstand challenge.

In the end whether explicit racism would be successfully forbidden by law does not seem to us a terribly important question. Explicit racism is and would probably remain rare. Where it occurs it may sometimes be effective, but often it must backfire. Even to the extent that it is effective, its impact is likely to wane in a free system; its credibility is partly a function of the very impediments placed before it by the larger society. Wholehearted toleration of such institutions might largely eliminate their *raison d'être*.

Were nonrich families given the choice between explicitly racist schools and quality schools lacking such an orientation, would many choose the former? Do lower income families who use or would like to use the most segregationist of today's Southern academies actually seek identification as practicing racists? At least *prima facie* it seems likely that families would sense that schools of this sort commonly would be weak in academic virtues—that few competent teachers would wish to be identified with such enterprises. Perceptions concerning the best interests of their children might move families to seek a more promising environment.

Implicit racism is the more important problem. It exists; it is widespread, though certainly not universal; it is probably effective in shaping children's attitudes, and it would exist in private schools operating under a system of choice irrespective of the legal safeguards imposed. What is more important, however, is that implicit racism is a feature of much of public education today. It is common in *de facto* segregated systems and even in systems that have, like Berkeley, California, been physically integrated by local political action. It is even more clearly visible in systems undergoing compulsory physical integration.

There is no reason to expect that implicit racism would be greater in schools of choice than in a system of compulsory integration; there is every reason to predict that it would decline. Hostility is the natural product of compulsion. What better hope to minimize racial conflict can be imagined than the right to attend the school one pleases and to leave it when one pleases? If a system of voluntary assignment were to achieve substantial physical integration, almost by definition implicit racism would decline. Whether such integration is likely to occur is the more complex question to which we now turn.

Chapter 7

THE ISSUE OF
RACIAL INTEGRATION

Building choice into the desegregation plans need not mean the postponement of integration for another generation, or allowing blacks to be intimidated and whites to avoid racially mixed schools, or embarking on a weak middle-of-the-road policy. It does mean taking the following into account:

1. The psychological power of self-determination.
2. The potential harm of conscription of all kinds and of school assignment in disregard of the diverse needs of individual children.
3. The danger of forcing the most hostile into a situation they resent.

. . . [W]hile schoolmen are learning ways of translating desegregation into integration, wise public policy, I believe, will allow parents and children, also, maximum choice among permissible educational alternatives.

—NANCY ST. JOHN, *School Desegregation: Outcomes for Children*

Incorporation of elements of choice in systems of integration eventually should achieve more than the current efforts of courts and legislatures. Successful white efforts at racial exclusivity through choice should be relatively few, and all-black schools should be largely self-selected. Most important, the integration attained would be stable and fraternal, hence more likely to beget further integration. The incidence of voluntary segregation should decline slowly to tolerable levels as voluntary integration proves possible and infectious. Furthermore, choice plans can be adjusted to stimulate or require physical integration in participating schools, though this would require a willingness to limit some specific elements of choice. What is to be kept in mind throughout is that choice can create opportunities for integration that lie beyond the reach of legal compulsion; it is in many instances the *only* hope for integration.

Our discussion will assume that the choice of any school by any family is genuinely free, yet we recognize that what is truly voluntary is rarely clear. By our definition those blacks who choose to ride a bus to the suburbs do so voluntarily; the sacrifice entailed only emphasizes the freedom of their act. It may be that black children will attend schools out of their neighborhood in greater numbers than will white children. But the concerns about "one-way" busing, quite valid under a compulsory desegregation plan, lose much of their force under conditions of choice. When the sole point of school assignment is interracial body mixing, it is fair that whites and blacks bear the time lost and the evictions from their neighborhood schools. But when all families can choose what they want, it is difficult to criticize the state if one part of town proves more popular.

The concern about the effects of choice should be directed at those who stay; was their decision freely made? Did they stay in an all-black school because they like the school; or was the bus too disorderly, or did they for good reason fear the whites at the other end of that ride? It would be foolish to expect clear answers. It is for us enough that the state provide the resources, encouragement, and protections that seem reasonable and that it remain vigilant to combat unfair pressures against the family's choosing any particular school.

Perhaps a larger number of blacks than whites will face the dilemma of having to trade off the burdens of distance against what is otherwise a preferred school. At least under a regime of choice, black families can make that trade-off for themselves. Moreover, under choice blacks can try to recreate on a local basis what they find attractive farther away. And if this includes the presence of large numbers of nonblack children, appeals to such children may be made as well. Where such appeals are not particularly successful, blacks must simply choose—neighborhood school or integration at a cost. This burden by itself would be insufficient to induce us to frustrate the choices of families of white children. We have, after all, never tried to desegregate eating establishments, hotels, clubs, and the like by forcing whites to use those formerly patronized only by black clientele.

BODY-MIXING AND THE INDIVIDUAL CHILD

Physical integration of the schools by race has been justified as good for the larger society and/or good for all of the children involved. The former we will assume to be true; the latter we cannot. Indeed, injury to many children seems a probable consequence of our current integration strategy and one of the reasons for its unpopularity. If integration is to succeed, it may be wise to modify our strategies in ways which take greater account of the needs of individuals.[1]

Since its inception in 1954, school integration has seldom been a "child-centered" undertaking. This inference is not drawn from social science about the impact of school integration on children. That research is in a chaotic and unhelpful state,[2] and is, in any case, nearly irrelevant. We will here assume, and in fact believe, what has not been demonstrated by science—that the majority of children have benefited from integration. The truth is that this supposed benefit has been but a supplementary rationalization of the policy. The driving force has been a moral imperative fueled by guilt, not a pedagogical proposition.[3] As a consequence, the achievement of integration has been deemed worth the unknown costs to individual children of all races.

We conclude that children have been unnecessarily and imprudently treated as objects to be used and not as persons to be protected. We draw this inference from two items of incontestable common sense. One is the significant differences among children in their capacities, perceptions, and educational needs; the other is the blindness of the current school integration techniques to those differences. When the judiciary is forced to confront and remedy school segregation committed by adults, the solution employed has typically ignored the ages, experience, school behavior, and academic and emotional needs of the children who are reshuffled, as well as the characteristics of the school and community to which or from which any particular child is sent. The transition from segregation has largely been attempted by a mere reversal of the traditional order. Formerly, in offending districts North and South, the child had been thrust by law into a specific segregated school; he is now thrust into a specific integrated school.

School officials do not consult individually with the families to be affected by the programs. The judges and school administrators make no inquiry whether the child or his parents prefer one integrated school over another. Nor does the law seek volunteers to integrate yet other schools beyond the zone of compulsion. This is not because the families are incompetent; nor is it because these officials lack the time and resources to make the sensitive decisions that individual differences would require (though they do lack them). On the contrary, their very objective is to make integrative racial assignment routine and impersonal and to ensure desired ratios in the schools by closing the door to families seeking a transfer from an assigned school on educational or other grounds. As a result, potentially better assignments for the particular child are simply disregarded.

Of course, the traditional policy of neighborhood assignment is no different in this respect; it is at least equally insensitive to individual needs. Compulsory neighborhood schools are based on a wide variety of corporate and social interests; administrative simplicity and transportation costs are the most obvious. Ordinarily no inquiry is made whether the individual child is served best by the assignment, and frequently he is not. Under either a neighborhood policy or compulsory busing for integration, to describe the assignment process as one adopted for the best interest of individual children is hypocritical. Obviously this is not to suggest that assignment by race for the purpose of disestablishing dual school systems is a moral or social evil.

EVALUATING THE SUCCESS OF FORCE

In the first generation after *Brown* v. *Board*, [4] force has been the principal instrument of desegregation. Choice has been little favored even as a supplement which could extend the range of integration. Private fancies have always been irrelevant to public school assignment; they remain so.

How well has this approach worked? Inadequacies of data and definitional uncertainties plague the attempt to discuss the effectiveness of efforts to integrate the schools. To begin with, data are usually based on reports from the schools themselves and may reflect incentives either to exaggerate or to minimize the pace of integration. Conclusions also vary depending on whether one looks at segregation among districts, within districts, or within schools. In addition, whatever the unit of analysis, the particular definition of segregation selected may determine one's picture of the world. Thus, segregation can appear to be more or less extensive depending on whether one counts the proportion of black children who are enrolled in 90 to 100 percent black schools or the proportion of the average black child's schoolmates who are white. It would be possible truthfully to report that at the end of a five-year period fewer blacks attended "black" schools but that the average black pupil had fewer white schoolmates; does that put segregation on the increase or the decline?

Whatever the measures used, all indicate that most blacks still attend predominantly black schools, and white students attend schools predominantly white.[5] Moreover, a number of studies suggest that the pace of integration has slowed and in a number of places has actually been reversed in recent years. A primary explanation is that whites are migrating from the city to the suburbs faster than are blacks and that urban whites who die or move to other parts of the country are seldom replaced by other whites. Using the percentage of black students attending majority white schools as the standard, Coleman found that in nine of the fourteen largest Northern school districts integration declined between 1968 and 1971.[6] Coleman also reports further disheartening news when integration is measured in terms of the proportion of whites in the "average black child's" school. Although a small increase in integration did occur nationally between 1968 and 1972, the regional patterns put the future in considerable doubt. During that period, integration in the Southeast region, where total segregation had previously been enforced by law, contributed substantially to the positive national figures. In the New England, Middle Atlantic, and East North Central regions, however, there was as much or more segregation in 1972 than in 1968.

There is no doubt that within-district integration has been slowed in many instances by bureaucratic design or neglect. Moreover, we have recent indications that the judiciary will no longer insist on full desegregation in offending Northern and Western districts, as the Supreme Court has retreated from its former position that discrimination in any one part of a district justifies a districtwide integration remedy.[7] Now plaintiffs must show that the racial isolation of which they complain was "caused" by unconstitutional conduct. Yet most within-district racial isolation in schools today is explainable in terms of segregated housing patterns and the assignment of children on the basis of proximity of residence. This kind of segregation might be alleviated even without court orders by busing within the district, imaginative revamping of school attendance zones, the location of new schools, and the choice of which old schools to close; but this is possible only as long as a sufficient number of whites continue to reside in the district and attend its public schools. Whatever the reasons, demographic trends make this unlikely in many places. Between 1960 and 1970, the proportion of blacks as a total of the suburban population remained stable at 5 percent, while the black population in the central cities rose from 16 to 21 percent.[8] The United States Commission on Civil Rights has predicted that if there is no reversal of the present city-to-suburb migration trends, by the year 2000 only 25 percent of the central city population will be white and some cities will be essentially all black;[9] its report for the Bicentennial year praising the success of desegregation in many communities does not modify this estimate.[10] The problem is magnified when it comes to school enrollments, since many of the white families who do stay in the city can, in effect, flee the public school environment by placing their children in private schools open to, but beyond the means of, most blacks. Moreover, a disproportionate number of the whites in the city are old or have no school-age children.

Civil rights advocates often argue that effectively eliminating existing school district lines through metropolitan busing is the only way to bring about school integration in many areas. This solution has been the subject of litigation affecting metropolitan Detroit, Wilmington, Indianapolis, and Louisville. In the Detroit case the Supreme Court held that the federal courts do not have the power to order multidistrict remedies unless there is proof that the school district lines were drawn in a racially discriminatory manner.[11] Predicting the course of metropolitan integration through judicial action is tricky and must account for differences in time and place. In the Wilmington case the Supreme Court allowed a metropolitan busing order of the lower court to stand.[12] It is, however, obvious that the Court has little relish for the encounter with interdistrict *de facto* segregation in the major population centers. We would be surprised if that posture soon changed to the advantage of the integrationists. In July 1977 the Court issued several opinions which emphasize that challengers bear the burden of proving segregative intent. In the *Dayton* case the majority opinion laconically understates the impact: "Findings as to the motivations of multimembered public bodies are of necessity difficult."[13]

Perceiving the unlikelihood of metropolitan solutions, strong integrationists have themselves begun to doubt the pragmatic value of compulsory busing within the district. They fear that in many cities "success" in that enterprise would be largely pyrrhic, as the exodus of whites might thereby be accelerated. Whether compulsory busing for racial balance aggravates the problem of white exodus seems anyone's guess; the statistics on residential change do not, by themselves, explain what motivates families to leave the city. The white diaspora could be nothing more than a continuation of a twentieth-century American trend for families to move to less congested areas as soon as they become economically secure. In any event, so long as attendance at public school is linked to district residence and the relative mobility of the races remains unchanged, hopes for integration in many cities are slim.

Although the courts choose to remain aloof, state and local legislative bodies are free to form metropolitan school districts. However, such consolidation seldom promises any benefit to the suburbs other than the achievement of racial integration; given the fiscal and human costs plus varying degrees of racial prejudice, such consolidations are politically unlikely. Survey data collected in late 1972 by the Civil Rights Commission indicate that, while almost 70 percent of the American public favors racially integrated schools, a large majority oppose the use of compulsory busing to attain them.[14]

If we want to use the schools to achieve the societal goal of integration, obviously we need new strategies consistent with political reality and with the Supreme Court's view of its role.

INTEGRATION UNDER CONDITIONS OF CHOICE

Those who oppose family choice of schools argue that if white migration from the city is not now a flight from school integration, the opportunity for the ordinary family to choose a school would make it so. Such a shift in policy, they say, would be interpreted by whites as an invitation to escape to whiter public schools, perhaps in the suburbs, or to new private schools catering to whites. Any answer to such a melancholy prediction is speculative; the way to find out how families would act is to try. Yet we should register our own optimism in this regard and explain its basis.

Many white and black families currently in segregated schools would like integrated education for their children and, given the choice, would select it. This is all the more likely to occur if families enjoyed the right to select the school at which the integration takes place. If choice permitted some white children to "escape" to suburban schools, black children could do the same. Moreover, perhaps the only way to achieve the cooperation and positive involvement of white suburbanites in integration is to open their schools to urban blacks who wish to join them. Conversely, the ability to select a school of the family's choice may keep more whites living in the city and even draw others back. They are not likely to choose predominantly nonwhite schools, but may quite happily choose integrated ones.

Integration that occurs by choice is stable and enduring. Indeed, the only intelligible meaning of "stability" is that those involved at the very least accept whatever integration has been achieved. Even "forced" systems of integration depend on choice for whatever stability they achieve; they are "voluntary" in the minimal sense that families who retain the bare and painful option to move from the district choose not to do so. Their decision to remain can be fairly viewed as a stabilizing act. Of course, the greater the degree of choice by which any integration is achieved, the greater its stability.

Family choice plans should promote more stable integration for the healthy reason that they expand the question of what school a particular child should attend beyond purely racial considerations to include the broader issue of the family's educational preferences. Ironically, integration might become more successful as families think relatively less about race and more about teachers, curriculum, and style. Furthermore, with choice it would be possible to turn to good use the individual tastes of minority families. For example, some blacks might prefer that their children attend schools with whites of a distinctive culture or social outlook or schools where black students comprise a larger (or smaller) proportion than they represent in the metropolitan area. Plans that rely exclusively on compulsion cannot harness the stabilizing influence of such preferences.

In the absence of experience with choice, factual predictions of family behavior must be mostly speculation. However, a few programs providing forms of open enrollment among public schools have been tried. The experience in these plans is consistent with the view that when choice is truly voluntary white families do not typically flee integrated schools, blacks seek them in substantial numbers, and (given certain conditions and regulations) choice promotes integration. To be sure, spurious open enrollment and "freedom of choice" plans have been used to preserve all-white schools;[15] and, in some instances by administrative neglect, blacks have lacked full information about the opportunities. However, where minimally implemented, voluntary integration not only has achieved some physical mixing but has mobilized community support in a way that contrasts sharply to the bitter polarization often generated by exclusive reliance on mandatory busing.[16]

Though no serious statistical studies have been undertaken, there are a number of suggestive examples. Two are from Northern California. Richmond, east of San Francisco Bay, is a rather large unified school district that comprises a number of cities.[17] The enrollment in 1968/69 was 44,000 students and in 1975/76, 35,000 students. In 1968/69, blacks, Asians, and Chicanos constituted 41 percent of that population; in 1975/76, 44 percent. Housing is substantially segregated, and the schools have historically mirrored that pattern. In 1969/70 the district inaugurated a program of voluntary transfer, with free transportation. Essentially it encouraged those transfers that would increase integration in the sense of moving each school toward the districtwide proportion of minorities. In the first year 1,105 students transferred, and in six years the number steadily increased to 2,474, despite the drop in total enrollment. About 200 of the transfers were white. As a result of the transfers, some schools have significant numbers of minorities where there were few before, and a few formerly minority-dominant schools now have a substantial proportion of whites.

Sequoia Union lies twenty miles south of San Francisco.[18] It is exclusively a high school district with an enrollment of about 12,000—9,000 white and 3,000 minority, mostly black. Most of the black population lives in one community, East Palo Alto; one of the district's six high schools, Ravenswood, is located there. Ravenswood was 94 percent black in 1970/71; the five other high schools ranged from 70 to 100 percent white. In 1971/72 the school district developed Ravenswood as a "magnet" school and encouraged white students from the other five high schools to transfer in and blacks to transfer out. Transportation was provided. In 1971/72 500 white students transferred to Ravenswood; with transfers out the black cadre fell to 51 percent. The transfers out effected substantial integration (from 12 to 30 percent minority) of the five other schools.

The subsequent pattern of voluntary shifts in Sequoia Union was complex and was affected by many factors, including a sharp drop in district enrollment apparently unrelated to school policy. Ultimately, it was decided to close Ravenswood altogether and to permit the students from East Palo Alto to choose among the remaining five schools under limitations which would maintain integration in each. In its last year of operation, 1975/76, Ravenswood had a minority population of 66 percent. The closing was generally opposed by the black families using Ravenswood, and a suit was filed to try to prevent it. East Palo Alto children now were required to bus to the five predominantly white high schools of the district. At one of the five considerable racial tension and upset has been reported.

The Minneapolis school district employs a transfer rule in one part of the district which attempts to go beyond body-mixing.[19] All families are given the choice among educational styles. The program locates three kinds of educational alternatives on various sites; families can choose to attend a traditional school, an open-classroom school, or a team-taught nongraded school. Every student is bused to the school of his first choice unless the integration criterion employed by the district requires him to attend his second or even third choice. So far, however, minorities are well distributed among the schools in that part of the district. Of course, Minneapolis is a far cry from Chicago or New York; its minority population, though heavily concentrated by residence, is miniscule by comparison. One of the curiosities of the Minneapolis experience is that in 1970 the district had rejected a "voucher" experiment, fearing that choice might increase racial separation.

There are other cities—Rochester, Portland, Milwaukee, Evanston—in which the experience with voluntary transfers has been satisfactory in terms of integration. At one time Rochester, relying on voluntary transfers, placed nearly 22 percent of its black children from minority-dominated attendance areas in integrated schools.[20] Evanston had a substantial white waiting list for admission to a formerly all-black institution reopened as a magnet school.[21] Even troubled Boston has for several years sent a few thousand volunteer blacks to white suburban districts which have made places available under the "METCO" program.[22]

Most important, we know of no instance in which a good-faith program has diminished integration. Of course, in no district has the number of students attending schools outside the neighborhood been very large as a result of voluntary transfers. This alone could account for the integrationists' hostile reactions to voluntary plans; they are viewed, perhaps properly, as the grudging concession of administrations opposed to integration. The point of the examples is not that these districts have done "enough." For all we know they are in other respects in flagrant disregard of the Constitution; indeed, a number of these districts—Richmond and Sequoia Union in California, Minneapolis, and Milwaukee, to name a few—have been the subject of a variety of civil rights lawsuits.[23] The lesson is that, even under difficult conditions, voluntarism has been relatively successful. There are families willing to make substantial sacrifices for integrated education. If those sacrifices could be reduced and the opportunities for individual choice expanded, this first wave of social pioneers might have company.

EXISTING LEGAL INCENTIVES TO INTEGRATION BY CHOICE

Perhaps the primary fear about integration by choice is that whites will collaborate to exclude blacks. This is a genuine risk, and we now consider what the law can do to prevent it. Without plunging into technical doctrine, we will try in this section to provide a rough sense of the existing law that would apply to discrimination by participating schools. In the succeeding section, we will describe new legislative models of "affirmative action"—particularly rules regarding enrollment—that might be adopted as part of a system of family choice. We are convinced that legal structures, existing and imaginable, could significantly affect the capacity of any system based on choice to advance racial integration.

Public School Integration. We will first consider how the law might affect segregation in public education, given the adoption of a voluntary assignment scheme. Plainly, under existing law "public schools of choice" could not discriminate on the basis of race. As a general proposition, however, at least under the federal Constitution, the existence of racially imbalanced—even uniracial—public schools does not amount to unlawful racial discrimination in the absence of governmental action promoting the separation.[24] Hence, where assignment is left wholly to individuals, any resulting *de facto* racial segregation would not be unconstitutional.

Hard experience, however, has exposed a broad range of informal devices that frustrate individual preferences for integrated education. In addition to racial manipulation of admissions, subtler forms of racism could both harm black children who enroll in a particular school and discourage them from doing so. For example, schools could discriminate in expulsions, class assignments, grading, counseling, and similar educational functions. These "second-generation" discrimination problems occur in public schools even today, perhaps particularly in those coercively desegregated by law.[25] The victims can employ political and legal responses, and this would remain true under choice. In any event such practices will be discouraged by the Supreme Court's decision in 1975 that the offending officials are liable to students for money damages under federal law.[26] Nevertheless, abuses are impossible to eliminate and should be expected to continue under a system of choice, even though we predict that on the whole self-selected integration would tend to diminish such practices. As is now true, private misbehavior could give particular schools informal reputations as places in which minorities (or whites) are not welcome. The law is helpless to prevent this whether or not choice is the policy. However, choice may at least make private racism more nearly bearable where a selection of popular integrated schools is available and where the rights of families choosing any school are vigorously defended. Moreover, the provision of choice may in itself temper the hostility of many whites.

The general proposition that the Constitution tolerates self-chosen racial isolation in public schools must be qualified. Many school systems that in the past discriminated by law on the basis of race have not yet disestablished their dual system to the satisfaction · of the courts.[27] These systems probably would not be entitled to adopt a plan based exclusively on choice if its operation resulted in a significant number of all-black or all-white schools. The Supreme Court has made it clear that free choice alone does not correct official segregation.[28] Nor should it; where blacks historically have been formally excluded, it is risky to presume that their choices have become truly free, at least where the selections are in fact segregative in their effect.

This does not mean that school districts with a record of unlawful segregation could never allow choice to anyone; nor does it imply that the judiciary should shy away from limited choice plans as part of desegregation decrees. The permissible role of voluntarism has never been clarified. Here, for purposes of describing the potential integrative uses of choice, we are willing to assume that the constitutional latitude is narrow—for example, that it would forbid any choice that diminished integration. This would still leave room for experimentation with a number of untried but promising judicial techniques. Some might be relatively simple. For example, rather than assigning students by computer, those families selected for busing to public schools outside the neighborhood could be given their choice among schools previously dominated by children of another race.

Perhaps more important, there would often be good reason to include private schools in the desegregation plans of public systems. Consider the Detroit example. Having found no state responsibility for the segregated demography of white suburban systems surrounding the central city, the Supreme Court refused to allow judicial imposition of a metropolitan busing solution.[29] As a consequence, the city has been left to desegregate itself by redeploying in its own schools the district's student population, now predominantly black. The apparent futility of that effort could be tempered by the employment of existing and future private schools in and around Detroit as agents of integration. Private schools now serve many Detroit children, white and black, who can afford them. Their tuition is generally less than the amount spent per pupil in the public schools. The federal district court might order the city district to provide black families a grant equal to tuition and the costs of transport to a nondiscriminatory private school. It might also make such grants available to Detroit blacks willing to travel outside the district to attend *public* schools that were willing to accept them.[30] The order could be coupled with intra-Detroit busing to integrate those whites still in public schools with a stable percentage of minority children. This complex solution would be incapable by itself of altering the basic pattern of a largely black Detroit public school system—unless the existing private and parochial schools rose to the occasion by supplying more space; unless new private schools formed to increase the number of places; unless the state became interested enough to help Detroit with the tuition; and unless some of the surrounding public schools found it efficient to fill unused space with visitors.

This easy talk overlooks a thousand difficulties. However, so long as no direct solution appears for the ills of our several Detroits, a court forced to draft an order might do worse than combine compulsory and voluntary solutions. We predict that the Supreme Court would approve a judicially created choice system where the objective is integration and the conditions imposed are intelligently conceived. Certainly if a plan were limited to integrating schools unreachable by judicial compulsion, it would be difficult for the Court to

object absent some separate constitutional barrier. This
conclusion is supported by the Court's approval in 1977 of
the latest court-ordered remedy for Detroit, which requires
remedial and compensatory programs to be provided for school
children subject to past segregation.[31] The broad discretion
thereby granted to the district court plainly should extend
to the solution we propose.

The question of choice in districts which, like Detroit, are
presently undergoing judicial desegregation, should be distinguished from the issue that eventually will arise where a
formerly segregated—but now officially desegregated—district wishes to shift in whole or part to a regime of individual
choice. The Supreme Court has said that prior segregation
will have been "remedied"at some point and that involuntary
assignment by race to produce integration will no longer be
required;[32] but the Court has not yet indicated clearly when
that point occurs, or what assignment policies would thereafter
be acceptable. Its 1976 decision in a case involving the
Pasadena School District leaves the matter for future resolution.[33] Presumably the Court will insist on a policy preserving
hope for continued integration. In many instances a gradual
withdrawal of compulsion would seem the most promising
route to a stable and self-regulating system. Under judicial
scrutiny such districts should be allowed at an early point
to experiment in a limited way with choice, as by designating
certain schools (perhaps previously all-white schools) as places
from which students may transfer into new and varied educational programs of their choice.

Private School Integration. The principal fear about the use
of choice for racial exclusion is that choice will stimulate
more private white academies of the sort operating in substantial numbers in the South since desegregation. This is possible,
but unlikely. Where a range of choice among good schools
is available, the segregation academies should have progressively diminishing appeal both to teachers and to the families
who seek them. As insurance, there are several effective legal
handles with which to discourage racial discrimination by
participating private schools.

For years after the law began to desegregate public facilities,
it was the common belief that private schools remained at
liberty to discriminate as they chose; today this proposition
must be closely qualified. It is probably true that the mere

existence of independent segregation academies—and even their capacity to satisfy state attendance laws—does not offend the Constitution: Such schools are sufficiently distinct from the state to escape the reach of the Fourteenth Amendment's equal protection clause, which is the doctrinal handle for the attack on governmental racism.[34] Yet it does not necessarily follow that such schools are insulated from the power of Congress to legislate against racial discrimination. According to the Supreme Court, that is precisely what Congress did in 1868 in a civil rights act since embodied in section 1981 of title 42 of the United States Code.[35] Section 1981 declares that all persons, regardless of race, have the same rights to make and enforce contracts. Since enrollment in private school involves a contract, section 1981 applies, and the Court has held that—with perhaps a few exceptions—minority children refused admission on racial grounds by private schools may have valid claims to money damages and injunctive relief. Section 1981 thus may provide a potent weapon against participating private schools that might hope to discriminate.

Furthermore, many private schools set themselves up as nonprofit, hence tax exempt, organizations; undoubtedly many schools in a choice plan would do the same. Such schools are required to seek tax-exempt status from the Internal Revenue Service[36] and are thereby subject to regulations which the I.R.S. has adopted under its authority to make rules within the general framework of the tax laws passed by Congress. At present the I.R.S. rules not only withhold tax exemption from schools which racially discriminate, but also place an affirmative burden on the school to prove that it does not so discriminate. More particularly, the rules provide,

> A school must establish that it has a racially nondiscriminatory policy as to students by providing in its charter, by-laws, resolution of its governing body, or other governing instrument that it will not discriminate against applicants and students on the basis of race.
> The school may use any method to publicize initially its racially nondiscriminatory policy so long as it effectively accomplishes the end of making the policy known to all racial segments of the general community served by the school. A school cannot limit the scope of its promotional activities to a specific geographical area if such a limitation precludes any racial segment of the general community in which the school is located from being made aware of the availability of the school.[37]

Assuming that this rule is valid, the Revenue Service would give tax-exempt schools a significant additional incentive to observe the rights of minorities that section 1981 guarantees.

Title VI of the 1964 Civil Rights Act, which applies to all programs or activities receiving federal funds, represents yet another statutory prohibition of discrimination.[38] Assuming that federal funds now provided to public school districts would remain available to schools participating in a family choice scheme (or that Congress would so direct), violations of Title VI would threaten the forfeiture of all federal moneys by the school, or even by the entire participating public entity (such as the state authorizing the experiment). The potential loss of funds gives the school an important incentive not to violate the rules, and gives the public agency motivation to police the system carefully. Furthermore, the Supreme Court, in at least one case, has allowed private parties to enforce Title VI in federal courts, awarding them injunctive relief as a remedy for discrimination.[39]

Finally, and perhaps of greatest significance, once a private school becomes part of the choice plan and the state finances the tuition payments of its students, this "state action" may well bring the school within the reach of the Fourteenth Amendment. Discrimination thus becomes a constitutional as well as a legislative problem. Existing legal theory suggests that if a school receives governmental support beyond general municipal services such as police and fire protection, this official involvement triggers constitutional protection for its students and applicants against discrimination, segregation, or exclusion by race. While the financial aid in any scholarship scheme would go to the family and only indirectly to the school, this does not seem to matter. A recent Supreme Court decision which stopped the State of Mississippi from giving textbooks to students attending private schools that excluded blacks illustrates the point that no public dollars can be used to help support private discrimination in education.[40] Once a violation of constitutionally protected rights is established, a range of remedies becomes available, including the right to challenge violations in private actions before the courts.

The impact of all these rules for punishing and constraining the misbehavior of private schools could be substantial, but their number and variety may exaggerate their killing power. In practice it is painfully cumbersome to bring the law to bear on offending institutions for their particular sins even when both individuals and government can initiate enforcement. Often the necessary procedures consume years, and the persons injured by exclusion or discrimination do not have years to wait before pursuing their education. Also, proving subtle forms of discrimination can be extremely difficult if schools have admissions criteria that can be manipulated so as to have the same effect as a forthright racist policy. In a comprehensive system of family choice, what may be needed are administrative controls and incentives that affect the school admissions apparatus even before the child is ready to apply. We turn now to consider the forms such systems might take.

FUTURE LEGISLATIVE DESIGNS FOR INTEGRATION

Maximum liberty rarely lies in the mere removal of official barriers. Indeed, it may necessitate new barriers. In education as elsewhere, one person's choice may depend on the restriction of another's. The family's choice to enroll can depend on the school's and other families' lack of choice to exclude. The constraints on admission policy and other devices described further on fall most directly on institutions, not persons; but it would be false to belittle the impact on individuals, both those who operate or teach in the schools and families preferring the kind of school which would be ineligible for subsidy.

Regulation to prevent or limit segregation can vary widely in its overall effects on the liberty of various persons. We will suggest three approaches that singly or in combination could produce integration beyond that obtainable through reliance on existing law. Each would have a somewhat different impact on the range of freedom enjoyed by schools, families, and students.

First, the plan might provide that wherever a school has room, all children not disqualified by relevant nonracial characteristics (age, physical abnormality, and so forth) are entitled to admission. This would strip the school of control over integration and place it in the hands of the users. Problems would arise only as to schools with more applicants than places; the simplest legislative model for that kind of situation would require random selection—in effect, a lottery—among applicants to each school. Under such rules, the state could easily run the entire admissions process. This approach has the virtue of utter neutrality. Its impact on integration would depend, of course, on the racial character of the applicant pool attracted by each school. Parallel regulation could further open the system by forbidding narrow recruitment policies. This enthronement of the consumer would entail the sacrifice of the school's right to select on the basis of nonracial factors important to them—for example, talent and interest. When we take up nonracial admission criteria in Chapter 8, we will argue that the elimination of such factors from admission decisions is a reasonable price of the expansion of consumer choice quite apart from racial considerations.

A second technique is to mandate minimum percentages of minority students. A school which, for example, failed for three years to achieve some minimum nonwhite enrollment— say, 10 percent—would be ineligible for future participation. Schools would thus be stimulated to affirmative action to ensure the necessary minority cadre. Note that as phrased this requirement would not apply to schools that are segregated all-minority schools; its purpose would be only to integrate otherwise all-white schools.

In setting the required minority enrollment percentage, the state in fairness and prudence would have to take note of the mix of the population from which the schools might realistically draw. In Minneapolis, for example, a rule of even 10 percent minimum black enrollment would mean that very few schools could ever qualify. In some cases it would be necessary for the minimum to vary throughout the state.

As a variant of this technique, the state could, of course, adopt a minimum proportion of both white and minority children as the criterion of school participation—in other words, a minimum integration standard. Such a rule assumes that, irrespective of their desires or special personal characteristics, homogeneous racial grouping is never helpful for minority children. It would also assume that those minority schools that try but fail to attract whites should close, even when the minority families supporting the school wish the school to continue as it is. Such a policy is not one we would promote.

Third, the state could use dollar incentives, "integration bonuses," to stimulate racial mixing. A number of payment schemes are imaginable. For example, the child's subsidy could be made more valuable if the school he chooses meets minimum integration standards. Alternatively, the value of the bonus could vary directly with some measure of integration; viewed from the other side, a relative lack of integration could trigger a financial penalty, although not total disqualification. A substantial bonus (penalty) would discourage families from choosing segregated schools and encourage schools to integrate.[41]

These three techniques—consumer choice (with random selection of buyers where demand exceeds supply), disqualification for nonintegration, and financial bonuses—can be combined in various ways. For example, schools could be required to meet a minimum integration standard, but could also be given financial rewards for additional integration. The random selection model could be modified to permit, encourage, or require a school to favor the minority applicants in its applicant pool. Our own preference is for the school to favor whatever racial group happens to be the minority within its existing student body. That policy could be implemented with the following rule:

> In cases in which a school has more applicants than it has places, admissions shall be random among all applicants to the school, except that the school shall first select at random from each racial group constituting a minority of its applications a number of students not to exceed 15 percent of available spaces.

Some might prefer that the schools be given the right to choose particular minority candidates to fill the 15 percent of their openings. Plainly, many variations are possible.

The practical effect of such techniques would depend on local demography, the history of racial attitudes in the given market, the character of the schools, and other variables. Given a well-designed system of transportation and information (to be considered in Part IV), it is entirely possible that a choice system employing affirmative action rules could initiate a process of stable integration. Obviously this would depend in large measure on blacks and other minorities perceiving the opportunity and being willing to seek an integrated experience. Whether a significant number of such families exist is something that cannot be demonstrated in advance of a substantial set of experiments, though as noted the experience so far with voluntary public school integration is encouraging.

A final related problem is the racial segregation of school personnel. Segregated teaching staffs may encourage racially segregated student bodies. We assume that participating schools would at a minimum be under legal obligation to hire on a racially neutral basis. It is not clear, however, that

an all-minority staff is in every imaginable case hurtful to
the ultimate values informing an integrationist policy—for
example, pupil satisfaction and achievement. Recognizing this,
the law may leave some room for the schools to maneuver.
For example, if Muslim schools are permitted to hire on the
basis of candidates' competency to teach the school's curriculum and message, that competency might be confined
principally to black teachers. If, however, it were deemed
important by the legislature to have all faculties racially mixed,
it would not be difficult either to require a minimum level
of faculty integration or to increase the value of the students'
grants where the school assembles an integrated faculty.[42]

IF WE DON'T ALL INTEGRATE

If America's schools do not become, by some standard, racially
integrated, would our society have failed? For us the answer
depends on the reasons that universal integration did not
happen. If the reason is that white America has deliberately
arranged it so, then by our accounting society will have failed
the test of justice. If the reason integration did not occur
is that well-intentioned government has been insufficiently
experimental and creative, the same conclusion follows.
However, if government has established and consistently
striven to maintain the conditions of free choice for individuals, we could not condemn those among us of any color who
have chosen by racial clustering in their education to preserve
special racial links they may value for reasons of their own.
These persons bear no duty to justify their preference; indeed,
such deeply personal values could scarcely be communicated
to those who do not already share them. For us it is enough
that someone holds these views.

One could imagine a time when the inheritors of "Western"
culture—assume them exclusively white—would constitute
a puny splinter among the peoples of the world. This cadre
of survivors might cling to a unique interpretation of human
experience and claim as a human right the opportunity to
educate themselves in that ancient tradition. We would hope
that their claim would be intelligible to the larger society
of their time, and it would be if that society shared with
its minorities a commitment to the sanctity of individual and
group belief. We understand such a commitment to be a
fundamental and defining feature of our own society. The
choice of racial separation, so long as it is free, should be

solemnly respected, even if the motivation of those (including ourselves) who promote this principle deserves close scrutiny.

CONCLUSION: ON USING THE CHILD

There is reason to believe that family choice could further both consensus and racial integration. This is consoling in view of our conclusion in Chapter 4 that, beyond a socially determined minimum, the interest of the child is generally best served by family dominion. We would be uneasy if we were forced to choose between one policy that advanced social goals and another that best served the interests of individual children.

This point deserves a last word. The use of persons who are physically weak, economically dependent, or politically disenfranchised as instruments of the strong always raises issues of fairness. And that is a serious problem with the existing structure of education. To suggest that in modern times social awareness and legislative intervention have greatly improved the lot of the child is no answer. That may or may not be true; but, however much the general affluence, child labor laws, and the welfare state may have assisted the young, to the extent that our society still uses children for its collective ends the fairness question remains.

Hence, society has the duty to be skeptical of broad policy measures that treat children as a uniform class. Applying this skepticism to the integration issue, we conclude that if the only practical options were compulsory busing for integration and compulsory neighborhood schools, we would prefer the former. Nevertheless, society should continually reexamine such apparent dilemmas. Using force and only force to mix children by race seems a failure of political imagination and a problem of justice, however convenient it may be to the adult regime. When it comes to using children to create a basic national consensus, society should be at least as sparing of duress. The legitimacy of government concern and involvement is unquestioned, but the quest should continue for political instruments more likely to be harmonious with the interest of the individual child.

It is plain, however, that treating the best interest of the child as an individual matter is not always possible, since that interest may lie in association with another person whose interest is to avoid him. Thus, when it comes to exclusion on the basis of race, it is inevitable that the admission rules must favor children in some families over what is seen by other families as the best interest of their own children. Even in the most thoroughly "voluntaristic" system, a number of such conflicts will occur with respect to enrollment rules; we attend more carefully to these impasses in Chapter 8.

Some seem to suppose that such conflicts could be avoided altogether by treating children as a group—that we could thereby eliminate every imaginable form of discrimination and achieve the best for all children. It is, of course, possible to treat children as a group; indeed, that is our common practice in education. It should not be imagined, however, that this avoids conflict or provides the best for all; it simply disguises the injury to competing interests by pretending they do not exist. It falsely assumes that children have identical needs.

Other educational critics with similar social instincts take the egalitarian theme in yet another direction. They recognize that children are different but would resolve their potential conflicts by aggressively favoring the interests of some over the interests of others. They complain that our society rewards "better" genes and environment and that this is unfair to those less favored by fortune. So far we tend to agree. We part company, however, when they infer from this a governmental duty to retard the development of the luckier children in order to close the opportunity gap fortune has created. Under this egalitarian regime, talent and home advantage would be visited with specific handicaps, including an inferior opportunity for education. This could, for example, be reflected in a system of choice that excluded the advantaged from options deemed superior.

A commitment to equality at the deliberate expense of the development of individual children seems to us the final corruption of whatever is good in the egalitarian instinct. It is a dog-in-the-manger morality of the most wicked and degrading sort. We concede that lifetime incomes should be made more equal through taxation and other forms of redistribution, but deliberately to deprive a child of his human potential as a way of achieving such equality represents the most vicious exploitation of a helpless minority.

IV
DESIGNING THE
INSTRUMENTS OF CHOICE

He who would do good to another,
must do it in minute particulars.

—WILLIAM BLAKE,
"Jerusalem"

Chapter 8

THE PROCESS OF CHOICE

That's not a regular rule:
You invented it just now.

LEWIS CARROLL,
Alice in Wonderland

Until specific regulatory structures are debated, the rhetoric of choice cloaks a good deal of conflict among reformers. Part IV describes the major administrative, fiscal, and equity conflicts among those purporting to speak for choice. It presents alternative solutions in distilled form and indicates those which are consistent with our own values. The discussion is divided into four chapters. In Chapter 8 we take up the process of choice—how the child and his schooling are to be matched, considering the sometimes conflicting interests of family and school and among families. Chapter 9 inquires who the providers of schools may be and how they should be governed. Chapter 10 looks at educational style—what life in school might be like. Finally, in Chapter 11, we explore the nature of the subsidy, the forms in which education could be state supported. By illustrating the various policy questions and their alternative resolutions, Part IV should demonstrate that the employment of choice, though requiring administrative skill and wisdom, is, as a technical matter, wholly feasible.

MATCHING THE CHILD AND HIS SCHOOLING

The broad theme of this chapter is the ways in which the child and his educational experience can be linked. In good part this becomes a matter of enrollment rules; however, the problem of consumer information is also explored here. We will assume in this chapter that the state will financially support the child's attendance at all kinds of schools, private and public.

In trying to imagine how a family choice plan would work, it is too simplistic to focus solely on giving each family what it wants for its children. In some situations interests will clash. One potential conflict is between the school provider and the family; the desire of providers to limit the number and kinds of children in their schools may be pitted against the applicant's desire to attend. Another conflict may arise between families; the Coonses want their children to attend school with children like the Sugarmans', but the latter want to avoid the former. These are the two major forms of discord to be reconciled in establishing enrollment policy. As long as tastes in clients and classmates differ, someone's freedom is inevitably limited. Whose should it be?

If the market for schooling were patterned after the "free" market, as it is conventionally viewed, the preference of the family would be constrained by the freedom of the school; that is, a child would be able to enroll only if the chosen school were willing to have him. Whether this power of exclusion should be eliminated is a complex issue; it requires us to examine separately three characteristics of schools— school size, admission policies, and expulsion policies. As we do so we shall weigh not only the interests of families and providers, but shall inquire how effectively educational regulation can be policed, how providers would respond to a restriction of their freedom, and what rules would be needed in behalf of children unwanted by schools.

SCHOOL SIZE

Should a school be able to limit its enrollment, or should it be required to admit all who apply? In the traditional private market, the ordinary supplier is entitled to restrict his volume. But for some suppliers society limits this right; for example, public utilities must expand to serve all comers. If individual schools were so treated, there would be some advantages. Every family could—in a certain sense—have its first choice. Such a rule also would make it unnecessary to face up to the difficult question of how applicants to schools should be screened. Moreover, it is at least imaginable that schools could live with unlimited enrollment. The California community colleges operate largely in this manner today. Most schools could probably predict the demand for their services reasonably well and plan accordingly.

Unlimited enrollment would, however, have serious drawbacks. A major concern is school style; providers might not be able to have the kind of program they wish if they were required to take all who applied. The family's concern would be similar; it would want to have a reasonably good idea of what the school it selected would be like. A popular school enrolling a hundred students one year and five hundred the next might fail to meet family expectations. Moreover, if the program must expand willy-nilly, quality would be ever at risk. Fluctuating demand would cause inefficiencies because of uncertainties about needed employees and facilities. Furthermore, because unlimited enrollment would preclude all screening, some providers would be deterred from entering the market, thereby making fewer choices available.

Enrollment ceilings, therefore, would benefit the children who actually enrolled in their first choice school. While the price of this benefit is the frustration of the families excluded for lack of space, popular schools are likely to be imitated, providing nearly equivalent second choices. Moreover, limitations on the size of enrollment do not by themselves discriminate against children on an invidious basis. Whether that occurs depends on the criteria used to admit and exclude.

Thus, on balance we conclude that the state should not interfere with the right of a school provider to put a ceiling on the size of its student body. This would apply to both private and public school managers, although the state might wish to designate some of the public schools participating in the experiment as unlimited enrollment schools. In any event, the state will have to assure each child access to a place in a public or private school.

ADMISSION POLICIES

Assuming that schools need not take all comers, we must consider methods and criteria that schools might wish to employ in making selections. Many aspects of this question have already been considered in our discussion of techniques for racial integration, and we will not reconsider all these difficult issues. There are two reasons for a school to distinguish among applicants. One is simply that the number of applicants exceeds the places available; the other is that the school prefers some applicants to others. This second reason may be relevant even where there are more places than applicants—the school may prefer having no one to having Jones. This motivation becomes all the stronger when Jones competes for the last available space with Kowalski, whom the school wishes to enroll. For the moment we will ignore the problem of making selections in schools where applications exceed available space and concentrate on the harder question of whether schools should in any case be permitted to prefer one applicant to another.

Traditional private markets again provide analogies. In America, customarily one may refuse to sell to any individual buyer; this right is circumscribed when the seller is a monopolist or a regulated industry and sometimes when the refusal is based on invidious classifications such as race or national origin. It is important to note, however, that whatever their legal right to do so, sellers of *products* usually do not refuse to sell. If their supply is limited, they sometimes favor certain regular customers or impose credit conditions; in addition, in order to build a reputation for consumer satisfaction, sellers sometimes counsel prospects against buying when the product and purchaser seem ill-suited for each other. However, the traits that prompt sellers to rebuff buyers are seldom personal. Rarely does the seller care if his buyer is smart, on the social register, or well-mannered.

By contrast, providers of certain *services*, especially personal services, do sometimes turn away business because of the individual characteristics of ready, willing, and able patrons. Finicky physicians, maids, lawyers, masseurs, podiatrists, and hairdressers are well-known examples. The reputation of providers of certain services may turn a good deal on whom they serve; the service may be outside the range of the provider's competence despite the confidence expressed by the would-be patron; the personal contact involved in providing the service may be disagreeable to the seller. Substantial sympathy supports the person who does not wish to seem just anyone's personal servant merely by having opened up his business to the public.

Even as to providers of services, however, the point should not be overemphasized. Because of the limited personal contact, dry cleaners and television repairmen, for example, seldom refuse to serve when they have the time. Moreover, even in the most personal of services, medicine, large-scale health maintenance organizations with the capacity to serve rarely turn away clients. Indeed, we suspect that, except for the most fashionable or unique services, there are few providers of anything who reject initial requests for service based on nonfinancial attributes of the would-be client. Even most landlords take the first tenant who seems reasonably certain to pay the rent. Of course, some providers refuse to serve after a bad experience with the customer, and we cannot know how many buyers avoid certain providers because the buyers assume they will be turned down.

Thus, before advocating governmental restrictions on refusals to admit students in a system of educational choice, it is important to ask what school providers would do if their right to withhold services were unrestrained. In the abstract one can say that individual school providers would be expected to enroll students based on criteria which maximize the school operators' particular objectives. In theory a school might admit all those who apply, restrict its enrollment to the first x number who wish to attend, accept only those students who meet or exceed certain criteria (academic or otherwise), select applicants by lot, or choose its students in some other way. Which pattern would be likely to emerge?

Education requires intense personal contact, suggesting some likelihood of refusals to serve; but looking at private education today, we see that—apart from individual music or language lessons and the like—the teacher having the daily contact typically does not make the decision to accept a particular person as a customer. This is because schooling is usually made available in bulk. Hence, the school may be seen as making available a package or product—much like hotels or restaurants, which generally serve all comers for whom they have room on a first-come, first-served basis. Furthermore, teachers who are finicky about their students may elect to work in places where they prefer the students who in fact attend, thus avoiding some of the problems of coerced personal service. This ability of teachers indirectly to select their clients, however, may influence school managers to cater to certain applicants and to treat schooling more as a personal service than a product.

Experience with elementary and secondary schools suggests no firm prediction about seller behavior under a system of choice. Today the public schools, by and large, admit all those in the attendance district, although a few children are excluded on the basis of their inability to benefit,[1] and some districts have established special schools with additional admission criteria.[2] Sectarian schools sometimes exclude nonbelievers; but many, particularly the Catholic schools which constitute the bulk, are willing to take substantial numbers of outsiders where space permits.[3] While most private schools probably impose informal minimum academic standards, few appear to employ complex admission criteria such as testing, prior academic achievement, talent, and family values. Of course the mere ability to pay tuition may effectively identify those who will "fit in."

Looking to higher education, the pattern of admission practices is mixed, as the California pattern illustrates. Stanford, a private institution with few constraints, applies strict admission criteria, presumably largely academic. At the other extreme the California community colleges take essentially all applicants, and proprietary postsecondary vocational schools typically admit all they have room for. Between these is the University of California, which stands ready to take as undergraduates all Californians who meet a previously announced academic standard—specifically that the applicant is among the top one-eighth of high school graduates.

This variety suggests that under a choice plan at least some elementary and secondary school providers would attempt to control more than maximum school size if given the opportunity to screen applicants. This expectation is reinforced when one considers the special features of education that increase the school's incentive to refuse particular applicants: These include student interaction and its importance to their educational experience; the weight given by employers and colleges to the school's reputation for "success"; and the fact that nonprofit institutions—which many schools would be— often pursue religious, ideological, and other special objectives unrelated to the client's ability to pay. Thus its character and quality may constitute very important aspects of a school.

In addition, while it is true that privately adopted admission rules would serve the interest of school operators, their interest would, at least, in part, reflect the preferences of their customers. Some families would see the children of others as assets or liabilities of the school, hence relevant to their own choices. A family may not want its child to go to school with children it perceives as disruptive, bigoted, stupid, or whatever. The family may seek to band together with families having children with certain characteristics it values, such as musical talent. Responding to such organized group action or the play of the market, school operators might in turn employ attendance rules catering to these wishes.

In short, if schools were unrestrained, some would give preference to students of particular kinds. Those left out would be aggrieved by a school's policy of exclusivity, either because they disagree with the criterion for inclusion or because they believe their child meets the standard. Recognizing the interests of providers and especially of other families in the school, society would have to weigh their importance against the injury to those excluded. On balance, some exclusionary policies might be thought justified.

Suppose, however, that children thought to be low in IQ, disruptive, ugly, or untalented were systematically relegated to second choices or even last resorts. This is a risk, because choice at the elementary and secondary level presents a special market problem: All children will attend some school, so there may be as much competition to avoid certain undesirables as there is to enroll students with special attractions. On this ground opponents of school control over admissions policies will argue that the right of refusal would result in pools of children that are unwanted by any of the places they would prefer. If no private providers appeared who catered to otherwise unwanted children, this could lead to enormous family frustration. Even if such providers did appear, this could lead to the establishment of special dumping-ground public and private schools, which would be sorry places indeed. While public schools of this sort presently exist in our society, they would now become highly visible and even more highly resented.

MECHANISMS FOR FAIR SELECTION

If the hope is to eliminate rather than merely to disguise such institutions of last resort, some restriction on the right of schools to refuse to serve particular persons is probably needed. Two general approaches are possible. The first is a presumption that schools should select their own students except in circumstances specified by law; the second is the counterpresumption that schools may not select among applicants by their personal characteristics except in circumstances specified by law. Logically these two approaches may be indistinguishable, but the practical differences are considerable because of the burden of proof in individual cases.

We start with the presumption that everyone is entitled

to be enrolled and consider plausible exceptions (none, of course, involving race) which would allow the school to exclude particular applicants. Given this presumption, what candidates for exception would we encounter? Let us begin with a relatively simple one. Suppose a group of families formed a small school in which they wished collectively to teach their own children. Assuming that this type of family initiative and that such intimate parent-child schooling were to be encouraged, permitting such schools to exclude others would seem fair. Otherwise the laudable initiative could be completely undermined. In a school consisting of one teacher, it also seems appropriate and fair for that teacher to select; otherwise this type of innovative and highly personal education might not materialize at all. In addition, these very small schools are likely to account for only a tiny portion of the total enrollment, pose no apparent threat to equity in the system as a whole, and would be difficult to police. Hence a special exception might here be recognized.

What about religious criteria? Would sectarian providers and believing families be unacceptably frustrated were such schools required to take all comers? As is true today, schools with a reputation for heavy religious indoctrination would be spared any significant impact of a nondiscrimination rule. If they wished to exclude nonbelievers, self-selection by applicants would solve their problems. But what of those schools now welcoming limited numbers of outsiders and often making religious study optional? Applications to these schools are likely to increase, but this could be less a problem than a solution to an existing inequity. Historically these institutions and their admission policies have often been based principally on altruism, and today the students are heavily subsidized by the private sacrifice of generous donors and low-salaried teachers. Under present fiscal arrangements it would seem incongruous if those who make such sacrifices to create, say, a Lutheran school were required to permit all comers to enjoy the private subsidy. Under a publicly financed scheme of choice, however, all this would change—in ways that are hard to predict. At a minimum, existing economic incentives to limit the number of nonbelievers admitted to sectarian schools would be substantially reduced. Many such schools under these circumstances would welcome open enrollment rules that assured nonbelievers that their religion would not stand in the way of their admission.

Whether or not the school is permitted to impose religious

criteria, constitutional questions arise. Conditioning the student grant on the child's enrollment in a school that does not discriminate on the basis of belief raises concerns about freedom of association and freedom of worship. On the other hand, permitting such discrimination by the school raises the issues of equal protection and establishment of religion. These problems are too complex to argue here, but the mere existence of the legal question should not interfere with experiments. For our part we would prefer legislation declaring the family's right to enroll in any participating school, leaving it to the school's religious character to limit the number of applications from nonbelievers. But we would not oppose experiments in which schools could establish entry requirements based on belief.

Schools seeking to specialize in one branch or type of instruction present similar problems. Sometimes, capturing pupil interest may be merely a matter of pitching the material at the right level of difficulty. Likewise, if one of the major reasons children tune out on school is lack of interest in most of the curriculum, many of them might be stimulated to learn by concentration on those offerings (art, music, drama, mechanics, advanced mathematics) which appeal to their individual tastes and talents. Furthermore, children who are gifted in a particular way—say, in music—would likely wish to attend a music school where they would have talented classmates. The same goes for children preparing for advanced placement in prestige colleges. Some exceptional children might wish to attend a school where most pupils are older than themselves; for example, a precocious eleven-year-old might wish to try junior high school. Such wishes are probably shared by school operators.

The admissions problem in such schools is not one of picking out the children with strong interest. Family choice, with counseling, should do this admirably. The problem, rather, is the identification of talent, a quality not always guaranteed by sheer interest. To what extent are the interests of providers and of those children they would select compromised by the law's forbidding all advance screening on the basis of talent? The family would, of course, sometimes overestimate the child's talent. However, we are skeptical about the competence of providers to judge ability, at least in reasonably close cases involving children they have not known before; and the experience with tracking in public schools increases our mistrust. In any event, the schools would have the opportunity to influence the decision where the facts support them. Even if the law forbade exclusion, it could allow the school to impose the taking of a test as a condition of entry. On the basis of such tests the school might be able to persuade the family in most cases of severe mismatch.

What happens if the family insists, and the child gets in over his head? It could be said that this is the family's risk and that the school should simply flunk him. But it may not be that simple. Even a school that is initially single-minded in its mission is likely to bend to the human needs of those in its charge; and too many improvident enrollments, even where rigorously handled by the school, can alter its entire character, worsening the experience of the talented. A school for budding opera singers cannot prosper when most of the students are tone deaf and have come hoping to learn from their talented peers. Moreover, the predicted impact of nonselective admissions on the ability to operate a challenging program might impede the establishment of certain kinds of new schools; and some existing academic prep schools would probably not participate unless they could do whatever selection they considered necessary to maintain their academic standards. Of course, some critics oppose the very existence of such schools, precisely because they may exaggerate the already greater lifetime opportunities of those with greater natural endowments. One need not be so egalitarian as this, however, to perceive that screening on the basis of talent can have undesirable results.

First, because determining the absence of potential is often a slippery judgment, a family that genuinely believes its child is suitably talented may very reasonably view exclusion on this basis as unfairness. Second, because of the nature of some entry tests, children of lower class families may be systematically admitted in fewer numbers to certain types of limited-focus, ability-based schools. Depending on the particular test, this class effect could be truly invidious. Third, some providers might employ entry ability tests for the very purpose of screening out the poor and certain minorities, and this would be difficult to prevent once testing were recognized as a legitimate basis of selection.

On this issue a compromise might be reached which precluded refusals to admit but which allowed schools to engage in a measure of selective recruitment and fair dissuasion of unpromising applicants. This would help the school to skew its applicant pool in the direction of the talents it seeks while leaving ultimate choice in the hands of families. Unquestionably counseling would sometimes be used to make the pupil feel not only unpromising but unwelcome, and such misbehavior would be difficult to police. If counseling created an inordinate risk of discrimination of this sort, the counseling function could be lodged exclusively in a government agency familiar with the schools' styles and academic expectations. This, however, would probably mean the sacrifice of school recruitment along with its advantages and would create another level of bureaucratic overlay. On balance perhaps the risks of leaving recruitment and counseling to the school would not be excessive. So long as schools were required to treat fairly those admitted, and so long as families were advised of their rights, implications that the child would be unwelcome would carry less force.

Other compromise solutions can be imagined for this problem. The state could, for example, allow the school to select a certain proportion of its students by announced talent criteria. Without systematic experience it is difficult to suggest the minimal proportion necessary for this purpose, but we would be surprised if a school would need to select half its places in order to assure the intended character and capacity of its student body. At least this would seem true of schools of any significant size. Something useful on this issue might be learned if schools in different experimental areas within a state were permitted to select different proportions of their students on the basis of talent.

Another solution would initially bar selection on the basis of talent. If substantial provider resistance and family unhappiness materialized in the early years, schools might thereafter be given carte blanche with respect to, say, their first fifty places and the right to select 20 percent of the balance on the basis of published criteria, the remainder to be filled at random from among all those who wished to attend. Such a rule, incidentally, would protect the small family cooperative and one-teacher schools discussed earlier.

Still other techniques are possible. A school might be permitted to reject arbitrarily a certain number of individual applicants—as with the peremptory challenges allowed in selecting juries. A fixed number of carte blanche preferences or arbitrary exclusions is attractive because of yet another problem. If schools were allowed to consider talent at all, a system for policing such decisions would be necessary. The state could scrutinize screening criteria and review applications, or it could simply allow individuals to challenge rejections and perhaps require the schools to justify their decisions. In any event, such review would be costly and difficult to administer; for small numbers it might be as well to forego regulation of the school's determination.

Finally, consider the regulation of refusals to serve by granting the school a general power to select, but proscribing decisions based on poverty, social status, IQ, talent, or whatever classifications were thought to be inappropriate. The use of certain admission criteria may be either unconstitutional or in violation of existing federal or state statutes, or simply bad policy. For example, if the federal Civil Rights Act of 1964 proved applicable to schools participating in a family choice plan, it would preclude providers from discriminating on the basis of race, color, or national origin. The equal protection clause of the Fourteenth Amendment, if it applied, might reach even further. Whether or not applicable to private providers, these legal rules provide models for policy makers.

In choosing between the two approaches to fair selection, it is crucial to consider on whom the burden of proof should fall. Who must demonstrate that the denial of an excluded person was or was not based on one of the prohibited or permitted criteria? Imposed on the applicant, the burden would often be difficult to carry and expensive even to attempt. In some cases the difficulty could be ameliorated by adopting an "effects" test; if the complainant could merely show a discrepancy between the percentage of all applicants to a school that share his relevant characteristic and the percentage that share it among successful applicants, the burden would be shifted to the school to prove that it was not selecting on the basis of the forbidden criteria.[4] This may work well with objective characteristics such as sex, in which every member of the relevant populations can be easily classified. However, if the state wishes to protect the child from exclusion based on the school's misestimate of his talent, interest, or other judgmental characteristic, an "effects" test would be useless. Once the school had gone through the motions of assessment, the applicant could seldom carry the burden of showing an unfair estimate. Therefore, if the state decides to prohibit selection on the basis of *any* judgmental characteristic, it should be willing either to put on the school the burden of proving a negative (of showing it did not use a forbidden criterion) or to ban all exclusions except for objective and acceptable reasons.

Having considered the two basic approaches and their variations, we conclude that perhaps the single most sensible balance of the interests of the child, school, and society is generally to ban refusals to serve but to give the school a small portion of its places with which it may, under minimal supervision, indulge its preferences for characteristics such as talent, interest, and possibly values. This solution is also consistent with discouraging racial discrimination as we explained in Chapter 7. Of course, we would welcome experimentation with a variety of policies.

THE MUSICAL CHAIRS PROBLEM

So long as schools are entitled to limit their enrollment, merely restricting the right of school providers to refuse service does not determine which individual students will attend. Where applications for a school exceed the spaces available, some mechanism for selection would be required, even if it were only a first-come, first-served system. Something more neutral would be desirable, however; preference by time of application would too often favor certain groups unfairly, even if it would sometimes be a reasonable indicator of family interest. The simplest neutral device would require all applications for every school to be made through the state agency administering the system. Where applications for the Jefferson School exceeded its announced capacity, this agency would make a random selection among them and inform the school who its students would be. Of course, a method for soliciting each family's alternate choices and for fairly assigning first-round losers to their second or third choice school would be developed.

Many problems remain. What should be the rule for those who come into the state or the experimental area during the course of the year or after the admission process has been completed? What about those who wish to change schools in the middle of the year? Will there be waiting list procedures? If so, should the schools control them, or should the state regulate or even administer the waiting lists? Presumably a student who attends a school one year will be given preference in the admissions process the next year, and such preference would help stabilize the school's style. Still such a preference might inhibit the growth of schools that specialize in serving students at particular ages or stages of development; families might fear that if their child attended a less than fully comprehensive school, he would encounter difficulties later in finding openings in a school of his choice. For example, a pupil finishing two years at a specialized grade 4–5 school might have a very limited selection of schools commencing at grade 6 or having openings for transfers at that level.

A choice plan must also consider what should be done about the rights of students who have been enrolled in schools already in existence when the system is introduced. Would it be necessary to give present private school students some kind of tenure in order to induce the school and its patrons to participate in the program? If so, should similar rules apply to public schools? Indeed, should the rules for public schools go even further and recognize an ongoing preference for those living in the neighborhood? These are issues a planning authority must consider and resolve one way or another before a program begins. At the same time, it should recognize that no final resolution of all these issues need be reached and that for purposes of experimentation a variety of solutions should be tried.

EXPULSIONS

Guaranteeing children access to schools is insufficient if providers can make their life inside the school miserable or can expel them on a whim. Under a conventional free market system schools—at least of the profit-seeking variety—would be unlikely to impose one-sided contracts which made students the serfs of the provider and subject to capricious expulsion. Schools would probably employ a standard contract of their own design, and consumer demand would probably require that its terms offer an attractive and secure school environment. Perhaps contracts of this sort could be relied on to protect the child even if the provider were compelled to deal with customers he would rather be rid of. We, however, are skeptical that families with unwanted children would be able to protect themselves by contract alone; enforcement would too often require litigation beyond the family's means. If the schools were successfully to push out unwanted students, this would probably mean a constant shift of the less desirable students to less desirable schools, and this shift would in turn undo in part or whole what regulated admissions had achieved. That seems intolerable.

On the other hand, when serious misbehavior by a student or his utter incapacity to cope with the work is destructive

of the school community, we think the school should have
the right through a fair process to rid itself of the problem
child. Others might disagree, believing that schools should
learn to deal with such children. Whichever view is preferred,
it should be clear that the concern is not for teachers or
principals but for children. To impose extreme restrictions
on the authority of schools would unduly expand the freedom
of one family's child to curtail the freedom of his schoolmates.
Some balance must be sought. We suggest that a school not
be permitted to flunk students out of the school for lack of
academic progress alone; as a corollary, however, it would
not be forced to promote the unsuccessful student.

These tensions between the interest of the student and the
interest of the school must be resolved, and that will require
policy judgments on two levels. First, if the school is permitted
under any circumstances to suspend, expel, require grade
repetition, or the like, the legislature or state administration
must establish *standards* confining the decision to particular
objective kinds of student failures. Many such standards will
probably be needed. In cases of misconduct, for example,
lines should be drawn between minor offenses for which
suspension is appropriate and serious misconduct justifying
expulsion. Second, the state must establish *procedures* for
determining the applicability of these standards in particular
cases. We will not repeat here our preferred standards and
procedures for each kind of case.[5] That no one set of arrangements is clearly best is illustrated by a question of crucial
importance to which there is no obvious answer: What should
be done with students who, for reasons of misbehavior or
utter inability to benefit, have been successfully excluded
from one school; do they become educational castaways, must
all other schools be open to them, or is there a middle ground?

A balanced solution to this problem might be to strip a
student who has been properly expelled of his *right* to enroll
in any participating school for one year. If during that period
no school would accept him, the state would be required
to provide him education in a special school. After the year's
exclusion he would again become as eligible as any other
child to enroll in any school unless, after notice and hearing,
an arbitrator determined that the pupil was not rehabilitated
(the burden of proof resting on the state). Even if he lost,
the pupil would remain eligible for yearly review by the
administering public agency. As a further protection, it might
be provided that if such a child were able to gain admission

to any other regular participating school, he would regain regular status except as against the originally expelling school.

The procedures today required of public schools by the due process clause of the Fourteenth Amendment provide examples relevant to many of these problems: Students have a right to tell their side of the story and to be given reasons before receiving short-term suspensions; more elaborate hearings, with the right to be represented, to cross-examine witnesses, and so on, appear to be required prior to expulsion.[6] Indeed, these procedural safeguards may represent the minimum legally required of all schools—public and private—participating in a family choice plan. The relevance of various procedural protections to the climate of freedom inside the school will be considered again in Chapter 10.

CONSUMER INFORMATION:
SUBSTANCE, DISSEMINATION, AND REGULATION

In a system with no options, ignorance might be bliss. In a system based on choice, ignorance is ruin. An effective mechanism for providing families basic information concerning available educational alternatives is crucial to the process of matching child to school. Yet unless artfully designed, information systems can themselves vitiate the variety that choice is intended to promote. It would be irony to encourage only conventional education by mandating the collection and publication solely of reading and math scores, average class size, and the number of credentialed teachers. To implement a policy of choice, the information reported to families should to the extent feasible reflect the full range of ascertainable family interests in education (including the more traditional information). In building the information system, the administering agency should survey the potential user population to determine what families wish to know about schools. This inquiry should be made a permanent part of the system; as families become used to exercising choice, they are likely to want different and additional information. Family concerns should form a principal part of the data to be gathered from the schools and disseminated.

This use of an information agency assumes that the information system would be in significant measure a government responsibility. It is possible to imagine leaving this function entirely to the market, as is today characteristic of private schools and colleges. That approach, however, seems prima facie unsuitable in the context of an educational system where private information networks could be employed to exclude unwanted families. The easiest way for a school to reestablish control over its applicant pool would be to control the list of those to whom information about that school is delivered. We believe substantial government involvement would be necessary to ensure effective dissemination to all classes of families. Private information services and advertising could, however, play significant supplemental roles.

There are costs in reporting, collating, and dispensing information, and hard choices will have to be made by agencies public and private. Furthermore, the range of school information to be included in any comprehensive publications by the public agency must be limited by consideration of bulk and reader capacity. The specific information to be required of schools could vary by region, but some items are likely to be common. These include curriculum and teaching style, the social and intellectual climate claimed by the school, the availability of support services, the commitment expected from parents, and, we suppose, achievement scores.

Beyond these, many families will want to know the system for governing the school and the process for inquiry and redress of grievances. Others will stress the present socioeconomic characteristics of the student body including patterns of income, education, and occupation for families now enrolled and for the alumni over time; these will seldom be available in any formal way, and some could be sought only at risk of offense. Scores on standard tests could be easily provided, and such items as career plans, racial and ethnic patterns, dropout rates, rates of college attendance, and the colleges attended would be manageable. Some of the socioeconomic characteristics of the staff could easily be provided—teaching training, experience, credentials, race, and perhaps any ideological commitments expected to be manifested in their teaching. Certainly the school's overall ideological commitment should be public.

An accurate picture of the financial structure of participating schools would be important to both consumer and regulator and should be exacted as a price of participation. Among the relevant items are net assets, value and character of plant, current costs, capital costs, other sources of income, the distribution of costs among school programs and personnel, and the expected rate of profit, if any. In Chapter 11 we shall indicate the possible uses to be made of such information in the economic regulation of schools.

Finally, it is conceivable that each school would also be invited to set its own criteria of success (for example, college admissions, employable vocational skills, commitment to the Baptist faith) and to report facts relevant to the evaluation of its performance by that standard.

We realize that this discussion has given casual treatment to several items of information that some regard as unmentionable in polite public circles. Test score, race, and social information about student bodies are certainly sensitive data. They are sensitive because people—for reasons good and bad—consider them important. We can understand how some would wish to deny families such information under the existing system of compulsory assignment. However, once it is concluded that choice is to be exercised by nonrich families, we see no reason at least in an experiment to interdict the disclosure by schools and private information services of whatever information families seek that neither defames nor invades the privacy of an individual.

For the ordinary family a comprehensive system for the dissemination of available and required information would be important. The public agency charged with general administration of the system would prepare a basic booklet to be mailed to all school families. Such a device has been employed with success in the Alum Rock experiment; the directory described the participating schools in terms of eighteen variables.[7] Such a publication for a large urban area would be no small responsibility and expense, but might effect a net saving by the efficiency imparted to the family's own processes of selection. For those families unable to understand written communications, personal contact seems necessary in order to assure access to information about all schools. The agency could arrange neighborhood counseling offices, telephone services, and home visits in areas of high illiteracy.

The agency should be prepared to collect information from schools in ad hoc and informal ways, perhaps on request of individual parents. Further, the family's own initiative should be encouraged in various ways, including a right of reasonable inspection of any school by a prospective applicant family. That is, on proper notice and subject to other sensible rules, the public should be allowed to visit schools, and the right must be established by law. The market would not cause

schools to open their doors to inspection by prospective
applicants the schools wished to discourage.

In addition to what government provides, information may
be made available to families by private services and by the
schools themselves. Just as information services thrive in other
fields, so evaluations and descriptions may emerge which
are organized differently from those disseminated by government. Fairly sophisticated private alternative school directories
exist even now in many urban areas.

Presumably some of the larger or would-be-larger schools
would advertise to increase their applicant pool. Some critics
find this prospect objectionable. We think media advertising
indistinguishable in principle from the present practices employed by public school districts to puff their successes; and
it would be surprising if public schools of choice did not
continue to advertise in a variety of ways. On the other hand,
if limits on market share and number of school sites were
imposed on private providers (see Chapter 9), we probably
would not see the kind of mass advertising now employed
by large sellers of products in a national market.

Mistakes, distortion, lies, and fraud are inevitable, as society
has learned from experience with schools public and private.
In a choice plan, because families would have to bank on
what is published, it would be especially important to try
to prevent such practices and to stamp out those that occur.
Without expecting miracles, the state should make a reasonable
investment in the discovery of false representation and in
the application of appropriate sanctions. For substantial deliberate violations, moderate criminal penalties would be appropriate, supplemented perhaps by a statutory right to civil
damages in a set amount for families who had enrolled on
the strength of the misrepresentation.

The most promising stimulus to candor by the schools would
be the authority of the administering agency to withdraw
the school's privilege to participate in the system upon a proper
showing that the school has been misleading in its advertising.
In short, an FTC-like regulation of unfair trade practices seems
needed. If the complaining family were authorized to proceed
before the agency as a private attorney general—and with
the resources of civil rights, consumer, and parent organizations behind it—such a system of regulation could be made
effective. True, not all seductive media ads can be challenged
as false or misleading, and the power of such ads to shape
tastes should not be discounted. Yet if the private providers

in the market are relatively small, mass image-building, brand-recognition campaigns would not seem efficient. Moreover, we think that in educational affairs people put great emphasis on local teaching personnel; hence, the promise to deliver a uniform product in many markets—perhaps impressive coming from baby food sellers—is likely to fall on unreceptive ears. In sum, given the potential for an effective system of information and counseling, the predictions of successful hucksterism seem overblown. We are confident that the average family and its professional counselors could make choices that would implement its values and serve its children.

Having said all of this, we do not wish to leave the impression that we anticipate that *all* families will behave as models of fully informed rational choosers as a result of the information scheme we propose. Some simply will not be adept at interpreting the information, matching it to their educational tastes, or even clearly formulating those tastes. The provision of personal advisers will help parents make educational choices; but we do not wish to push this too far. There is a risk that advisers invested with too much power and too many opportunities to help may replace families as the real choosers; in the chronicles of education, the role of school and vocational counselors has not always been a neutral one. Perhaps, however, this problem can be avoided by the creation of diversified and competing counseling services. This might be done by subsidizing the advice that families seek (up to a modest amount) and allowing families to choose where to obtain that advice—doing for advisers what we are proposing for schools themselves. We also believe that the family's experience in making successive decisions will over time tend to make those decisions better. Perhaps families, like children, can "learn by doing."

Chapter 9

SCHOOL PROVIDERS AND
SCHOOL GOVERNANCE

The case for hope rests on the fact
that ordinary people are often able to
take a wider view, and a more "humanistic"
view, than is normally being taken
by experts.

—E. F. SCHUMACHER, *Small is Beautiful*

SHOULD PRIVATE SCHOOLS BE INCLUDED?

The idea of family choice in education does not logically
require the involvement of private schools. A few years ago
we described how family choice could be confined to publicly
owned and administered schools competing with one another
for the patronage of families.[1] If properly structured, such
a system could satisfy most families reasonably well. This,
in fact, is the approach adopted in the experiment with
educational vouchers in Alum Rock, California. Nevertheless,
most family choice proposals would include private schools.
Indeed, under Milton Friedman's plan, the public sector would
begin to withdraw from the business of providing education,
at least in urban areas.[2]

There are a number of reasons for including private providers
in the program, and surely the idea is worth an experimental
try. Private schools are the only potential source of religious
education and may be the major hope for offbeat education
in general. In a choice plan including both private and public
schools, it is probably inevitable that the former will be less
constrained legally and politically.

Moreover, the economic survival of private schools requires
a sensitivity to family demand that a public institution finds

153

hard to muster so long as it is protected from private competition. Public schools today are rarely permitted to die of unpopularity. Thus, their incentive to innovate is meager, and their capacity to terminate unsuccessful programs is as bad or worse. Above all, the public system needs the prod of good example, but there will be no prod unless there is an alternative. Of course, public schools could actually become competitive with one another. For this to happen without private competition, however, the public school must somehow be made to risk the loss of its fiscal support if families do not choose it. The relationships among public schools in such a system would probably be similar to those reported among the factory units of Yugoslavia; they are state owned but must survive by their ability to produce and sell their products. Taking a lesson from Marxists about competition could prove a blessing to our public enterprise. Still, the possibility of improving the public sector through internal competition seems an insufficient reason to foreclose the choice of a private provider the family prefers.

The inclusion of private schools would also fulfill the need for a margin of extra space. Choice systems assume that there will be more than adequate space for all students. Otherwise the first choices of many families would be frustrated, and the basic objectives of the system would be largely lost. Although extra space could be provided within a purely public model (and school enrollments are declining), in the early stages of operation at least the space made available by private schools would probably be needed.

By what principle the proper mix of private and public schools should be determined remains unclear. An obvious possibility is to allow the users to determine this by their choice. Another possibility is that instead of an open and equal competition for students, the state would designate a particular quantitative mix of public and private schools. One device for achieving that objective is the issuance of licenses to a specific number of private schools. This device is simple in concept, but less so in practice. The manner of selection would be a tender issue and could raise difficult constitutional questions regarding equality of treatment among applicants. This problem could be avoided if a lottery were held for the licenses, so long as the state did not exclude individual aspirants from the pool. We would prefer that no limits be imposed on the number of private providers or the share of the students they could serve.

WHO MIGHT BE THE PRIVATE PROVIDERS?

If permitted, religious groups and others now offering private elementary and secondary education would no doubt participate in a choice plan if the conditions imposed by law were not incompatible with their goals. The plan could, however, stimulate providers quite different from those who run today's private schools. For example, ethnic community groups of the sort which led the community control movement might wish to start schools. Since the meaning of "community" in a family choice system is radically different from that in a geographically and politically defined system, however, it is difficult to predict how much grassroots support these leaders might have.

A second potential source of providers is private industry, although the brief experience of some business enterprises with performance contracting is not especially encouraging.[3] In many quarters the contracting experiments are thought to be failures, inasmuch as providers were unable to demonstrate sustained gains in achievement on standard tests over what is accomplished in ordinary public schools. Whether the participating children would have nonetheless chosen to remain with the experience offered by the private contractor, if given the choice, is another question. Still, the episode may have soured many large enterprises on the opportunities for profit in the school business.

Some supporters of family choice would simply exclude profit-seeking organizations from the system on several grounds. They argue, first, that students are always short-changed by those with dollars as their objective. They also fear the growth of a private monopoly that would replicate the present monolith in a new form; and they warn of undesirable political effects from the transfer of an unpredictable portion of the enormous economic power of the education industry to new hands. We take up these three objections one at a time.

The charge that some children are ill-treated by those with one eye on the cash register is a truism supported by anecdotes. We are willing to assume that this sometimes occurs in private vocational schools and franchised day-care centers. Yet one sees little to justify the flat exclusion of profit-seeking educators; particularly in an experiment to determine the effect of choice, we should be content to rely on required disclosure and other regulation of private providers. On the positive side, there is substantial empirical evidence that private vocational schools are at least the equal of their public counterparts in terms of job placement.[4] Recent studies have shown that, while student and public expectations of benefit from such training may be unrealistic, as a general rule there is no reason to prefer the public providers and much to be said for preserving their private competition. Many continue to prefer it despite the availability of a tuition-free public option.

There are some suggestive analogies. Bad experiences with private nursing homes are surely matched or exceeded by the dismal record of many state hospitals. And the use of food stamps in retail markets by the poor can be seen only as a release from the misery of commodities distribution schemes. No system, public or private, will be free from failure and frauds, and programs for the delivery of human services are peculiarly subject to disaster. Yet even with all its problems, Medicaid is an improvement for many now freed from reliance on public hospitals or the private charity of doctors. In sum, broadside condemnation of the private sector, as compared to public provision, is generally based on isolated episodes and, on the present record, is quite unjustified. Of course only an experiment including such providers can give us the experience needed to judge.

It has been suggested to us that the retail grocery industry exemplifies the evils of encouraging private education: Supermarkets render the economy of nutrition too impersonal and uniform and also tend to market food of marginal nutritional value, giving us white bread instead of wheat bread made of organically grown natural ingredients. We are not convinced. On the contrary, the grocery industry with its defects seems to us a vast improvement over today's elementary and secondary education industry. In the first place, in addition to supermarkets, small personal service shops, markets with eccentric hours, and specialty food stores are available in nearly all urban and suburban areas—for those willing to pay the typically higher price that those extras require. More important, an extraordinary variety of food items is available within the total market, products designed to satisfy—and in some cases, create—a great diversity of tastes. To prefer the distribution of food through agents of a public monopoly such as the local post office (to use Milton Friedman's favorite example) is to us incomprehensible. Anyone who has shopped in a government store in Eastern Europe will appreciate the point. One portion of the critics' complaint, the junk food indictment, does trouble us. We are continually told that parents are seduced into buying for their children food that is useless or worse and that children are in fact being injured thereby. The same scenario is then predicted for a system of educational choice. We believe, however, that controls on advertising, required disclosure by schools, and the devices for family educational counseling proposed in Chapter 8 should deal adequately with the issue.

The second risk said to arise from admitting private enterprise to the system is that education will become a private monopoly. There is nothing to support such a prediction; and there is good reason to predict that no single firm, or handful of firms, would achieve or even seek a dominant market position. Market entry would be easy, since start-up costs for new schools (possibly excepting certain vocational schools) would be small; the primary cost for most schools is faculty salaries. In addition, the small school would in itself be especially attractive for many families. Therefore, while our own criticisms of the existing school system for its bulk, uniformities, and constriction of choice would apply to a private monopoly, there is little reason to expect such an outcome. The only reason monopoly survives in the present school system is the absence of competition and the coercion of the clientele.

If monopoly were a widespread fear, rational or not, its prevention could be easily guaranteed by regulation limiting the market share of participants. We would support such limits. Regulation could take one of several forms. It must be decided first whether to restrict a firm's power only within each local market or whether also to set limits on aggregate size. Various techniques are available, and some of our long national experience with the antitrust laws might be helpful here.[5] For example, each private provider could be formally limited to 20 percent of the students and any eight firms to 50 percent of the students in any substantially populated geographic area, yet even if smaller percentages were used, we doubt that the need for their application would arise; that is, such market power is unlikely to be accumulated in any heavily populated locale. Attaining a significant (say, 10 percent) position in a number of markets is more plausible, particularly if national firms and, especially, makers of school books and supplies entered the business; this is even more likely if such firms adopted a system of franchising for prepackaged forms of education. In itself this seems harmless. A decision to frustrate families simply because an educational plan has—like Montessori—achieved a national appeal must rest on political considerations. On that ground, however, we could understand limits on the number of students served by a single private enterprise both locally and in the aggregate. On the same ground the state might choose to limit vertical integration; for example, ownership of schools, direct or indirect, might be limited to persons or corporations whose sole activity is education. Thus manufacturers, publishers, and service companies could be excluded. However, we are not eager to waste resources on enforcement costs, and they could be substantial—for example, the sorting out of interlocking economic relations could be quite troublesome.

The imposition of a limit on private market share should be enough to dissipate the third concern about the political implications of including private providers. Essentially this worry is that big business will gain a new lobbying foothold. Considering the influence of oil and auto executives on government decisions, the fear is credible; the changes in campaign financing, the growth of consumer groups, and the development of public interest organizations have only begun to right the balance. Nevertheless, the problem seems much less serious in the case of less concentrated industries. Of course, as with the farm industry, medicine, and other decentralized activities, political power can be aggregated through trade associations. Presumably this would occur in private education on a larger scale than today and at all levels of government. This behavior, however, would merely parallel that of the public school establishment. The political power wielded today by teacher unions, school superintendents' associations, and the like is no secret. If government is to proceed by log-rolling and interest-bargaining, by what principle are particular groups to retain a monopoly of the lobbying forum? If there is in fact a political danger in the power of educators, choice would appear more a remedy than an aggravation.

Finally, there is a practical problem about excluding profit-making schools. Profits are very difficult to prevent without massive regulation, since managers can prune money from corporations with nearly invisible techniques including high salaries, management fees, and development contracts. Hence, the principal effect of excluding profit-makers may be the multiplication of nonprofit organizations. Based on the experience in higher education and hospitals, we doubt that conventional proprietary enterprises would dominate anyway, even if their entry were freely permitted. The typical private providers would probably be organized as nonprofits such as Stanford, Swarthmore, Mount Sinai, and St. Joseph's, with "public" boards of trustees. If these too were banned, most of the potential private suppliers would be eliminated.

What could remain, even in the narrowest of reforms, are schools controlled by those families who form the school's community. The model here is a nonprofit voluntary membership association whose voting members include the parents of children attending and, perhaps, the children themselves, their teachers, administrators, and other school staff. By giving those served an official voice in ongoing school operations and not simply the power of original choice and exit, such an arrangement provides special assurances that those managing the school have the children's interests at heart. Such user-controlled schools are an attractive idea and an additional source of school providers; surely they should be allowed and even encouraged. But we do not find the case for their exclusivity compelling;[6] schools that provide other forms of internal voice would surely be preferred by some. It would be ironic if the only tolerable alternative to educational vassalage were a school based on precisely the opposite principle. We agree that the matter of in-school choice and voice is important, however, and we return to it in greater detail further on.

Let us assume, then, that private schools would not be limited to voluntary membership associations. In that case, teacher groups, universities, and other existing community organizations are further candidates for forming new schools of choice. Indeed, teachers are probably the most promising source of new school providers. In addition, municipal governments may decide to compete with the conventional public schools now supported by their citizens through the school district. Other variants may be provided by federal government schools and army schools. As reflected in our discussion in Chapter 6, ideological groups of various types may also wish to experiment. There would no doubt be a few Communist and Buddhist schools as there have long been in miniscule numbers in Denmark, where families are supported in their choice of education.[7] Mainstream political parties and religious groups such as Republicans and Methodists, not now in the private school business, may toy with participating. Whether all of these are good ideas or would attract any families is not the point. We wish simply to illustrate the wide variation in potential new providers that might represent competition for one another and for today's public schools. Ultimately "private" and "public" are probably not very good labels. What may matter is the extent to which the style and content of state-supported educational experiences are permitted to differ.

STIMULATING PRIVATE PROVIDERS

Merely to decide that private providers may participate is probably not enough to enlist them in significant numbers. Government incentives for the formation of schools would probably be necessary. This would be true especially for teachers, nonprofit education groups, and other impecunious types. Their primary need would be sufficient credit for financing capital acquisitions and hiring the staff. At least in the beginning, traditional private sources of funding might view these ventures as too risky to justify large-scale investment or low equity loans.

In the case of existing schools, the present private credit market might prove adequate if the grants to students were substantial. Even here, however, the economic picture would probably vary from school to school. Catholic parochial schools, for example, have been marked by extremities of wealth and poverty in cities where they have been orphaned financially by the diocesan structure and left to depend largely on the pockets of the local parishioners. Unless that structure were to be radically reformed, or the diocese were to act as guarantor, it is unlikely that the schools in poorer parishes would be any better off in the private money market than the new secular schools.

Probably the most promising form for maximizing the impact of limited state resources on private operators is the governmental loan guarantee. Its historic impact on the housing market demonstrates the fecundity of government resources turned to the creation of riskless or near riskless private loans.[8] Of course, the FHA has been criticized for the race-specific and class-specific effects of its structure and administration, some of which seem to have been intentional.[9] Now that these discriminatory and segregative characteristics are understood, an alternative loan structure can be designed to stimulate more variety in education for all classes of families.

Another approach to consider is the leasing to private providers of public space, particularly public school buildings. The decline in school enrollment has forced school systems to abandon a large number of school buildings, and we suspect that there is little demand for such buildings other than as schools. Of course, because the aims of some private providers will be to provide physical environments strongly contrasting to existing school buildings, such providers may not want to make use of this possibility.

CHOICE AMONG WHICH PUBLIC SCHOOLS?

Any system of choice must define the range of schools open to selection by each family. The scope of the market will depend on the geographic area from which families are permitted to select schools and the flexibility of choice allowed among public and private schools. Three examples will illustrate how the design could vary: The family might be permitted to choose among (1) private schools and the student's neighborhood public school, (2) private schools and any public school in the district, and (3) all schools, public or private, within a defined area larger than the school district.

The first example seems much too limited. Most families are likely to prefer public school, and public schools will provide most of the seats; therefore, competition among public schools is an important feature. Although the competitive threat of a private school option for all families might by itself induce public schools to respond to family concerns, extending that choice to the public sector would both ensure that response and make more options available to families.

The third suggested design would create additional options valued by urban families. If families in Chicago were asked their preference among high schools, probably more would name New Trier Public High School in suburban Winnetka than any private school existing or imagined. Clearly there are social and educational advantages in the employment of geographically larger areas of choice. A population more heterogeneous than the central city's would make possible a greater mix of children from different family backgrounds than could otherwise occur. A larger population also means that those with exotic interests are more likely to find a sufficient number of like-minded peers to form the critical mass needed to start a school.

TRANSPORTATION

If there is to be equality of access to all the schools in the system, and if financial considerations are not to cripple a family's choice, an adequate system of free transport is necessary. At some geographical perimeter for each child, however, the provision of free transportation becomes too costly. The desire to extend equality of opportunity to the poor may suggest that the area of choice be limited for everyone; whether those families willing and able to pay the *extra* transport costs should be forbidden to send their children to schools of choice elsewhere is a difficult question.

The cost of transporting residentially concentrated ghetto children to scattered suburban schools and scattered Buddhists to one centrally located school, although significant, would be justified. But this does not say precisely how it should be financed (we assume the family will not pay). Should the state pay separately for the bus, or should the school provide the cost out of its tuition proceeds? Differential transportation costs may argue for state payment, since schools might otherwise see students living at a distance as an economic burden. The attractions of creative en route education designed by the school may cut the other way. And a decision that the school pays may induce schools to cooperate in various ways, including locating and sharing of facilities in educational parks. Of course, sharing of facilities or programs might occur independently of the influence of transportation costs.

An equally serious problem is the administration of such a system. In comparison, our current public busing systems are extremely simple. This is not to say the problem would be insurmountable; thousands of private schools manage it every day, and many cities have had substantial experience with complicated busing-for-racial-balance programs. Moreover, we would expect that a number of schools would turn the bus ride into a competitive selling factor. Experiments of the last decade with en route education might be expanded.

GOVERNANCE AND FORMATION OF
PUBLIC SCHOOLS OF CHOICE

Today states delegate much of their power over education to geographically based school districts, which are usually independent governmental agencies whose policies are set by locally elected boards of education. These boards in turn delegate some of their power to central administrators (typically a superintendent and subordinates) and to their school site personnel (principal and teachers). This structure is probably incompatible with family choice, at least where families may choose public schools outside their district of residence. The overall governance unit would have to be expanded to encompass the full range of choice, and there may be no logical stopping point—except for experimental purposes—short of the state itself. Thus, local school districts, as we know them, may no longer be functional.

Even if experiments were confined to existing or expanded districts, important issues concerning the governance of individual schools would remain. Family selection seems inharmonious with an elected board of districtwide trustees holding the power to decide what is provided in individual schools; under such arrangements public schools of choice would respond too little to the demands of individual families or even of groups of families that attend any particular school. Nor could the issue of governance be satisfactorily settled by dividing each school district into as many separate conventional districts as it has schools, since to have neighborhood voters controlling schools which serve parents outside the neighborhood makes little sense. A different model for the allocation of power between the school and higher authority is necessary.

One solution would be to establish each public school as an individual nonprofit corporation with a charter spelling out its independent power and duties. The terms of that charter would have to attend to a variety of matters, and all schools need not have the same charter. When we discuss alternative structures for curriculum and teacher hiring in the next chapter, we will, in effect, be considering potential charter terms for public schools. As we will explain there, in general we favor substantial autonomy at the level of each public school.

A related and difficult problem concerns the launching of new public schools. We assume that private schools would be organized where founders expect sufficient demand and are willing to risk their investment, but there is no comparable self-policing aspect to the public sector. It will be important, therefore, that no public school be founded without some basis in family demand or be protected from failure by overcapitalization or by a continuing subsidy from the state. Otherwise they will tend to survive irrespective of their capacity to serve and will provide "unfair competition" to other public and private schools. Perhaps all new public schools should arise as subsidiaries, split-offs, or branches of existing public schools that are motivated by their own faculty's perception that through expansion they can provide better service.

The public sector must do more than divide responsibility between its individual schools and the larger public regime; it must consider allocation of power inside the school itself. One possibility is to give each school's principal power over all matters not otherwise provided for by law. Such a model is widely employed in England, where the headmaster enjoys a strongly authoritarian role. Another approach is to create for each school a board of trustees which would exercise all the school's charter authority. Such a board might be composed of the faculty members chosen in a variety of ways; or it could include some teachers, the principal, representatives from the administering state agency, and perhaps independent public trustees. User parents and students chosen in a variety of ways—by election of parents, by appointment of the principal, or by lot as in jury panel selection—could also be included on the board. Indeed, students and parents representing all user families could be given exclusive responsibility for all of the public school's charter functions, thus moving public schools toward the voluntary membership model earlier described for private schools. The school's charter could also allocate different functions to different parties. Teachers might be given the authority to determine curriculum, principals the authority over budgeting, and a parent council control over class assignment. Various other possibilities for internal division of authority, pariculary those involving a role for the family, are discussed in the next section; this is an issue for private as well as public schools of choice.

FAMILY PARTICIPATION IN SCHOOL POLICY MAKING

It has been argued that the problem with public education today is that the rich can exit; if they were forced to remain, they would exercise their voices and such complaints would bring about needed change.[10] Our interpretation of the problem is the converse. The problem is that only the rich can exit, and that it is the extension of the right of exit to the nonrich that will induce educational improvements. There is, of course, some force to the notion that an institution suffers when those who would demand of it the highest standards depart rather than remain and struggle from the inside for reform. Yet we are skeptical about an argument which implies that higher education in, say, California would be improved if the public university took over Stanford, the Claremont colleges, USC, and the like. We reject the view that blocking exit rights will improve elementary and secondary education, but we concede—indeed, insist—that voice can be very important. Hence, an important policy issue is the appropriate role for parent and student in their chosen school's decision process. Specifically, the question for us is should formal structures, such as a family council, be mandated for schools?

If the forms of participation were left to the free interaction of family and school, a variety of models would probably emerge. Some private schools would likely employ a governing board made up of parents elected by the parents. If such a board held ultimate power over the school, it would be very much like the voluntary membership association earlier described. While such arrangements would probably be common among parent-initiated schools, as just noted they might also be adopted by the public sector for some of its schools. Rather than hold ultimate power, this parent board might be given specific, limited powers—perhaps to hire and fire the principal and to set policy for building use and hours of instruction. Again, this parallels the possibilities for shared authority in the public sector that we noted earlier. Of course, such a board could be intended only as a source of legitimation, a sounding device, or an advisory council with basic governance lodged elsewhere. Yet even then the parent board would be a mechanism through which all parents could learn of controversy involving the school. Note that, whatever their role and power, boards of these various sorts could also have student members, or separate student boards could be employed for appropriate functions.

Another form for emphasizing universal participation is the "town meeting." Potential changes in school policy could be presented in writing by the manager or principal to parents (and students) beforehand and voted on at scheduled meetings, not unlike the conclaves of corporate stockholders. A variant of this would follow the mutual fund model in which the families would periodically vote on whether to continue the management. In either case ultimate power would rest formally with the users, whether the school were private or public. Most of the real power, however, might gravitate to the administrators. A third and quite distinct arrangement might emulate the collective bargaining model: School operators— public and private—would be required to bargain in good faith with a client union or consumer league.

This variety of arrangements and of potential preferences suggests the wisdom of leaving the issue open to development at the individual school. Many families, having confidence in a school's administrators, will want no voice at all and will choose schools precisely because they wish to place responsibility in such professional hands. In fact, they would object if other families were to influence the judgments of the school officials; likewise, many administrators may insist on full authority as a condition of their serving. Hence, if too much family voice is legislated as the condition of a school's participation, schools which some families desire would not come into existence. Again, flexibility and variety in the family's role would be important in both public and private schools. In the public sector the state authorities could decide to set the rules for some of its schools while creating procedures for other public schools to fix the family role for themselves in different ways.

Suppose that, despite their aggregate market power, disorganized consumers were unable to induce the creation of enough private schools in which they have the voice they desire. Substantive and procedural mandates could be legislatively enacted to ensure whatever governance forms were thought to be basic. Three forms come readily to mind. First, parents (and perhaps students and teachers as well) could be guaranteed representation on the school's board of directors, a strategy reminiscent of consumer groups which have tried to place directors on the boards of industrial concerns. Second, families might be given the right to force the school into collective bargaining with them by obtaining sufficient signatures from users desiring this type of family voice. Finally, in order to stimulate family participation in policy making, schools might be required to make information available about school affairs and school policy on particular questions (in addition to that made available annually as part of the process of school selection by the family and described in Chapter 8). Of course, these provisions could be applied to public schools as well.

Chapter 10

EDUCATIONAL STYLE

In my State everyone may be saved
after his own fashion.
Ascribed to FREDERICK THE GREAT
by Victor Gollancz

Politically, any proposed model in which families could send their children with state funds to any institution that called itself a school, there to receive any form of service or attention which that school was inclined to label "education," is simply a pipe dream—or, perhaps, nightmare. The state will decide that the use of "mind-expanding" drugs on children does not qualify as education. The only doubt is where it would cease to interfere. In any experiment some universe of activity which qualifies as education must be defined. In this chapter we focus on four major areas requiring specification: curriculum, teachers, school environment, and the climate of freedom and fairness to students.

CURRICULUM

To the extent that schools of choice must conform to state-imposed curriculum requirements, the principle of family choice is compromised. Each centrally imposed curriculum prescription or prohibition tends to shrink the proportion of families which can be satisfied. If the state demands too much, the chilling effect will go beyond simply adding or eliminating specific courses; entire schools will be excluded. For example, some existing private institutions would refuse to participate if sex education were required; others would refuse if it were forbidden. It seems sensible to us for the state to impose very few restrictions or mandates. In general, schools should be free to please themselves and their customers.

Given a liberal scope for curriculum, schools which are privately owned and managed would simply decide for themselves what to offer. How would that decision be made for public schools? Here we must revisit the issue of governance. One approach is to leave curriculum decisions to the individual public school; depending on the general arrangements by which each school is to manage its own affairs, the principal, the faculty, or some other authority specified by the school's charter might decide.

The state might, however, wish either to assure a diversity of offerings or, to the contrary, to protect the availability of a "standard" program which offers less adventuresome families security in their selection. It might, therefore, give curricular direction to at least some of the participating public schools. This could be done by giving the administering state agency plenary power to regulate curriculum and style in public schools. Since regulation by such an agency ordinarily tends toward uniformity, we would hope that at least a substantial segment of participating public schools would be controlled at the school level. While a variety of arrangements should be tried at the school level, giving teachers collective control over the subjects taught and the style of education would be especially interesting; through such "faculty schools," the state would officially invite public professionals to experiment and diversify.

Regulation of participating schools might or might not emulate current state curriculum requirements for private schools. These state laws vary and are differentially enforced.[1] Thus, if some states held participating schools to existing requirements, innovation might be inhibited. Schools usually have considerable leeway, however; what qualifies as "English" or "social studies" is conveniently vague. Still, a school's wish to concentrate specific work in certain years or semesters could be frustrated by regulations requiring a diversified subject matter at all times. For the elementary years to require only that a set number of hours of instruction be provided over the school year with a significant portion devoted generally to reading and mathematics might be enough insurance.

Especially at the high school level, outside forces may affect curriculum offerings. Colleges, for example, currently demand that their applicants have mastered certain subjects; so do some employers. Moreover, employers and colleges seem increasingly to rely on scores on norm-referenced standardized tests as a way to screen their applicants. ("Norm-referenced" tests are designed to display the *relative* abilities of those tested, not whether one knows something or knows how to do a certain thing.)

To the extent that these threshold requirements are more narrowly drawn than necessary to serve legitimate objectives of colleges and employers, they may have the practical effect of narrowing the curriculum—indeed, even the educational outlook of the school—hence the range of opportunities open to teenagers. That is, families would to some degree emulate the present behavior of high school authorities who kowtow to predictions concerning the labor market. Families concerned about employment prospects for their children could not ignore their need to acquire credentials and test-taking ability, however unfair or irrational these might be. This is not to suggest that families would prove as pliant to employers and colleges as today's schools have been. Indeed, precisely because families may represent a broader spectrum of values than do professional educators, systems of choice could be viewed as a promising mechanism for prodding colleges and employers to reexamine their entry requirements.

This pressure from below is not likely by itself to dominate course requirements and testing, but it could play an important role in reform. It would augment the impact of other reform efforts on the credentialing system. Tests and degree requirements are already under fire because of their alleged discriminatory impact on minorities.[2] That pressure will continue and will independently force employers and colleges to reconsider their screening criteria. Moreover, to overestimate the influence of college and job requirements on diversity in the schools may be a mistake. An experiment with choice may disclose a toughness of family commitment to a diversity of values, views of history, pedagogical techniques, levels of informality in the school, and other options that is wholly independent of the criteria of the labor market.

Diploma-granting is a related issue, particularly since colleges and employers often specify "high school graduate" as one entry criterion. If participating schools control their award, diplomas ought not greatly to affect high school curriculum offerings. To the degree that the meaning of diplomas becomes ambiguous, colleges and employers are less justified in requiring them. Whether this is promising or threatening depends on the system of evaluation that replaces it. If achievement testing or other such standards were employed in their place, but proved to be as arbitrary as diplomas, the state might insist that particular courses be passed for the diploma.

If such requirements had any real bite, however, they too could impede school variety. One resolution to this dilemma would be the adoption of a state-administered examination that a student must pass to qualify for a high school certificate, leaving diplomas to the schools. The high school graduate equivalency examinations now given in many states provide a model for this approach. In this regard, the details of the test and the demand for such certificates in addition to high school diplomas are important variables. Thus, we view askance the new California High School Proficiency Exam, passage of which is supposed to be equal to a diploma;[3] in fact, this test is designed so that one-half of high school seniors will fail it, rather than testing the amount of knowledge or skill that is thought to qualify a high school graduate. Still, at least such examinations are not likely to constrain curriculum as much as tightly drawn curriculum requirements; employers and colleges wanting additional specific skills or learning will have an incentive to devise tests more appropriate than diplomas.

As this last statement implies, we believe it fair to allocate jobs on a merit basis. Whether higher income should also go to the more talented—whether it is fair to gain income advantages from the luck of being born talented—is a question we need not address here. Whatever one's answer, it provides no justification for the view that the way to deal with inequality of talent is to arrest the development of "lucky" children.

We are not indifferent to the charge that many jobs in America are boring and dehumanizing. One does not advance the solution of this problem by leaving schools boring and dehumanizing. Schools can be better places for children independent of changes in the nature of work; changes in education might produce children who themselves will bring about an improvement in the way workers feel about and are treated at their jobs.

TEACHER CERTIFICATION

Teacher certification—the acquisition of a license from the state—is an issue closely related to curriculum control. The use of certification to exclude personnel from the school labor market limits the spectrum of program and style which more diversity in training, preparation, and professional outlook would be expected to provide. Because of teacher credentials, public schools have been staffed by persons trained in certain sets of methodologies. However competent, such personnel would not always be the ideal agents for satisfying family choice.

This is not to imply that today the faculties of private elementary and secondary institutions are significantly more diverse. Although the law in most states has given private schools broad discretion in staffing, most have responded by striving to reproduce the certification patterns of the public schools. The administrators of private schools generally have considered the acquisition by their teachers of both the traditional college degree and graduate school training to be primary indices of progress for their institutions. Historically, the teaching nun went to Columbia rather than to Harlem for the summer, though this is changing.

Even under the present American school structure, this private school pattern seems likely to shift; indeed, we sense that already it is changing, and not merely in the "free" schools. Skepticism about the value of traditional teacher education and confidence in the teaching ability of many persons lacking formal credentials seem on the increase. This suggests that, in a choice plan, certification requirements applying differentially to public and private schools could affect competition between the two sectors. If so, should credentials be required of all teachers participating in the choice plan, of teachers in publicly managed school only, or of no teachers?

Those who favor "higher" minimum standards would seek to impose credential controls on participating private schools. The fact that private education historically has been largely unregulated in its hiring practices might be considered irrelevant. Arguably, private schools have escaped the full measure of professional attention only because they represented so small a fraction of the total pie of dollars and power. Moreover, it is naive to suppose that advocates of credential requirements could be turned aside by arguments that private education has in the past performed as well as public education and at a significantly lower cost per pupil (if that is the case).

Given the current surplus of teachers with credentials, the teaching profession and the powerful organizations representing them are likely to favor requiring credentials of all who teach in a family choice system. Moreover, others within the public school confederation—schools of education, administrators, and textbook sellers—are likely to support them. Although the issue is often sincerely cast as protection from the educational charlatan for the gullible parent, the professionals have important personal interests at stake. For teachers these include the limitation of competition for jobs, the validation of their own career preparation, and the protection of their professional culture against the invasion of those lacking the shared experience and orientation of their forerunners. Similar considerations can motivate the other professional education cadres.

If teacher certification requirements were fastened on participating private schools, the effects would be profound. Unless a grandfather clause were included, many of the faculty now performing well in private schools would be out of jobs; families happy with such teachers could not continue to employ them without forfeiting state financial support. Perhaps more important, many potential new and experimental schools would fail to materialize. The total effect would probably be a diminution of variety sufficient to cancel out much of the advantage from a family choice experiment.

But perhaps this unhappy prospect is only a consequence of starting at the wrong end of the credentialing issue. Many professionals—perhaps the best—are restive with the current constraints and would argue that not only should private schools be free from certification restraints, but the public system should be liberated as well; obviously this group could harbor significant support for family choice. Many of these professionals are themselves certificated but are prepared to accept a modest risk. Relaxation of certification controls would not mean that formal training would become irrelevant, only that it would now compete in the job market with other indices of ability such as energy, personality, knowledge, experience with particular types of children, and social background. On behalf of families who thought credentials important, the plan could require disclosure of faculty qualifications by participating schools. An experiment that removed credential requirements from public schools might also help test whether present restraints merely interfere with school effectiveness, as critics claim, or whether they provide a useful index of the more competent employees.

One imaginable compromise on the credentials issue would simply maintain the existing distinction between public and private schools in regard to credentialing. The educational purpose of this choice would be unclear, but its political virtue is plain—doing nothing is generally easier.

UNION POWER

Quite apart from the credentials issue, teachers' unions have consistently opposed proposals for family choice.[4] Some readers may find this surprising, since family choice might give individual teachers unprecedented control over their classrooms and the opportunity to innovate in ways now enjoyed by other professionals. Hence, today's teachers could find it both an attractive personal possibility and a boon for their professional successors. Still the reaction was predictable. The most widely advertised proposals were often promoted on the very ground that teachers could be brought to heel by the parents. An increase in accountability to consumers and job jeopardy is seldom embraced voluntarily by the labor establishment or any other.

Both the individual teacher's fears concerning competition and the union's reluctance to risk its present influence are understandable anxieties. Individuals generally prefer competition only among those on whose services they depend. Perhaps most teachers would always prefer to be relatively insulated from and dominant over the families whose children they educate; they are no more authoritarian than the rest of us, but simply prefer to retain their liberty to structure their work as they think best for themselves and their pupils. Yet many other teachers would no doubt welcome the growth in professionalism implied in family choice, and if choice plans were put into effect, over time their numbers could grow.

The union's ultimate attitude is perhaps more promising. If the provision of choice proved to increase the public's level of satisfaction, education might experience an expansion of fiscal commitment—a dim prospect while the current malaise endures. A larger fiscal pie would expand the union's potential power in a market economy of education. From that perspective, unions may become more eager to support and run the new machinery than to smash it.

Absent additional legislation, the rules of the National Labor Relations Act would apply to private schools in a system of choice. Although many schools would probably be too small to trigger NLRB jurisdiction of their union-management relations, presumably the employees would at least have the legal right to strike,[5] a right denied public school teachers today by the law of most states.[6] While teachers' unions often flout the law and strike, the outlaw character of their conduct adds to its unpopularity and diminishes its effectiveness.

Nonetheless, in the short run the objections of Luddite school teachers' and administrators' organizations to the augmentation of family choice probably cannot be erased, only moderated. It is likely that economic guarantees will be the minimum necessary to defuse the resistance of labor. Therefore, for the moment we focus on the pragmatic problem of job security for public school personnel in the switch-over to a family choice system. In short, choice plans would alter teacher expectations that today's contracts, school district policies, and other sources of employees' "rights" have created, and the question is what to do about this.

CONTRACT AND STATUTORY RIGHTS OF TEACHERS

If the school district ceases to exist as the basic unit of authority for public education, and if individual public schools begin to compete with one another as well as with private schools, at least two kinds of teacher rights questions arise. First, to what extent must the managers of a public school honor guarantees made by the preexisting district? Will new criteria for making decisions about promotions, salary, hiring, firing, and the like apply only to personnel with no previous connection to the school or the district? Second, what should be done where such guarantees have a diminished value because they are now enforceable only against an individual school and not against a district? Tenure rights and retirement benefits illustrate this problem.

Obviously, the specific expectations of teachers vary in legal status and practical importance. Tenure, for example, may be considerably more significant than a particular position on the school transfer list. Furthermore, some teacher guarantees may be rather easily maintained without inhibiting the decentralized flexibility associated with choice. For example, responsibility for retirement benefits contractually guaranteed by a district could be assumed by the state. Still, if each public school is to be able to hire most efficiently, some delicate policy choices must be made. We will look at alternative resolutions in three of the more difficult areas, suggesting what seems fair and feasible without trying to estimate precisely what would be politically necessary to reduce teacher group hostility toward choice plans.

Teachers would vigorously, and let us suppose properly, oppose elimination of tenure rights. We will therefore simply assume that at the point of switch-over to the choice plan, the staffs of individual public schools will include all those employed at the school the prior year who wished to stay on. Moreover, we will assume that these teachers retain job security vis-à-vis their school to the extent of their previous tenure rights; the school managers could not adopt new and inconsistent termination criteria. Nevertheless, as the unit in which the teacher has tenure rights shrinks from district to school, the practical protection it affords would be reduced. If the school fails to attract students, it would be forced to decrease the size of its staff or even to close, and the employee would have lost an important part of the status achieved during his prior employment. This danger could be tempered, however; for example, the new system could guarantee priority access to available teaching positions in other participating public schools to those tenured employees discharged as a result of a reduction in force or the closing of their public school. This solution would, of course, tend to keep inefficient employees in the system and to frustrate the ability of public school managers receiving such teachers to satisfy family tastes. (Notice that as long as the sending school actually survives, because of seniority rules receiving schools would tend to get the newer teachers from the sending staff; this, of course, could be an advantage or a burden).

To avoid giving private schools a competitive advantage with respect to teachers, perhaps the private schools in the system could be required to accept their share of the discharged, but tenured, employees. Alternatively, the state could provide a substantial amount of severance pay—say, one or two years—to tenured teachers who lose their jobs because of their school's loss of enrollment. During that period most should be able to find another teaching position or retrain for alternative work. In any case the inefficiencies of such special protections could be minimized by phasing out the old relationships over the years. All this assumes that such employment guarantees would be limited to those employed by school districts prior to the starting date of the new system. Thereafter, teachers would gain tenure rights only against individual schools. Indeed, whether the state should insist that teachers newly hired be given the opportunity to work toward tenure as a universal rule is unclear. If public schools are to be innovative, a great deal is to be said for leaving to each school the decision whether to employ tenure rights as part of its structure.

The hiring preferences of individual public schools may conflict with other teachers' rights claims. In many districts today, teachers presently employed in one district school have first call on positions that open in the other schools. If individual public schools were to control the character of their staff, plainly these transfer rights could be recognized only in the beginning year or two of the choice plan. Senior teachers would thereby have a fair opportunity to choose the school they prefer. Thereafter, open spots would be filled without such preferences.

Salary arrangements present similar problems. Existing employees have their current salary to protect plus, commonly, a contract right to periodic increases. If individual public schools must abide by these but are permitted to hire new teachers on a different wage ladder (either more or less generous), dual employment status problems would arise. On the other hand, if the new teachers must be paid on a scale that emphasizes seniority and graduate school, individual public schools wishing to try merit pay plans would be stymied. We would leave the schools free to bargain this out on their own.

At some point the role and nature of collective bargaining under choice plans must be faced. Conventional collective bargaining by teachers is a reality in most public schools today (regardless of its legality), and we will assume that it would continue under a regime of choice. Unions could view choice as an opportunity to expand the number of workers under their umbrella since there is little collective bargaining in the private school sector today. Choice might also increase the unions' power, particularly if they were able to whipsaw individual schools, just as unions today pressure small or vulnerable districts one at a time. As in the private sector today, this could lead to multi-employer bargaining by schools in nearby areas or with similar philosophies. It might even result in statewide bargaining between most schools of choice and their teachers over the main terms of employment.

Coupled with a tendency of teacher unions increasingly to treat educational policy issues as proper subjects of bargaining, centralized negotiation could threaten the variety which is the very object of reform. Plainly some system of checks and balances would be needed to maintain system flexibility while ensuring adequate representation for the economic and professional interests of teachers. However, strengthening the bargaining status of teachers could diminish their impulse to strangle the system in the name of security. Teachers may be less worried about legal tenure, transfer rights, or statutory salary schedules if they are assured strong collective representation.

TEACHER FREEDOM OF EXPRESSION

One of the most interesting features of choice is its potential effect on teachers' freedom of expression in the classroom. To a large degree, choice would solve the intractable problem of promoting this aspect of academic freedom within a compulsory public system. Historically, the reconciliation of the teacher's claims to liberty with the captive status of his audience has been difficult. While some have argued that the First Amendment interests of the students themselves require that teachers be allowed to dissent from majority views,[7] there is probably more force in the counterproposition. When the child is compelled to give his attention to whatever is dispensed in the classroom, there is strong reason to control the teacher's own expression through majoritarian processes. And in fact and under law teacher expression in the classroom has been controlled by political authority to a very considerable degree.[8]

As long as the monopoly endures, the only serious question in public schools will be who shall be allowed to teach whatever the system permits and requires to be taught. Thus, the law of teacher liberties concentrates not on classroom behavior but on hiring discrimination, and in public schools everyone is eligible to teach irrespective of belief; freethinkers, Catholics, and Communists all share the protection of the Constitution.[9] They are free to teach, that is, so long as they stick to the script and do not teach their private beliefs. Academic freedom under the present regime is essentially the right to teach whatever the school board permits. The teacher must be given adequate notice of the boundaries, and often there is considerable leeway, but it is a matter of grace, not of right.[10]

Choice would free the captive audience and the equally captive teacher from each other, rendering the range of the teacher's expression a matter of contract for both speaker and listener. Obviously contract is no perfect instrument of academic liberty; the teacher must find a school that will offer him a platform, and one can imagine that individual schools would seek by contract to impose on their teachers limitations far exceeding the existing constraints in public education. Yet the general prospect is a hopeful one. Once the average family has become an effective actor in the educational process, it will be possible to increase in-class teacher freedom by the expansion of two kinds of institutions. First, for the first time many schools should appear with vivid and singular commitments both as to style and content; second, schools would arise whose very distinguishing feature was the broad license guaranteed their individual teachers. Each of these types—the schools with very particular means or objectives, and the schools whose motif is the independence of its teachers—would provide opportunities for teachers hitherto saddled by the political constraints of public education. There would at last be a market for the services of the nonconformist now excluded from a public system that by its nature must trade in commonalities.

Probably more teachers would be interested in the second type of school—guaranteeing by contract a wide range of individual teacher freedom. If such schools did not otherwise appear in the market, teachers could create their own. Further, even in a system including schools that have strong value commitments of many different sorts, there would be a greater chance that the offbeat teacher could find a school representing his own values. If a socialist teacher could not find a school that gave him personal freedom, he might at least find a socialist school in which he would feel at home, an institution made possible for the first time by choice.

If the opportunity to bargain for academic freedom were thought insufficient protection, legislation ensuring the teacher greater classroom freedom could no doubt be adopted. Just why this would be socially desirable or even thought to be libertarian, however, is unclear. It would, in the name of teacher liberty, curtail the liberty of the school and the family. The school could no longer stand four-square for anything in particular, nor could families be guaranteed the character of the education for which they had contracted. Fewer schools would wish to participate in such a system; thus the net effect even on teachers' freedom would very likely be negative. We prefer to leave the teachers, schools, and families free to negotiate their relationship.

This, however, does not dispose of the question whether a participating *nonpublic* school may refuse to hire simply on the basis of an applicant's beliefs. It is one thing to propagate communism in class; it is quite another simply to be a devout Marxist. One who dissents from a school's ideology might nevertheless wish to teach mathematics, art, or even history to its students in a manner consistent with that ideology. As a matter of legislative policy, should the school be permitted to exclude him? The argument for the private school's right to employ ideological criteria would be based on the plausible relation between belief and teaching performance. One opposing consideration is fairness to the public school, which could not impose a belief test upon job applicants. Another is the argument that accepting government money should render the school "public" for this purpose. Legislatures would differ on this question, which we find very hard to answer.

The present law on the subject would put the private school's use of belief tests in some jeopardy. If family grants were to bring private school hiring under the Constitution, issues would arise parallel to those involving the use of loyalty oaths in public systems, and most restrictions would fall. Moreover, quite apart from the Constitution, the Civil Rights Act of 1964 would seem to protect academic job applicants from certain forms of discrimination; it is significant, however, that religious organizations that hire on the basis of belief are specially exempted from that act.[11]

Academic freedom encompasses more than teaching, of course; the experience of teachers in some institutions, public and private, has been that their behavior outside school becomes the subject of their employer's interest. How would the advent of family choice affect the teacher's liberty to choose a private life style inconsistent with school values? How would it affect his liberty to criticize the school outside the classroom? Both questions have arisen frequently in public education. For example, the homosexual teacher and the teacher who publicly criticizes the principal have sometimes found their job security threatened.

The courts have recently shown signs of a willingness to protect public school teachers in the extraschool segment of their lives.[12] These gains in freedom seem worth preserving and extending to teachers in nonpublic institutions, and perhaps the application of the Constitution to participating private schools will simply do that. If not, would permitting such extraschool activity to be regulated solely by contract provide satisfactory protection for both teacher and school? We suspect it would in most cases; yet we are concerned that, in a depressed market of the present sort, teachers could in some instances be pressed to accept unconscionable limits on their private lives that would not today be tolerated by the courts if attempted by public systems. The ordinary solution for such entrepreneurial misbehavior in our society is collective bargaining; however, we would not oppose the added shelter of legislation designed to protect both the private behavior of teachers and their freedom to criticize their employer without fear of retribution. The drawing of lines in this area is a complex matter. Protection of out-of-school expression may require that all schools be prohibited from using the teacher's beliefs as a criterion for predicting teaching performance except where the course is explicitly ideological.

ADMINISTRATORS

Under choice, problems having to do with public school administrators are similar to, and perhaps more difficult than, those relating to teachers. To begin with, a family choice scheme should require fewer administrators, at least above the school level. The case for choice, however, does not rest on financial savings in the bureaucracy, and we do not wish to overemphasize its potential in this respect. At a minimum someone must determine which students are eligible for subsidy, assign the students to their chosen schools, approve schools for participation, and control the transfers of funds. The Department of Agriculture has not run the food stamps program on a shoestring. Still, we expect that central staffs may be whittled, although some of these extra employees might be needed at the school level as it took on more independent administrative responsibility.

The more difficult problems are those concerning the school site itself. In addition to the parallel problems with teachers which have already been discussed, there are problems peculiar to the school's administrative head. To what extent should an ineffective principal be financially and professionally protected at the expense of the school? Conversely, to what extent should principals of *public* schools of choice be shielded from ongoing interference or from removal by a central public authority? These questions are necessarily tied up with the other public school governance questions discussed in Chapter 9. If the individual public school has its own board, that board should probably have the authority to hire and fire the head administrator within the limits of the contract it negotiated with him. Whether the state should to some degree set the conditions for discharge to be incorporated in such contracts is a difficult question. Moreover, those who are presently principals should perhaps be guaranteed the right to return to teaching positions if they are dismissed.

SCHOOL ENVIRONMENT

Some see family choice systems as a way of creating novel institutions such as living-room schools and other kinds of schools with intimate environments, or schools without buildings at all. Schools having an environment other than that associated with the conventional school building may require special provisions to assure that they qualify as a state-subsidized educational experience. They also face many barriers erected by state and local building and safety codes.

If experimentation with novel environments is to be permitted, the proponents will have to overcome stiff opposition. To pose an extreme example, suppose that Mrs. Jones, a ghetto mother, decides to start a school in her apartment for her own four children and half a dozen neighborhood children. Depending on the choice system adopted, Mrs. Jones could qualify, let us say, for from $5,000 to $20,000 in tuition payments from the state. In short, the incentive to operate such schools would be strong, and unless discouraged by law they could become common.

At the present time, the interlocking housing, building, and other codes, which were drawn with larger enterprises in mind, would probably prohibit Mrs. Jones's school. It may be argued that safety rules serve as an educational quality control—that schools of this kind would typically be fraudulent disasters. We find it easy, however, to imagine learning systems that might operate brilliantly under amateur direction in private living rooms, and a central purpose of encouraging choice is to diminish automatic and heavy-handed paternalism. Therefore, existing physical standards should probably be relaxed in the interest of stimulating the entry of private minischools. The safety element can be exaggerated. After all, these children already spend most of their time in these same homes with the blessing of the state. As long as families know what they are getting in for, the state need not be too fastidious. One effective administrative reform would simply withdraw from the municipal government the authority to fix physical standards for schools and give it to the agency responsible for the experiments with choice. With minischools in mind, the agency could develop a set of appropriate safety standards.

Single-teacher schools, whether held in living rooms, store fronts, or museums, are only one potential type of minischool. To us, a more attractive idea is matching up a child and a series of individual instructors who operate independently from one another. Studying reading in the morning at Ms. Kay's house, spending two afternoons a week learning a foreign language in Mr. Buxbaum's electronic laboratory, and going on nature walks and playing tennis the other afternoons under the direction of Mr. Phillips could be a rich package for a ten-year-old. Aside from the educational broker or clearing house which, for a small fee (payable out of the grant to the family), would link these teachers and children, Kay, Buxbaum, and Phillips need have no organizational ties with one another. Nor would all children studying with Kay need to spend time with Buxbaum and Phillips; instead some would do math with Mr. Feller or animal care with Mr. Vetter. This system for arranging a personally tailored education through state subsidy has the additional advantage of easily accommodating part-time teachers.

While we have assumed that education in a minischool setting would be private, this need not be so. Atypical forms of shelter could as easily house public education. Under a plan designed to give public schools the ability to respond to new forms of competition, public units might operate in unusual settings or at odd hours or seasons.

The mobile school—public or private—could also prove a useful variant of the minischool. Obviously, there is no point in trying to conduct every form of instruction while moving. Certain courses of study, such as art, however, could profit from an ability to expose the children to what there is to see in the municipal area, including the local museums and art studios. Peripatetic schools are ideal for such purposes.

At the opposite extreme, family choice might lead to the creation of large educational parks. Since giantism in schools has been criticized for its tendency to classify pupils unfairly and to treat children impersonally, we do not suppose that many families would prefer single schools of several thousand pupils, particularly for younger children. But a complex made up of many kinds of separate public and private schools would have the advantage of some economies of scale without the disadvantages of organizational hierarchy. Each child would be admitted to one school as his home base, but he would have the opportunity to make use of the others to serve his individual needs. Such complexes could also rent rooms appropriate for single-teacher minischools whose students would then have access to the general facilities as the independent teacher chose. Indeed, such complexes could become beehives of minischools cooperating and competing with one another in the manner of medieval tutors.

HOME INSTRUCTION

Finally, family choice might also permit a family to provide its own education. Recall that Mrs. Jones's living-room school was to include her children; assume now it would include *only* her children. This home instruction should not be confused with tutoring in the home by outsiders, which we will assume would also be allowed. Some existing compulsory attendance laws do not recognize parentally provided home instruction as satisfactory.[13] Others permit it only when the parent doing the teaching is a credentialed educator.[14] The rationale for the restriction relies either on the need to police the quality of education and the child's safety or on the state's interest in socializing the child through exposure to things or persons outside the home. The restriction rests uneasily with the constitutional right of the family outlined by the Supreme Court in the *Pierce* case. Moreover, if the state is concerned about simple exposure to other people, belonging to the Boy Scouts or singing in the church choir ought to suffice. Furthermore, there is no reason to believe that those rare families who are actually willing to carry the burden of home instruction will not do a good job. On principle, flat prohibitions against home teaching should be dropped if workable means can be found to assure that the parents in fact are providing instruction.

If the plan not only permits but actually subsidizes the family for its efforts, the problem of policing the adequacy of home instruction is substantially increased. Parents might simply pocket the subsidy without bothering to provide the promised education. Obviously it is not the objective of a choice plan to give cash grants to families, much as they might be needed; and it would doom future experimentation with subsidized home instruction were this sort of dishonesty thought to be widespread.

Before coming to grips with this home instruction dilemma, we must make clear that it is related to a potentially larger problem. Suppose a participating school, private or public, attempted to attract a following by providing money or goods to its students. In the grossest form, a school might agree to kick back 25 percent of its state subsidy to any family enrolling its child. Criminal penalties might be adequate to deter kickbacks in such blatant form, but more subtle mechanisms for giving the family cash or equivalent benefits present some sticky line-drawing issues. Could a school provide free lunch? What if the school provided great quantities of school supplies or numerous books for home reading? A related problem would arise if the school hired its pupils to perform bona fide tasks in return for cash. A school might, for example, pay its older students to tutor younger ones, or to perform maintenance functions around the building.

The appropriate standard for judging such activity must be reasonably broad, although administrative machinery, including financial disclosure, would probably be needed to deter families from using the school as a means for converting the state education subsidy into cash. In most schools families which were not being cashed out would complain; offering rewards would stimulate such behavior. If a school gave a kickback to all enrollees, the magnitude of the fraud should help the policing agency discover it.

In the case of home instruction, more supervision may be necessary. Parents might be required to file with the administering agency proposed objectives for their child, plus a plan for achieving them. If the agency accepted the proposal, the subsidy would be released; if after a specified time the objectives were met, the family could submit a new plan and continue their subsidized home instruction. As a safety measure the funds, or some of them, might be withheld until after the objectives were met. The subsidized home instruction privilege would be lost—at least for some while—if children failed to meet the stated objectives. If the parents simply flouted the agreement, the family might lose its right even to select the place of the child's future education.

The definition of acceptable objectives would be a delicate matter. In principle, a family with a child plainly capable of achieving more than the societally determined "minimum" would be required to have "higher" objectives. Thus, the agency would be compelled to scrutinize content (would learning to ride a horse count?); quantity (the child might already know most of his multiplication tables); and the technique proposed. The objectives would also have to be somehow measurable. We suppose that at the beginning standardized tests, traditional methods, and conventional subjects would be stressed by the state agency. While there is clearly a risk that the agency would be too rigid or biased, and that the educational programs proposed by some families would be rejected, at least there would be some room for creative parents to mark out unique at-home programs for their children that would be subsidized.

The idea of using "results" as the basis for state subsidy of home instruction suggests the further possibility that families could receive a state subsidy for *whatever* private experience they call education, so long as their children make sufficient learning gains. Plainly, individualized objectives for all children—rather than the few who would be expected to choose home instruction—would be administratively overwhelming. We think it conceivable, however, that general outcome standards in basic areas might eventually displace control over curriculum, environment, and teachers.

This possibility parallels our suggestion in Chapter 4 to treat education like child-rearing generally and to accept family discretion until sufficient lack of progress—outcome—indicates that the child's interest lies in turning over some or all of the choice to others. In such cases the state could impose restrictions on family choice, but in different ways depending on the degree of the child's failure on the tests. A modest shortcoming by the child might limit but not eliminate the family's discretion. Progressively more serious failure might limit the family's choice to public schools, give public authorities a veto on its selection, or give to such authorities the choice of school.

THE CLIMATE OF FREEDOM AND FAIRNESS: STUDENT RIGHTS

The right of students to be protected from unfair and arbitrary action by school officials is a growing edge of the law.[15] As a substitute for full control of admission policy in a family choice scheme, schools may be tempted to employ harsh internal policies, including capricious expulsions of those whose only sin is to be unwanted by their school. As previously noted, it is not clear whether private schools under a state scholarship plan would be constitutionally bound to recognize those claims of their students that are protected in public school settings. Even if the constitution applies fully to participating private schools, student rights may deserve more than this minimal protection.

The specific rights that student activists have typically sought in recent controversies include free expression (speech on school grounds, student newspapers, handbills, speakers at school, armbands and other symbols), free assembly (clubs, rallies), and personal choice as to appearance (dress and hair codes). Some of these demands are already constitutionally recognized by judicial decision; others may soon come to be; still others remain improbable; and some have been rejected.[16] Systems of choice would continue to involve these issues of "civil liberties" as well as those raised by academic insufficiency and by all forms of behavior offensive to the administration. A choice plan could contain a legislated code of prescriptive and proscriptive minimums on top of which each school and its users could develop local standards.

The handling of expulsion, suspension, and failure raises both substantive and procedural questions. We have already explained that a school must be permitted to expel intolerably disruptive children, so long as it follows fair procedures in determining whether the behavior warrants this classification. Likewise if a child is demonstrably incapable of benefiting from regular education, we would allow him to be excluded; again fair procedures are essential. In appropriate cases we would also permit graded schools to require a child to repeat. Others will prefer different substantive rules; for example, an experiment could be tried which forbids exclusion for inability to benefit.

The process employed in applying the substantive standards, while fair to the student, must not burden the school intolerably. Whether or not the rights at stake are constitutionally protected, a sensible balance of the competing concerns must be the objective. Thus, decisions involving threat of expulsion will demand more of the system than will suspension cases, simply because more is at stake.[17] Yet even in trivial matters the spirit of the rules should not become niggardly in the name of efficiency. Even though decisions on grades and grade repetition are difficult to fit into an adjudicative model, at the very least the family should be consulted and given an explicit written explanation. On the other hand, it is inappropriate to require a hearing with confrontation of witnesses on every petty issue of discipline. The plan should not try to carve out optimal rules for every school; rather, it should encourage as many procedural variants as family choice generates.

A crucial students' rights question is that of compulsory attendance. This long-existing practice is presently under attack in the courts, and there is no reason to believe that the extreme opponents will be satisfied by the provision of options unless virtually anything a child does qualifies as school. The degree to which the compulsory attendance laws are currently enforced varies from place to place and perhaps by family circumstance. Most suburbs go through the motions of enforcement and give the appearance of taking these laws seriously; the reality is more difficult to assess, because parental excuses are typically accepted without question. Big city schools are content with the half-hearted cajoling of truant officers. Private schools are generally left to themselves to enforce the attendance rules. Some deviant groups, such as the clientele of certain unaccredited "free schools" or exotic religious schools, do find the compulsory attendance laws invoked against them.[18]

Several legislative options would be consistent with a system fairly labeled "choice." Compulsory attendance could be eliminated, could be left to the judgment of each school, or could continue as at present subject to whatever changes come through constitutional attack. As one form of experiment, we favor requiring children of school age to enroll in an approved program, leaving day-to-day monitoring of their attendance to the individual school. A school could use unexcused absences as a basis for disciplinary action and even expulsion, so long as it acted in a nondiscriminatory manner. We think absences would decline in view of the child's increased opportunity to find something attractive. The state would still have to concern itself with the extreme cases. At some point a child's nonattendance should be deemed dropping out, thereby cutting off the right of the school to receive the state funds earmarked for him. Without such a rule the school would have no legal incentive to woo regular attendance from the reluctant participant, though the family would often exact diligence from the school as the price of its enrollment.

Throughout the student rights area sensitive problems might

arise from intrafamilial clashes; parents may side with the institution and be willing to waive their child's individual rights. Whether parents ought to be able entirely to waive the free speech rights of six-year-olds is problematic; whether they should be able to waive all such rights of their high school children is not. Just as we think it important for the child to have increased power over the choice of his school as he matures, it is equally important that the right of political expression in the school he selects by stages become his to exercise. Again, however, one must recognize that "rights" of unemancipated children are strongly affected in their practical exercise by parental preference.

Fair procedures for handling expulsion or retention could become meaningless, particularly in large schools, if families have no rights within the school to select their child's classes, teachers, and resources. There are two different kinds of problems here. First, a family might desire that its child attend a certain school only if he can experience a particular third-grade teacher, take a particular class or course of study, or—in a school that has multiple locations—be assigned to a particular site. Should a choice plan insist that families be permitted to make these within-school selections? If so, could a family with an eight-year-old demand his admission to a school's sixth grade? In short, this is the problem of school admissions revisited, but here within the school.

Perhaps the legislature should wait to see what intraschool guarantees market and local political forces would generate. Presumably, some schools would offer the right to select individual teachers as an attraction; others would announce class selection procedures in advance. Smaller schools would present fewer problems; although their limited program would mean fewer options, families would presumably have understood this when they chose the school. If the market mechanism gave the family reasonable confidence about what it was buying for its child, additional regulatory supervision might well not be needed.

Unfortunately, if schools are stripped of control over admissions, the market would not work for those students who had been unwanted applicants. Their threat to withdraw from school would be no lever on the school, particularly if it had a waiting list; indeed, the school would have the incentive to encourage their departure. However, the appropriate type of in-school protection to be afforded such children is difficult to determine. The degree of policing and state intrusion required to operate the process could make this problem more difficult than that of basic school admission. Requiring preannounced school policies and even-handed application of the school's own standards would help, but enforcement would be difficult. Perhaps schools should be forbidden to track students by ability or, if permitted, tracking might be limited to classes whose students have been enrolled in the school at least one year. If the problem of mistreatment of certain students became serious enough, and if the state's commitment against educational refusals to serve were strong enough, some regulation of the allocation of in-school opportunities would be necessary.

A primary protection for student and parental rights lies within the general power of the administering public agency to disqualify individual schools from participating because of substantial failure to observe the rules of the system— including respect for the rights of users. This standard administrative stick, however, ordinarily has haphazard impact unless one of two further conditions is met. Either the agency must have a well-staffed inspectorate or the consumer must himself be armed with the capacity to initiate the sanctioning process and have resources to carry it through. The former is generally too expensive. The latter could work if private voluntary organizations were permitted to appear before the agency and represent those families that had complaints against the school. Such a system of private attorneys-general might tap a rich lode of volunteer energy and resources. One can imagine the happiest marriage of the ACLU with the PTA, the combination producing an epidemic of honesty and fair dealing among the school fraternity.

Chapter 11

THE NATURE OF THE SUBSIDY

Get it beforehand and in cash.

—HILAIRE BELLOC,
Cautionary Verses

Any large-scale experiment with choice will include "subsidizing" most or all families. Political reality would dictate that the middle-class families who now receive "tuition-free" education not be required to pay directly the full cost of their children's education. This may also be good policy, as we noted in Chapter 1. We take this reality into account in describing the technical decisions to be faced in designing the financing. We will also continue to assume that society's objective is to give families of all incomes as nearly equal access to participating schools as possible. Family circumstance should not unfairly affect choice of school. What that proposition means—or what different things it might mean—is the subject of this chapter.

TUITION ADD-ONS: THE PROBLEM OF RICH AND POOR FAMILIES

Milton Friedman has proposed that each school-age child be given his per capita share of the public budget for elementary and secondary education in the form of a redeemable education voucher. The child's family could use the voucher to purchase education only from state-approved schools. Each family could, however, add its own dollars to the voucher if the chosen school charged an additional tuition.[1] This freedom to add on private dollars makes the Friedman model unacceptable to many, including ourselves. Unless the amount of the voucher were so large as to preempt all interest in further spending for education by all but an insignificant number of families (an outcome economically and politically unthinkable), the effect of Friedman's proposal is plain. Families unable to add extra dollars would patronize those schools that charged no tuition above the voucher, while the wealthier would be free to distribute themselves among the more expensive schools.[2] What is today merely a personal choice of the wealthy, secured entirely with private funds, would become an invidious privilege assisted by government. Isolation and excellence would be purchased by the rich with public assistance. Both wealthier classmates and the schools they might prefer would be foreclosed to the poor—all with the help of the state. This offends a fundamental value commitment—that any choice plan must secure equal family opportunity to attend any participating school.

Even under a choice plan which allowed tuition add-ons, poor families might be better off than they are today. Friedman has argued as much. Nevertheless, however much it improved their education, conscious government finance of economic segregation exceeds our tolerance. If the Friedman scheme were the only politically viable experiment with choice, we would not be enthusiastic. Conceivably many wealthier families would not select schools with tuition charges in excess of the voucher amount; conceivably the poor would be able to scrape together extra funds. Friedman says society should experiment to see if his plan would produce economic segregation in enrollment patterns. However, it would be a curious experiment; the outcome hoped for is wholly inconsistent with Friedman's own model of human behavior. Rational economic theory predicts economic class segregation within such a model; if a parallel is needed, consider the housing market. Moreover, the political impact on education appears wholly negative. If tuition add-ons are permitted, the nonpoor will have no stake in assuring that the voucher amount increases as inflation pushes up the cost of education. We would support a plan which allowed tuition add-ons only as one among many experiments, the remainder of which were designed to diminish or remove the effects of wealth.

Our objective, however, is not to level the wealth of families. We assume here that even huge differences in personal wealth are inoffensive so long as their impact is confined to the private financial sector. We assume also that wealthier families will always be free to supplement formal education with the purchase of private learning experiences for their children. The effort here is to eliminate the influence of family wealth only in the limited arena of "publicly financed education." That objective is nevertheless an ambitious one. It would help ensure that rich and poor in substantial numbers would, by choice, experience the educational process together.

Initially it might appear that our objection to the Friedman plan could be eliminated simply by forbidding participating schools from charging tuition in excess of the voucher amount. Let us suppose, however, that the amount of the voucher were fixed at only $300 per child per year—or that over time the grants purchased annually only $300 of education at today's prices. In such a case, the rich would probably desert the system altogether in favor of purely independent schools, and they would be better able to do so since their tax burden for education at this price would be relatively small. The middle class might resort to using part-time voucher schools— say, three mornings a week—and pay for additional instruction at private nonparticipating institutions out of their own pockets, once again leaving the poor to enjoy one another's company. For this reason, the family subsidy must be large enough to ensure that most families use the plan to provide the bulk of their children's education.

Of course, it might be possible by law to require all children to enroll full time in participating schools which charged no extra tuition. Later we will look briefly at the desirability and constitutionality of such a "preemptive" system. For now, we want only to note and put aside this device for putting the rich in the same boat with the poor. Until otherwise indicated, we will assume that choice experiments will be designed so that most families will find it desirable to use full-time participating schools and that such schools will not be entitled to accept privately funded tuition supplements.

GEOGRAPHIC DIVERSITY: THE PROBLEM OF RICH AND POOR PUBLIC SCHOOL DISTRICTS

Our states have long tolerated a system of education finance based on local school districts with widely differing taxable wealth. As a consequence children in poor districts suffer from lower spending levels. Often these children are from low income families as well and cannot escape to private schools.

We will briefly describe the typical scheme.[3] Today in most states, public school finance relies on local property taxes. School districts raise a significant portion of their money by taxing property located within their borders at a rate set by the school board or the local voters, sometimes constrained by limits established by the state. The state supplements this local money with funds it raises through income, sales, and other statewide taxes. The state distributes its funds according to various rather complicated formulae, typically allocating a larger share to "poor" districts—those with lower taxable property values per pupil. Despite this state aid to poor districts, districts with more taxable property per pupil can and do spend much more per child than do poorer districts, even when their local tax rates are identical. Far from being a policy objective, this state-created economic privilege of families in tax-rich districts has consistently been excused as an inevitable evil—the price of decentralization. This is a gross misconception.

Indeed, this system of haphazard privileges and penalties has been held to violate a few of our state constitutions. The California Supreme Court, for example, in 1976 recognized the constitutional norm of "fiscal neutrality"—that spending for public education may not be a function of wealth other than that of the state as a whole.[4] Although the United States Supreme Court has held that fiscal neutrality is not required by the federal Constitution,[5] one of the five majority justices conceded that the existing school finance systems are "chaotic and unjust."[6] In recent years, even without judicial intervention, legislatures in a number of states have begun to eliminate state-sponsored wealth discrimination.[7]

Reforming legislators have many alternative policies open to them. Those that follow the California norm of fiscal neutrality are free to adopt either a fully centralized fiscal system for education or to make all local units equal in their capacity to raise money and spend according to taste. Several states have put decentralized schemes of this sort into operation.[8] Though imperfect, these reforms are important as experiments; they have demonstrated that wealth-neutral plans encompassing decentralized decision-making about expenditures are possible. Shortly we shall show the relevance of this possibility for family choice.

In all states, the existing structure of finance will affect family choice plans. Under the typical unreformed systems, wealth discrimination will be reflected in choice plans adopted within single school districts; some choice plans would be well funded, others impoverished, depending on the property wealth per pupil in each district. Furthermore, the continued existence of poor and rich districts will impede the formation of multidistrict compacts. Efforts to extend choice beyond a district's boundaries or to create regional plans will encounter problems with varying wealth, tax rates, and spending per pupil. Therefore systems of fiscal support for areas of experimentation larger than districts will often require significant state involvement.

SHOULD EACH CHILD RECEIVE THE SAME SUBSIDY? FOUR MODELS OF FINANCE

The purpose of this section is to describe and evaluate four different models for distributing the financial subsidy or scholarship. Each model is consistent with the minimum fairness requirements described in the previous sections but represents a distinct outlook on the issue of equal educational opportunity. The idea of equal opportunity is sufficiently plastic to support arguments on both sides of nearly every practical issue we have faced in this book. Not surprisingly our fiscal models represent a spectrum of views that strongly conflict, yet all claim egalitarian roots. They range from mere uniformity of the power to spend to uniformity of spending itself.

(1) *Uniform Grant Model (UGM)*. Under this model each child would receive a scholarship or voucher of equal value. The greatest virtue of the UGM is its simplicity. If no extra tuition can be charged, and if the schools must fundamentally rely for funds on their students' grants, UGM approaches a "Uniform Spending Model." UGM does not necessarily mean that all schools would spend exactly the same amount per pupil (for example, some might invest, others take profits), or that the same would be spent on every individual pupil (the school might allocate its total resources unevenly over its various programs). Still, UGM approximates uniformity in spending, a quality often seen as a political advantage, and certainly one common definition of equal educational opportunity.

(2) *The Needs Adjustment Model (NAM)*. The second model is a variation of a scheme first proposed by Theodore Sizer

and Philip Whitten.[9] Their original idea was to compensate
for the discrimination inherent in the unregulated Friedman
model by making larger grants ($1,500) to the poorest families
(under $2,000 income) and progressively reducing the grant
to zero for families of average income. In a system in which
schools controlled their admissions (which Sizer and Whitten
assumed), the disadvantaged child would become a more
attractive applicant, since he would bring substantial funds
with him. At the same time, although the plan is clever in
conception, it is nearly inconceivable in political terms because
it forfeits the support of the middle class.

The Center for the Study of Public Policy (CSPP) has
published a modification of this scheme which seems more
plausible.[10] Under the CSPP proposal, all children would
be given a basic grant, and the grants to poorer families would
be augmented by an amount inversely related to income, as
in the Sizer-Whitten proposal. The children of the poorest
families might, for example, receive a $2,000 grant, with that
amount diminishing to a flat $1,000 for families at and above
the average income level. Tuition add-ons would be forbidden
in the CSPP model.

The CSPP authors used family poverty as shorthand for
educational need. Since the schools could not charge tuition
beyond the grant, they would determine their income by the
degree of educational need (wealth) of the students they
selected. The consequence for all schools could be seen as
the equalization, not of spending, but of the *true quality*,
because two major determinants of quality education—dollars
and the abilities of the students—would be "in balance" in
every school. The more the school admitted educationally
needy applicants (using family income as the standard), the
more the school would have in dollars to spend on education,
but the less it would have in the abilities of students and,
thus, their capacity to teach one another. (The NAM might
well be styled a "Uniform Quality Model"; curiously its
authors seem never to have perceived this feature of their
system.) Looked at from the user side, this model presents
the family with an interesting option. Assuming that needier
students are not evenly distributed among the schools, the
model allows families to choose between two kinds of schools
of presumably equal quality—those with more generous bud-
gets and those with more able classmates.

There are grave difficulties, of course, with balancing lower
income students against extra money. One of these is the

equating of the level of family income with the child's contribution to the school; given our limited understanding of how peer influence operates, family income is a very crude indicator of desired pupil characteristics, even if no better measure is readily available. The second problem is quantifying the relation; how many extra dollars are needed to balance out the supposed negative impact of the needier students? Clearly there is no education production function on which this judgment can be based. Any conclusion is just a hunch.

In fairness, since the authors of NAM did not perceive it as a uniform quality model, it should be evaluated in their terms. They intended the differential subsidy as a way of assuring, first, that even if they continue to control their admissions, schools would have an incentive to choose the less attractive students, and, second, that extra funds would be spent on such students to offset the educational disadvantages they suffer. Unfortunately the NAM disclosed nothing about how the extra dollars that come with needier students are to be spent by the school. Let us assume that, absent regulation of within-school allocations, these extra funds would be spread evenly over the school population and program. In that event the holders of bigger grants may be attractive to schools, but they have no claim for extra spending on themselves. Conversely, if the school's own spending is regulated to require that resources are spent on each child in proportion to those he brings with him, disadvantaged children may no longer be so attractive to the school.

(3) *The Cost Adjustment Model (CAM).* One does not deliver education in the form of greenbacks; they must be converted into goods, salaries, and so on. But it may be argued that these inputs do not *cost* the same in every school. A number of things might be meant by this statement; for example, it does not cost the same to build a school in San Francisco and in Petaluma (because of weather, land values, vandalism, or whatever); the cost of living in Oakland is higher than in Eureka and so teachers' salaries must be higher; the equipment needed to teach vocational education makes it costlier than college prep; specialization in teaching makes high school more expensive than primary grades; it costs more to get the same teacher to teach in the urban ghetto than it would to get him to teach somewhere else. The Cost Adjustment Model (CAM) would modify the value of the

voucher in order to account for factors that are beyond the school's control. In this way CAM might be seen as an Equal Offering Model—the purchase of equal educational inputs—another version of equal educational opportunity.

What cost differentials are beyond the school's control? Certainly some of the examples given fail to qualify. Why does it cost more to provide an offering in high school which is "equal" to that available in elementary school? The answer lies in history, not in nature. For various contingent reasons, society has acquired the habit of devoting more money per pupil to higher grades. One reason may be that we have thought high school is more important, though today many urge that this spending pattern is one of the prime evils of our current system; elementary school, they say, is more important, and therefore we should concentrate resources on the younger students. Viewed broadly, then, a CAM system would operate so as to increase the amount of the family grant in accord with officially approved criteria. This qualification does not forfeit CAM's egalitarian claims. When all the policy preferences are worked in, the resulting vouchers, though of different values, are an attempt to provide equality of offering within each category of school. If all categories are open to all persons, the system retains democratic credentials.

Because of the need to resolve value questions and to put dollar figures on them, CAM means intensive political haggling. A legion of educational factions would arise to lobby particular dollar adjustments in recognition of their special burden or special contribution. Cost adjustments also raise difficult definitional and policing problems. If an extra grant is to be given when a child pursues vocational education, what is to qualify as vocational education and what are vocational schools? If Chicago is a high-cost-of-living area, should the larger grants be available even to children who choose to attend schools taught by unsalaried computers? Finally, CAM, to the extent that it ignores important personal differences among students, treats them as inputs much as does UGM. Of course, there is nothing to prevent adjustments for such personal differences by combining CAM and NAM. Students of different sorts may be thought of as costing more to educate. Just which sorts, again, is largely a matter of one's values. It would be easy to argue that our resources should be concentrated on those likely to learn the most and be most productive.

(4) *The Quality Choice Model (QCM).* The fourth fiscal model is intended to promote variety in the quality of schools rather than uniformity. While we have elsewhere called this Family Power Equalizing,[11] or FPE, here it will be styled the Quality Choice Model (QCM). In simple outline QCM would allow participating schools to charge whatever tuition they wished within a stipulated range, say, from $800 to $2,500 per year. Each family would select from the various priced schools the one it thought best for its child and pay a portion of its income toward tuition; the state would subsidize the rest, with the subsidy based on family income. Hence, for example, a poor family might be expected to pay $200 per year for a $1,600 school, while the state provided the remaining $1,400; by contrast, a middle-class family might pay $800 to send its child to a $1,200 school while the state provided the remaining $400. Subsidies would be set so that the poor, in some meaningful sense, could afford the high-priced schools—indeed, any school—as easily as the rich. Even the desperately poor would be required to pay something, however, if only $10 toward a $1,000 tuition and $20 towards a $2,000 tuition, to establish a personal stake in the choice.

A family with more than one child presents an interesting policy issue. Probably, as is true of the existing school finance system, no extra cost would be imposed on families with more children. Hence, once a family paid its assigned share of the tuition for one child, the rest of its children in school at that time would be fully subsidized at the same tuition level. If the family wished to send different children to different priced schools, its total financial obligation would be an averaged amount.

QCM would function in a manner similar to the way in which the federal food stamp program operated through 1977—with important differences. In the food stamp plan, families put out their own money to acquire the stamps used to pay for groceries. They were given a choice as to how many stamps they wished to buy. The amount they paid was scaled both to income and to family size. QCM and food stamps are quite similar in these respects. Indeed, the family's ability to divide up the food stamps and use them at different markets parallels our earlier proposal for divisible educational experiences under which a family could package together a number of independent teachers.

There are two crucial differences, however. First, the food stamp program is available only to the poor, and, second,

even the maximum value of stamps which can be acquired
will provide only the *minimum* food budget the government
thinks necessary. It is no wonder that most food stamp
participants purchased all the stamps allowed to them. The
nutritional analogue to QCM would be a program in which
the maximum value of food stamps obtainable was raised
to the level of a high quality food budget, and families at
all or nearly all income levels could acquire food stamps
at some discount.

While some may shrink at "subsidizing" the food bills of
the rich, note that through the taxes they paid they would
support the food subsidy program and on a net basis enjoy
no subsidy after all. The same can be said of QCM. Moreover,
even assuming that the public were to finance choice in
education so as to provide the rich a net subsidy while their
children are in school, it could scarcely equal the bonus now
enjoyed by most rich families using public education. Today
a family with a $40,000 income, a $75,000 home, and two
children in the public schools of San Francisco receives a
net yearly subsidy of about $3,000. Under a QCM system,
for the first time such families would pay tuition directly
on the basis of income.

The expanded food stamp parallel may be puzzling at first;
Americans are unaccustomed to government benefit programs
which apply a wealth standard at all income levels. Furthermore, we suffer a traditional unwillingness to use such
programs to provide anything beyond the bare minimum.
However, in the case of education this society's aspiration
for children has generally reached higher than the bare
minimum—and for all children. How much higher is hard
to say because of the chaos in school finance; however, one
safe inference from the present pattern is that there are many
opinions concerning the proper level of spending. If education
is to reflect all these opinions, and if families are to have
reasonably equal access to schools, then income-conditioned
subsidies for a wide variety of tuition levels are needed.

The complications of QCM are made necessary because
its objective is not to equalize school spending, school offering,
or school quality but only each family's economic ability to
select cheaper or more expensive schools; it aims to make
the family's choice depend only on its interest in education
(compared to other items it buys) and its evaluation of what
its child will gain from a particular school. QCM emphasizes
this option among spending levels as one element of the

"choice" which the state should strive to provide its families.

Variety in quality is ordinarily viewed as the problem, not the goal in public education. But it is a problem largely because education is imposed, not chosen. In an involuntary system justice may require uniformity of quality; when there is choice, the rationale for such uniformity becomes tenuous. We assume there is a variety of family preferences concerning how much money should be spent on the education of their children. And a system which allows these differences to be expressed represents a very valuable type of equality. The other models would sacrifice this equality of choice among spending levels for equalities of other sorts.

Recent social science research has taught us to be skeptical about equating cost with quality.[12] QCM is in harmony with that outlook; it would encourage families to exercise their own judgment about the efficacy of extraschool purchases compared to other goods and services. It would also satisfy providers who prefer to offer programs at a price above or below the norm, and might stimulate kinds of choices that otherwise would not be available.

At this point in any discussion of QCM an objector usually surfaces who simply does not trust poor families to spend enough on education and fears that their children will inevitably end up clustered in the cheapest schools. Such skeptics must—like all of us—hold their beliefs in the absence of any relevant data, since the poor have never had the opportunity to make any choice, much less an equalized choice of spending level. We suspect that, if anything, the risk is not that the poor will underspend, but that, unduly optimistic about the value of education, they will overspend. Even if, as a class, the poor prove to have preferences for lower priced schooling, there will be many individual exceptions. It is not clear that we should frustrate these aspirant families who are willing to sacrifice in the hope that their children will enjoy wider opportunities; only by providing some form of quality choice can that impulse be given reality. In any event, the situation is ideal for experimentation. For the first time society may obtain reliable insight into class-specific commitments to education.

In the broadest sense, however, choice among spending levels (above some adequate minimum) must be defended on the ground that if the family is to be relied on to determine what is in the best interest of the child generally, it should also have something to say about how much that education should cost. Children's needs differ, and QCM avoids the unrealistic assumptions of uniform and cost-adjusted grants, which treat children as homogeneous; in our judgment it is also superior to needs-adjusted grants where need is centrally determined for masses of children defined by abstract conceptions. QCM allows the child to be viewed by the family and its supporting system of counselors as an individual for whom an educational investment is to be tailored according to his wishes, his needs, and his aspirations.

A number of very difficult decisions must be made if QCM is to be implemented. QCM seems to require that the state determine precisely the income of every participating family in order to specify its liability for tuition. Most state income tax programs (or the federal returns) could perform this function, although some might think the tax definition of income inadequate for the purpose of determining educational subsidies as it fails to treat as income various items (including welfare) that might be appropriately included. Adjustments would not be too difficult to administer and police, however, particularly because there are ways to simplify the QCM plan. One technique would be to require schools to charge tuition rates at one of several levels—for example, $1,000, $1,400, $1,800, and $2,200—and then to group families in relatively large income classes. This would permit the publication of a simple table showing the payment obligation of families in each income class for each of the four school tuition amounts. In this way officials would have to worry only about families with large amounts of income not treated as such for tax purposes. Objections could be raised regarding the inevitable "notching" effects at the borders of the categories and the diminution of progressivity in the prices charged, but on the whole these are minor points.

Since user families would, for the first time, pay direct tuition in a public system, QCM could significantly alter the present distribution of the education burden between users and nonusers. This may be viewed as either a threat or an opportunity, and many legislative responses are plainly possible. The aggregate burden on the separate classes of users and nonusers might, for example, be reestablished on its present basis by adjusting the size of the dependency deduction (or credit) a family can use in computing its state income taxes and by altering the child allowance distributed through existing welfare and social insurance programs. Although QCM is the only one of the four models requiring a direct financial outlay by the family, an income-scaled user fee could be imposed under the other models as well. As under QCM, direct payment for the UGM, NAM, or CAM voucher could give the family a greater psychological stake in the selection made.

Several conceptual and policy problems must be faced in determining the appropriate price schedule for the various tuition options. First, if it costs a $10,000-a-year family only $25 to move from a $1,200 to a $1,600 school, perhaps all such families would choose the higher priced school, but if it costs $375, perhaps none would make the choice of the more expensive school. In either case the formal choice has been made meaningless because of the price charged. Hence, the relationship of the change in the amount paid to the change in the amount of the subsidy gained must be given careful attention. Second, rates need to be set so that they make sense across income classes; should a $16,000 family pay ·twice what an $8,000 family does, or three times that amount? If the family tuition payments will be interpreted as a tax that is deductible for federal income tax purposes, the rates charged to different income classes should also take this into account. Note that if tuition is nondeductible for tax purposes, it becomes a type of reverse revenue sharing; that is, other things being equal, families will pay higher federal tax bills than they do today since school property taxes are now deductible.

The crucial test of a family's interest is its willingness to sacrifice other goods and services for education. If education had to be purchased completely with private resources, of course, the poor by necessity would express a preference for less than the wealthy. The real question, however, is not how much the poor would buy unassisted, but how much variation in spending for education there would be if price counted but individual family wealth did not. By equalizing educational purchasing power through QCM, society would identify those families with stronger preferences by their willingness to pay more. It may be difficult to assure that the power to purchase education is effectively equalized. But the objective is clear: to approximate equality of educational purchasing power by adjusting the price of education according to family wealth. How to do this with reasonable precision could be learned through experimentation and monitoring.

Finally, QCM encounters an interesting but manageable difficulty in its application to the education of older children. Earlier we stressed the importance of granting teenagers considerable independent power over their own education. Assuming this were done, under a QCM system would children be allowed to choose an expensive school and force their parents to pay the increased family share? We suppose not. Unemancipated older children would have to be limited to a selection from among those programs offered at a price level the family is willing to support, and we concede that this financial power may give the parents an additional informal bargaining tool with which to influence the child's choice. It seems a reasonable trade-off. Only QCM would satisfy the family in which both parents and teenager agree on a costlier than average education.

It would be a mistake to single out one of these four fiscal models as the exclusive subject of experimentation. Each has its theoretical strong points and drawbacks, and each should be tried. If nothing else we may be able to learn whether the fiscal arrangements matter very much in a choice plan. For example, if substantially all families in a QCM experiment opted for essentially the same priced schools, the result would approach that of a UGM experiment. The same might be said about an NAM trial in which needier students are relatively evenly distributed across participating schools. Whether such outcomes would call for restricting future experiments to UGM (or CAM) is a more complicated matter. Deliberation about which empirical findings would be significant in the statistical sense exceeds our purpose and capacity. However, the focus of any experiment is clear; it is the discovery of the modes of education preferred by families with children.

Regardless of the fiscal model, attention must be directed to three further matters relating to finance—transfers, the regulation of competition among the providers, and the possibility of restricting the grants to fewer than all children.

TRANSFER POLICIES

It would be possible to permit a family to contract with a school for the education of its child for however long each side agreed desirable; under such a rule a family could commit its child's grant to one institution for a number of years in advance. People are known to buy dancing lessons on this basis—a compact they sometimes regret. In the ordinary case, however, there would be little advantage to the family in long commitments, and they would create potentially serious detriments both to the individual child and to the plan as a whole. In our view it is desirable to diminish the importance of the original selection of a school and to maximize the freedom to transfer at any time from a school that proves unsatisfactory for whatever reason is sufficient to the family. This policy objective is buttressed by the frequency with which family responsibilities—such as parental employment—make transfers a necessity. Families should, of course, be under an obligation to give the school adequate notice when they decide to remove their child. And perhaps certain newly formed schools—especially small cooperative schools—should be entitled to an initial longer range commitment from a nucleus of families in order to justify the risks of organization. In general, however, both consumer protection and the interest of the state suggest that the system of transfer be fluid, forbidding long-term contracts and permitting families to exit, even during a school year, and to take the unconsumed portion of their grant with them.

Current federal government regulations affecting private vocational postsecondary schools point the way toward liberal transfer policies of this sort.[13] Federal authorities are beginning to insist on liberal tuition refund policies for students who drop out or transfer from schools of cosmetology, accounting, and the like. This development may provide helpful guidelines on which the choice plan could be modeled. It may also provide experience with respect to the possibility, feared by the schools, that users would combine their power and threaten to withdraw *en masse* to force the school into making drastic policy changes. We generally applaud families using their economic power to stimulate responsive providers. No doubt there are limits to the organized pressure that may properly be visited on an entrepreneur, but school providers like others would enjoy the protection given by the common law against boycotts and other restraints of trade; in some states they would have statutory rights as well.[14] We suspect these are sufficient protection for suppliers. Experience with the postsecondary school controls may soon be available to help confirm or rebut this.

REGULATION OF COMPETITION AMONG PROVIDERS

Even if schools were not allowed to charge extra tuition, there would remain the question whether they must operate entirely on the tuition grants received from students, whether—or to what extent—a school may use outside wealth to support its operations. "Outside" may encompass many kinds of financial support, including (1) income from interested sources, for example, voluntary contributions of the parents of enrollees or gifts from supporters such as alumni and groups affiliated (say, ideologically) with the school; (2) disinterested donations, such as grants from independent foundations or federal aid; and (3) initial assets, such as the existing physical plant or endowment of a participating school plus the income earned on such school assets, including proceeds from the leasing of facilities and interest or dividends on endowment.

We would be very concerned about outside wealth if it enabled schools to discriminate against the poor. This could occur, for example, if parents could make "gifts" *and* the schools had control over admissions. In that case even if a plan formally prohibited tuition charges in excess of the state-subsidized amount, it might be converted into a Friedman plan by selective admission of those who could be counted on to make donations. This can be prevented most easily by the admission policies earlier discussed. However, the poor could also be put to an intolerable disadvantage if the school tracked its students and allocated resources on the basis of whether the child's family was a big giver. If the package of student rights, including guarantees against gross misallocation, proved adequate, it might be unnecessary to forbid contributions of a disinterested sort.

An important independent argument for placing strict limits on "outside" wealth grows from the special character of the educational market to be created. The philosophers of competition are not ordinarily offended by a mere diversity of economic power among competitors—at least where the differences do not threaten monopoly. However, an educational grant system is not the classic market of free enterprise theory, the function of which is essentially exhausted in the production and distribution of goods and services. A principal purpose of a choice plan is the fair competition of ideas; much more than economic power is at stake among the suppliers. The fair contest which is its object is frustrated if the grant a child brings to school A can be supplemented by an affluent religious or political group, while school B with no rich sponsors has to survive on its tuition. This is, after all, a system of public finance we are proposing. That government might be used to provide a foundation upon which ideological interests with the deepest pocket may erect the most inviting programs and institutions is for us a problem.

The practical conclusion that flows from this viewpoint

is that justice to the nonrich school, its students, and its values may require a flat proscription of the acceptance and use of interested income; gifts to a school from any allied source, whether a parent corporation, a friendly church, or an individual, would be barred. The proscription, of course, should include special outside income from the state to public schools. There is no reason to discriminate economically in favor of their message. This would require special steps to assure that participating public schools received no extra support from the state. For financial purposes each public school should operate very much as a separate nonprofit corporation, including the susceptibility to bankruptcy. Earlier we suggested that such independence might be desirable from a governance perspective.

One could imagine a prohibition of donations even from disinterested outside sources. Such donations, if allowed, might also upset a fair competition of ideas. In the first place, it would be difficult to separate "interested" from "disinterested" donations. Even grants from foundations, and this includes tax-exempt foundations, often have ideological bias. Furthermore, when the foundation funds are given for a wholly neutral purpose, this ordinarily would be for experimentation; the same, we suppose, would be true for the other main sources of disinterested funds—state and federal governments. But singling out specific schools for experimentation seems unwarranted; the whole choice program is an experiment, and the introduction of new variables could only complicate its interpretation. It would seem wiser that such added resources go toward either the overall funding or the evaluation of the plan.

Restrictions on a school's initial assets and their fruits might also be needed; otherwise preparticipation accumulations would circumvent control over interested income. One approach to this problem is to impose a ceiling on the per pupil assets of schools entering the plan. While this is easily understood and probably could be simply administered if only cash or equivalent endowments were at stake, it becomes complicated because existing physical plant and other tangibles are involved. It would, of course, be possible to forbid private schools from bringing any tangible assets of its own into the program and to require each public school, over time, to pay the state for the present value of its existing plant and assets out of its tuition profits. Thus private schools that own buildings might, on entry into the program, be required to buy or lease them at state-approved rates from a holding company set up for this purpose, and the income of such a company would not be allowed to benefit the school.

Requiring schools with existing plant to pay for it may be thought especially unfair to public schools, and singularly odd for private schools. First, such a rule would give an advantage to new schools that would not be stuck with outmoded facilities. Second, supporters of private schools, who have worked hard for years to build and pay for a school building, would be terribly deflated to learn that it must be paid for again. And what would be done with the proceeds of the second purchase? Finally, public educators, even if they would own most of the best plant, might need a grace period in which to adjust to the unprecedented competition; allowing them to start out with their buildings may be a reasonable cushion to support them while they strengthen their survival capacities. Hence schools owning buildings at their time of entry might be exempt from an assets test with respect to those buildings. Moreover, the disadvantage this would impose on new schools should not be overestimated. Schools can be organized and operated without enormous start-up costs. Store-front and residential facilities are, for many purposes, superior to the gaunt and expensive architectural relics now inhabited by city pupils.

Some proponents of choice would oppose any wealth limits, even in an experiment.[15] To them, it is already sufficiently clear that the more we spend on education the better, and that the advantage of affluent ideologies is irrelevant so long as all families have equal access to participating schools. Certainly in the marketplace of ideas outside the schools wealth counts, and the line between public and private action is for them a distinction without a difference. Moreover, the opponents of wealth controls have practical objections. They would argue that parental contributions in kind—in the form of part-time volunteers in the schools—cannot be policed and in any event will be and should be bestowed, and therefore money gifts might as well be allowed. Administering wealth controls may also be expensive. However this issue is resolved—and it is not easily settled on principled grounds— each choice plan must confront it.

COMPREHENSIVE VERSUS PARTIAL PLANS

Most of the discussion has assumed a program that, within the geographic area of the experiment, is available to all children, used by most, and accounts for the bulk of a child's formal education. This need not be the case. An experiment might, for example, encompass only children within a particular age group.

Other limitations on scope can be imagined that view choice as a solution to particular problems. Grants could be limited to children who, because of certain individual characteristics, are inadequately served by the public schools. Indeed, in some states today vouchers are provided for handicapped children, because the public schools cannot educate them. Non-English-speaking students are another example. These children and their parents are primarily interested in learning English, but existing public school programs designed for the bulk of children do not well serve this need. Grants which could be utilized in more individualized programs chosen by these families might correct this deficit. Similarly, the grants might be limited to children with educational objectives in which the private sector has more expertise than the public sector. Vocational training is the most obvious candidate for this approach.

Still another approach would provide subsidies for children who, for whatever reasons, are failing. Different ways of measuring failure would imply quite different programs. If, for example, the average reading score of students attending a particular public school fell a specified amount behind national or local averages, or averages of students matched by background, the school would be declared educationally "bankrupt" and its revenue turned over to the families of the students in that school in the form of grants to be used in other schools.[16] This approach could also be adapted to classes or grades within a school. Of course, any set of criteria, not merely reading scores, could be developed to trigger this special "bankruptcy" status. Alternatively, failure might be measured on an individual basis; if a student were sufficiently far behind his peers in basic skills, the family could be given a grant and permitted to enroll the child elsewhere. Whether other public schools were willing or required to take children from failing educational situations might have a lot to do with whether this type of partial grant plan would help either the failing children to obtain better schooling or their assigned schools to prevent failure in the first place.

A final possibility for a partial system of educational grants would support services supplemental to the present public school system. "School stamps," for example, could be spent for after-school, weekend, or summer educational experi-

ences.[17] There may be good reasons for making such supplemental aids available only to the poor. An important way
in which the lives of children of poor families differ from
the norm is their use of out-of-school time. Typically they
have little or no access to music, art, or dance lessons, private
tutoring, or the summer camp experiences characteristic of
the lives of children from wealthier homes. Since these
nonschool experiences (or their lack) may account for some
of the in-school achievement variations between rich and poor
children,[18] a supplementary stamp program restricted to the
poor seems just. Such a plan might provide a uniform number
of school stamps to each poor child or perhaps, like food
stamps and QCM, the family would choose different amounts
at fees graduated by income. An extraschool subsidy proposal
has the political advantage of avoiding the direct confrontation
with the existing public education establishment. Its disadvantage is that it may have little effect on the major portion
of a child's educational experiences.

A PREEMPTIVE MODEL?

In this part we have examined most of the major policy issues
a choice program must resolve to become operational. The
strength of our personal preference for particular solutions
varies. As a working rule, however, we would handle the
subsidy problem by equalizing the power of participating
families to select what they think is best. In general this
means striving to open up a far wider choice of educational
experiences than is available under current public school
arrangements.

However, this broad conclusion finesses a fundamental
issue. One important family option that we have assumed
will continue is viewed by many critics as itself an enemy
of liberty because practically it is not available to most families.
This is the option to use private schools not participating
in the scholarship system. The question is whether the state
should eliminate the right of those who can afford it to opt
out of the state-funded plan entirely. Should the rich family's
choice of such schools be foreclosed? What can be said for
the desirability, workability, and constitutionality of a preemptive scheme of family choice in which all institutions
that wish to qualify as schools must operate within the system
of state control and support?

While some Western nations have largely preempted private

formal schooling, and in this century one of our own states attempted to create a public monopoly, such historical parallels are distinct in motivation and structure from a proposal for preemption under any family choice scheme of the sort we have described. A preemptive education policy has at least two justifications that harmonize with the values we have ascribed to family choice and are consistent with diversity in curriculum and style. First, the society might place such a high value on the ability of the poor to attend with the rich that this policy would transcend the interest of the rich in the freedom to exit. Second, it might conclude that the necessary support of the upper classes for adequately financed education for all children can be obtained only by forcing all to use the same system. These objectives are quite consistent with freedom of choice *within* the system. All that need be added to the family choice models already described is a legal requirement that each child of school age attend an institution qualifying to receive his grant.

A preemptive system might not work, however. The well-to-do might undermine its objectives by using their public grants for what amounted to part-time formal schooling, supplementing the experience by the purchase of substantial formal and separate education. Whether this emphasis on after-school experience would frustrate the central purposes of the scheme would depend largely on the controls imposed—such as required number of hours of instruction—which could diminish the opportunity of the rich to buy "bootleg" education. Of course, the state could never eliminate this opportunity altogether without eliminating private wealth. Nor should it wish to. The basic objective cannot be to stymie such private action but only to coopt to a fair extent the energy and capacities of the upper classes and to focus their primary contribution within a system in which all children share.

For the immediate and foreseeable future a preemptive system seems politically inconceivable. It is well outside the cone of vision of either the traditionalists or the reformers. It would be risky to argue, however, that preemption would never be the choice of the electorate. It is quite possible that in states notable for the defection of the wealthy to private education the mass of blue- and white-collar middle-income groups could eventually perceive its interest to lie in dragging the rich kicking and screaming into schools to which all have access.

The constitutional issue is interesting and deserves fuller

analysis than can be given here. The problem is fundamentally different from that faced by the United States Supreme Court in 1925 in *Pierce* v. *Society of Sisters*. [19] It is one thing to require a child to come into a system designed expressly to eliminate choice, to prohibit variety, and to stamp out private education. It is another to require him to enter a system in which choice and private education flourish. The *Pierce* case forbade the state to require the child to attend a public school. The sytems we are considering actively encourage children to attend private school by making it possible for more to do so. In short, preemptive family choice systems of the sort here considered would tend to carry out rather than frustrate the central values represented in the *Pierce* rationale. Of course, all this assumes that the state stands ready to license schools irrespective of their ideological or religious bent and not to load them with requirements to such a degree as to render them incapable of carrying out their ideological mission; a system which is preemptive both in the sense of being mandatory *and* ideologically exclusive would rather clearly offend *Pierce*. The real question, then, is whether *Pierce* requires that families be given a right of exclusivity—to be able to attend schools where the children of others may be refused entry. This associational interest, while it could prove to be constitutionally protected, surely is not so strong as the interests asserted by families in *Pierce*.

CONCLUSION: SIGNS

The year's at the Spring
ROBERT BROWNING,
"Pippa Passes"

This concluding chapter makes three points. First, small-scale examples of family choice in education exist and can be observed; these "experiments" hint at the feasibility and promise of choice, but by no means tell us enough about the effects of broad experimentation. Second, outside of education, social intervention in children's lives seems increasingly to rely on the family as the decider; the overall trend threatens to make education policy an anachronism. Finally, we suggest that the family as primary protector of children ought to be considered for broad support in every aspect of children's policy.

EDUCATIONAL CHOICE AT WORK

Examples of state-supported educational choice already exist. Experience with these varied programs demonstrates that the family choice experiment we propose is not a wild dream. This experience has also revealed a number of pitfalls that planners of family choice schemes can anticipate in the design of their programs; indeed, the feasibility of some of the regulatory proposals we have advanced seem's confirmed. One should not assume, however, that the existence of these other choice arrangements makes broad experimentation of the sort

212

we have advocated superfluous. They differ too widely from what we propose.

In certain parts of Vermont and New Hampshire there is a very long tradition of nonoperating public school districts. Instead of running their own schools, these communities pay tuition for their students to attend elsewhere. Sometimes this is merely a contractual arrangement with one nearby public school. Often, however, nonoperating districts will pay tuition costs at whichever of a number of private and public schools the local family prefers. To be sure, this practice seems to have arisen and is maintained in large part because of local fiscal concerns. Yet the importance of choice to the families involved should not be played down.

The nonoperating districts that have given their families a fair range of choice tend to be clustered in certain parts of the state. One area is in and around St. Johnsbury, Vermont.[1] In the town itself is St. Johnsbury Academy, a long-established, college-preparatory, private school. While most families in the town have elected to send their high-school-aged children to this school, about 6 percent have not. Moreover, 20 percent of the Academy's enrollment comes from children living in nearby nonoperating districts; their families have chosen the Academy and are provided with public funding in the form of tuition payments. St. Johnsbury youngsters not attending the Academy go to a variety of other high schools at public expense. Two that have received much of this business are Peacham School (a small private "alternative" school) and Danville High School (a traditional public school). These two schools also draw publicly supported students from a variety of other local places. About 20 percent of Danville's more than 200 students are public tuition recipients; nearly all of Peacham's—about 60 students—are publicly supported. Two other public schools that participate in this "market" are Blue Mountain Union High School, with about 25 percent of its more than 300 students as tuition recipients, and Hazel Union High School, with 7 percent of its more than 500 students as tuition recipients. Some think that Blue Mountain and Hazel fall somewhere between Danville and Peacham on the traditional-alternative scale. Not all the families in the greater St. Johnsbury area have educational choice, but among those who do the family decision process is plainly a reality.

We are talking about a very few children living in rather thinly populated areas of states whose citizens are probably relatively homogeneous by national standards. Still, the perseverance and seemingly smooth functioning of this state-supported choice arrangement for elementary and secondary schools pupils are heartening. This is especially so since the replacement of nonoperating districts with consolidated districts is the traditional American way.

The education of handicapped children illustrates another tradition of educational choice. In a number of states, rather than provide public schooling for certain (often many) children in need of special education, public school resources have been made available to parents of such children to permit them to buy the needed schooling from the provider of their choice in the private sector.[2] And from one perspective this choice has well served many of those handicapped children. Compared with what public schools were prepared to offer, tuition aid for private schools was a godsend to the family. However, there are some less savory aspects to this tradition. Frequently the public officials seem moved primarily by a desire to have the public system rid of these handicapped children and their high-priced needs; in turn, this has meant that to be a voucher student has carried some stigma. Moreover, while it is acknowledged that the education of handicapped children almost by necessity must cost more than the norm, the tuition aid granted often has not been a realistic amount. On top of that, private providers have been permitted to charge whatever additional tuition they desired—with the result that handicapped children from poor families frequently had no desirable program available to them.[3] For those reasons and others, including recent educational claims that many handicapped children should be placed in regular classes, these choice programs seem on the wane. Yet this tradition is by no means dead; just recently an organization of California parents whose children are in state mental hospitals has demanded "vouchers" to be used to send the children to private facilities.[4] In sum, while the experience with educating the handicapped has shown that once scholarships are made available private providers are likely to respond with educational offerings not provided by the public sector, we think little else about a universal plan may be learned from this very limited experience.

A systematic attempt to learn about family choice through experimental programs was proposed by federal officials in 1970. Armed with a report from the Center for the Study of Public Policy advocating an education tuition voucher tryout for elementary school children, Office of Economic

Opportunity and later National Institute of Education leaders set out to convince localities to try one specific choice plan— the Needs Adjustment Model described in Chapter 11. Unfortunately, despite the fact that a substantial economic sweetener was offered, their powers of political persuasion were insufficient to the task they set for themselves—convincing all portions of the local school community, including teachers' unions, public school principals, and public boards of education—to endorse the experiment. As a result, only one community satisfactory to the federal program leaders was selected for the experiment—Alum Rock, a district of approximately 15,000 pupils located in the San Jose, California area.[5]

Alum Rock is a predominantly Mexican-American and highly transient community. Racially it is well integrated. For four years the district, with the aid of federal funds amounting to more than $200 per pupil, experimented with a substantial choice scheme for grades kindergarten through 8. More than half of the district's schools participated, with the faculties in those public school buildings dividing themselves into a number of "minischools." Families who would otherwise have had their children assigned to the participating schools were, in general, given the opportunity to choose any minischool located in any building in the program. This gave families a large number of choices. In the fourth year of the program, for example, the thirteen participating buildings offered more than fifty minischools—although, of course, a child in a particular grade had fewer choices. As a result, a significant percentage of families chose to send their child to other than what would have been his assigned school; the numbers making such election became sizable as the program matured—5 percent of the children in the first year, but 15 percent in the second and third.

Some minischools were plainly more popular than others, and, by the third year, distinctive self-images were evident in a number of the programs. District officials speculated that teachers were doing "market research"—that is, deliberately seeking to discover and satisfy user interests. Thus, it is perhaps revealing that more than half the families chose minischools that labeled themselves nontraditional. More interestingly, many families with two children eligible for the same program chose to enroll them in different ones. At the height of the experiment, the level of reported parent satisfaction with the education at Alum Rock was very high (though it was also quite high before the experiment began).

No signs of racial isolation appeared, with the possible exception of the bilingual-bicultural programs aimed at one ethnic minority. As a result of the experiment much practical learning was acquired about enrollment logistics, school site budgeting, techniques for informing families about choices, and transportation problems under choice.

However, Alum Rock was hardly the full experiment we propose. First, no high school students were included. Second, families could not choose public schools outside the district. Third, teachers were, in effect, guaranteed their jobs; the experimental rules provided that they were to be passed around to other programs if and when their minischool lost its popularity and had to cut down on staff. Thus, no real opportunity arose to hire noncredentialed teaching personnel, and effective accountability was minimized. Fourth, minischools were not allowed to take all comers, and efforts to expand facilities or to create satellite campuses for popular programs were not enthusiastically supported. Indeed, counter to the spirit of decentralization, school principals were allowed to maintain substantial control at the level of their building. Thus, while teachers who formed minischools enjoyed unprecedented professional opportunities to develop their own educational ideas, these teachers, their pupils, and parents never managed to seize anything like full governance control.

Finally, no private schools participated in the experiment. Although the district formally committed itself to the federal government to permit private schools to enter the plan and to compete for students, nothing ever materialized. At first the district took the position that state law barred private school participation. As a result, substantial time was taken to enact new state legislation and to obtain legal interpretations supporting participation. During that process, one group of outside teachers emerged with a plan to start a participating private school. However, having no preexisting base of community support and frustrated by the number of delays, including footdragging by the district, this private initiative collapsed. Whether because of this one unhappy experience, or because there was simply no substantial family or community group interest, no other serious effort to include private schools was made. Certainly the district officials did not seek out private providers.

We applaud both federal and Alum Rock officials for carrying out the experiment. In many respects, we are encouraged by the results of even this truncated plan. If nothing else, it appears that providing family choice will become a permanent part of Alum Rock's operating procedure. Yet the failure to include in the plan either private schools or public schools outside the district necessarily meant that the full effect of competition could not be felt by the participating schools: as a result, the diversity of a more open plan was prevented. We conclude that if the variety of offerings we have imagined is to be allowed to develop, new experiments must have wider scope.

Choice plans also exist at the postsecondary level. For example, California provides state scholarships to a number of academically meritorious college-bound high school seniors.[6] These scholarships may be used at private institutions of higher education. And the G. I. Bill is a much larger national program of a similar sort.[7] Under it, certain veterans are given both tuition aid and living stipends to permit them to attend the postsecondary public or private school of their choice. These programs differ quite significantly from what we propose, however, because the student is typically an independent adult, and thus he is very much the chooser. This is surely true for most G. I. Bill recipients and probably so for most college-bounds today. Thus, such programs are irrelevant as devices for solving the problem of which adult sovereignty ought to be given the power to make choices with and on behalf of children. Still, these postsecondary programs do illustrate the willingness of society to provide public funds for use at a range of private and public institutions—a recognition that the opportunity is more valued by the recipient where it is a scholarship instead of merely an opening at the local state college or university. It should also be noted that through the administration and observation of these plans and related ones (such as college student grants and loans from the federal government) government has learned some things about consumer (and Treasury) protection efforts that seem appropriately to go along with choice plans. Some of this experience is represented in recent regulations requiring certain disclosures and, in some instances, tuition refunds from private providers.[8] Unfortunately, federal agencies have not yet seen fit to insist that the range of public providers disclose fully the success of their programs in preparing students for jobs.

CHOICE IN CHILDREN'S POLICY

In 1976, in a variety of settings, Congressional committees debated federal day-care policy. In the end, the most important program adopted was a federally subsidized family choice day-care scheme—the tax credit provisions of the 1976 Tax Reform Act.[9] In general, this law provides that the federal government will pay for 20 percent of a family's day-care costs, if these costs are incurred so that the children's parents (or parent, if he has only one) can work.

This is not the place to debate whether the federal government should encourage parents to work rather than rear their children, or whether it is fair for the subsidy to go only to those who use child-care in order to work. Moreover, we will only have a few words to say about the financial dimensions of the plan. A 20 percent subsidy for all is obviously better for the poor than the arrangement which obtained under the previous tax deduction scheme that subsidized a greater proportion of a family's costs the richer it was.[10] Yet plainly the new law is not a power-equalizing scheme. Thus, richer families will more easily take advantage of the full $400 per month subsidized spending maximum (an $80 per month tax credit) than will poorer families. Equally obvious, poorer families will not as easily be able to place their children in as costly facilities as will richer families. Finally, the law does nothing for those too poor to owe federal income taxes at all.

But the point we wish to emphasize is that the program adopted was not tuition-subsidized public provision of day care. Instead, it was a subsidy for the purchase of day care of the family's own choosing. Indeed, there are really no restrictions on the kinds of facilities and day-care workers chosen. Relatives and neighbors may be hired, for example, and children may be cared for in or out of their home.

This policy stance toward the care of children—providing public money but relying on the family to see to the child's interests—might be seen as consistent with the shifting tradition in social welfare legislation of this century. Welfare payments are an example. At the end of the nineteenth century the dominant public rhetoric—and often practice—favored institutionalization of the children of impoverished families in the poorhouse, so-called "indoor relief"; other alternatives of this era were apprenticing or auctioning off the children to masters in whose households they would live, and placing them with foster families.[11] In the early twentieth century, however, stimulated by the resolutions of the 1909 White House Conference on Children, the rhetoric shifted toward "outdoor relief"—the provision of funds to needy families so that children could remain in their homes. In the next twenty-five years, nearly all states enacted Mothers' Pensions programs; these were designed to provide cash to deserving mothers—mainly widows—who were husbandless and poor, so that they could rear their own children at home. While the motivation for such programs was in part fiscal, the lower cost of outdoor relief, the major theme was the welfare of children. And when the federal government, as part of the 1935 Social Security Act, revived state relief plans from bankruptcy by enacting what is now known as the AFDC (Aid to Families with Dependent Children) program, it agreed to provide financial support for needy and dependent children only if the child lived with relatives, preferably a parent.[12] It was not until the 1960s that federal AFDC funds were available for foster-care placements.[13]

In recent years the call to universalize AFDC—to make it available to all poor families and not just those with an absent parent or unemployed father—has continued to be clothed in family-strengthening rhetoric. For example, one serious concern of policy planners under the existing program is the incentive for men to desert so as to make their remaining family AFDC-eligible.[14]

The major federal policies adopted in the 1960s for the feeding and health maintenance of poor children have also been increasingly family-centered. From 1935 until 1964, the federal strategy for assuring food for the poor was the distribution of commodities. Parents and children got what the government had to give. Starting in 1964 (and with increasing funds since 1970), the federal government came to favor family choice through the adoption of the food stamp program. Now children from poor homes are more likely to eat what the parents and not government officials decide they should have. Similarly, the passage in 1965 of Medicaid—federal assistance in the funding of health care for the poor—has increased family options. Previously, the poor were largely restricted to health care provided by charity hospitals. Now when their children are ill or injured, the poor through Medicaid can take them to any public or private physician or hospital accepting Medicaid patients.

To be sure, the heavy paternalisms have not altogether passed. Especially where the welfare rolls are not bulging, with the cash often comes an intrusive welfare bureaucracy seeking to make the recipient the kind of mother that the professional welfare worker wants her to be.[15] And food stamps in any case do not leave much room for choice. They allow the family to satisfy minimum dietary needs and then only if it shops very efficiently. In addition there remains the phenomenon of school lunch; this is in-kind assistance given directly to children, even though there seems to be no evidence that children are nutritionally better off than they would be were the funds used for increasing food stamp allotments or even cash grants to poor families. Finally, Medicaid too suffers from choice-limiting features—among others, the ability of doctors to charge more than Medicaid reimbursement levels, thereby excluding many Medicaid patients altogether.[16]

Even in day care the picture is mixed. AFDC working mothers are eligible for a subsidy in their choice of virtually any day-care arrangements they wish.[17] They are in fact more generously treated than working parents paying income taxes, because the government pays the full cost of day care for welfare mothers and only 20 percent for taxpaying families. And the governmental resources committed are substantial. Yet of late larger amounts of federal monies have been put into in-kind provision of day care in the form of centers to which welfare mothers are increasingly encouraged to send their children.[18] Most of these centers are run under the direction of public school authorities. Still, there is no reason to anticipate public domination of day care. Overall, indeed, it is fair to conclude that family choice in child policy areas is becoming the norm.

THE FUTURE OF FAMILY POLICY

These examples—both in and out of education—indicate the administrative and fiscal feasibility of experimentation with choice. What remains wanting is recognition by legislators of the strong public aspiration for more family responsibility and—what may be the same—legislative perception that choice represents a living political option. The hope must be that the visible success of choice in other areas will at last impel the political system to confront the social costs of sustaining the present monopoly in public' education. Indeed, if society continues to move in a variety of ways toward freedom and responsibility for the family, the present world of schools will increasingly appear an anachronism. We are tempted to conclude that serious experimentation with educational choice is inevitable, and recent developments encourage the hope. National figures such as Governor Milton Shapp, Senator Daniel P. Moynihan, and Congressman Richardson Preyer have all advanced large-scale proposals for educational reform grounded in family choice.[19]

Yet the hints of a broad public enthusiasm for the generation of responsible family roles could prove but a cyclical retreat from New Deal enthusiasm for large-scale solutions—a temporary loss of confidence in giant, publicly administered programs. In the current search for a different social anchor, alternatives to the state and the family are few in a society that has largely neutralized the mediating communities of preindustrial civilization.[20] Public rediscovery of the family may prove but a minor epicycle in our journey toward the omnicompetent state. Ultimately, many may prefer the security of well-run and uniform government programs to the challenge of personal responsibility.

Whether this occurs will be affected by the quality of intellectual support the family receives. The significance of the current political favor for the family is that it provides a respite—a breathing space in history—during which arguments about the family as a responsible political unit can expect a serious hearing for the first time in a century. While this opportunity lasts, there is hope that the protagonists of family responsibility will discover a justification more enduring than the current level of distrust of bureaucracy.

There is much room for improvement in the quality of the national dialogue concerning children. Reviewing the exchanges in Congress, the states, and the media on proposals such as day care, we are struck by the relative impoverishment of our public philosophies when they are applied to the concerns of children. Such debates lack one of the ordinary assurances of candor and intelligibility—the self-regarding participation of those whom the policy is intended to affect.

Children are excluded from direct participation by their youth, inexperience, and incapacity to communicate to policy makers. Worse, their indirect participation is also feeble, for they are usually unrepresented by anyone whose self-interest is linked to their own. Parents as individuals can and do contribute little to the process. And their lobbying organizations tend to be puny for at least two reasons. First, children differ from one another in their needs and are perceived so to differ by their parents. Hence, few parents (or others) see "children's lobbies" as truly representative of any distinct clientele. Second, even where the interests of many children are perceived by their parents to be similar, parental support of a truly representative organization is seldom an efficient use of those family resources which otherwise would be spent directly on the child. This is one form of the "free-rider" phenomenon that cripples many a would-be lobbying effort.[21] The family gets the benefit of the organization without supporting it; hence, few in fact support it.

Thus, the policy maker must rely principally on two sources of intelligence that are of minimal accountability. One is the altruistic volunteer who has ideas but no economic or social stake in the outcome; the other (and more prominent) is the professional whose vocation is to minister to children in need and whose economic and social interests may be advanced as effectively when children suffer as when they prosper. The debate thus features such protagonists as teachers' unions, day-care associations, medical societies, social welfare leagues, and other lobbying groups who assert that the best chance for children lies in the government buying some of whatever service each group has to sell. While these groups may differ somewhat over policy, they seldom lobby for increased family authority, tending to view parental independence more as the problem than a potential solution.

These circumstances impose on lawmakers a duty to doubt the reliability of their sources when shaping childhood policy. This principle extends beyond education to other areas in which the child's best interest is indeterminate; it is our observation that conflict and confusion about the child's interests are widespread. At the very least, it would be dangerous for the lawmaker to assume otherwise.

Unfortunately, confronted with indeterminacy the legislator and executive face two strong temptations. One is to adopt a substantive answer even though none is convincing or commands a consensus; the other is to vest decisional authority in the professional cadre from whom he hears rather than in families from whom he does not hear. In order to resist these temptations, lawmakers must be helped to understand that conflict, confusion, and ignorance respecting the child's interest are not a disaster but the stuff of which a rich pluralism can be forged.

For this reason we hope that the manner in which the basic issues were posed in Part II may have an application broader than education. Specifically, the development of childhood policy should become an exercise in applied humility that begins with the presumptions that our sources of information are impure, our aspirations for children are diverse, and our technology and ability to predict the consequences of intervention are generally weak. Whenever such a chastened political process encounters indeterminacy of fact or value, this commitment to intellectual modesty should help to counter the twin temptations of the uniform answer and the unthinking delegation to professional judgment; such calculated diffidence should shift the question from what is the best interest of the child to who is best qualified to decide his interest for him. The real issue is not substance but jurisdiction, and on that question no presumption should favor the professions merely because they dominate policy discourse.

What is needed, then, are intelligible arguments—theories, if you will—about what kind of units should be recognized as having authority in those cases where society is deadlocked by indeterminacy but remains eager to serve the child. In the case of education we have here begun the outline of such an argument based on specific value premises and assumptions. This has led us to prefer families or familylike units—supported by professionals—as the appropriate locus of the authority over the child's education. As yet we have neither discovered nor imagined a relationship more likely to ensure that the interests and needs of the individual child will be given the best of both amateur and professional attention.

We suspect that the argument would hold as well for many areas of the child's life other than education. Whether this is so is worthy of serious inquiry by all who would do justice to children. If in due course there is to be a political economy of childhood, it must rest on an assessment of the capacity of the modern family to speak for its children. It is a fascinating problem. The institution has been declared vestigial by some and dysfunctional by many. If, indeed, it is in serious trouble, the hope to limit the family's impact on the child seems humane and progressive. Bondage to a bankrupt institution would be a patent injustice.

Yet there are aspects of the modern family that are unprecedented and represent new hope for children. When the industrial revolution made children burdensome and when medicine made children avoidable, a new economy of the family was born. Although these influences seem to threaten the basic function of the institution, in fact they may be the sources of new life and a fresh career. Today those who choose parenthood display the only reliable token of craft and mastery known to the ancient vocation of child-rearing—the readiness to sacrifice.

NOTES

For journal article references, the number preceding a journal title refers to the volume; the number following the journal title refers to the beginning page of the article. The year is in parentheses.

INTRODUCTION

1. John Coons, William Clune III, and Stephen Sugarman, *Private Wealth and Public Education* (Cambridge, Mass., Harvard University Press, 1970).

CHAPTER 1

1. Stephen Sugarman and David Kirp, "Rethinking Collective Responsibility for Education," 39 *Law and Contemporary Problems* 144 (1975).
2. See generally, Kenneth Phillips and Michael Agelasto II, "Housing and Central Cities: The Conservation Approach," 4 *Ecology Law Quarterly* 797 (1975).
3. See generally, *Handbook of Public Income Transfer Programs;* Studies in Public Welfare, Paper #20, a staff study prepared for the Subcommittee on Fiscal Policy of the Joint Economic Committee of Congress (Washington, D.C., Government Printing Office, 1974).
4. Mario Fantini, *Public Schools of Choice* (New York, Simon and Schuster, 1973), pp. 82 and 247.

CHAPTER 2

1. Thomas Paine, *Rights of Man* (New York, E. P. Dutton, 1915), pp. 252–253.
2. Adam Smith, *Wealth of Nations* (Chicago, Great Books Edition, Encyclopedia Britannica, 1952), p. 340.
3. John Stuart Mill, *On Liberty* (Chicago, Great Books Edition, Encyclopedia Britannica, 1952), Ch. V.

4. 268 U.S. 510 (1925).
5. Milton Friedman, *Capitalism and Freedom* (Chicago, University of Chicago Press, 1962). See chap. 6, p. 85.
6. See, for example, "Teachers Told to Wage War on Voucher System," *The Oregonian*, June 30, 1973, p. 21, where the views of New York City teachers' union leader Albert Shanker are reported as follows: "Shanker says the plan's appeal is to 'a new coalition of forces in America': parochial school interests who see it as a source of money; political conservatives who feel nothing should be public if it can be private; Southern whites trying to weasel out of desegregation; black separatists; businessmen looking for a new market in education; middle-class parents who want a subsidy for their escape into private schools in suburbia; and 'liberal new left anarchists.' 'Against this anti-school coalition you have relatively few groups—primarily the teachers and some parents groups,' Shanker said." See also Shanker, "Parental Choice of School? Some Words of Caution," New York *Times*, July 21, 1974. For other criticisms, see Eli Ginzberg, "The Economics of the Voucher System," 72 *Teachers College Record* 373 (1971); Maurice Berube, "The Trouble with Vouchers," 3 *Community* 1 (Nov. 1970); and see generally, Henry Levin, "Educational Vouchers and Educational Equality," Occasional Paper 74-2, School of Education (Palo Alto, Stanford University, Aug. 1974).
7. See, for example, Virgil Blum, *Freedom of Choice in Education* (New York, Macmillan, 1958).
8. See generally, Ronald and Beatrice Gross, *Radical School Reform* (New York, Simon and Schuster, 1971); Paul Goodman, *Growing Up Absurd* (New York, Random House, 1956) and *Compulsory Miseducation* (New York, Horizon Press, 1964); Edgar Friedenberg, *The Vanishing Adolescent* (New York, Dell, 1959). See also John Holt, *The Underachieving School* (New York, Dell Delta, 1969); Jonathan Kozol, *Free Schools* (Boston, Houghton Mifflin, 1972).
9. Everett Reimer, *An Essay on Alternatives in Education* (Cuernavaca, CIDOC, 1970); Ivan Illich, *Deschooling Society* (New York, Harper and Row, 1971).
10. John Coons, "Law and the Sovereigns of Childhood," 58 *Kappan* 19 (1976).
11. James Coleman, "Toward Open Schools," 9 *Public Interest* 20 (fall 1967); Christopher Jencks, "Is the Public School Obsolete?" 2 *Public Interest* 18 (winter 1966); Henry Levin, "The Failure of the Public Schools and the Free Market Remedy," 2 *The Urban Review* 32 (June 1968).
12. Dennis Doyle, "The Politics of Choice: A View from the Bridge," in *Parents, Teachers and Children* (San Francisco, Institute for Contemporary Studies, 1977), p. 227.
13. See, for example, Edward Banfield, *The Unheavenly City* (Boston, Little, Brown, 1970) and *The Unheavenly City Revisited* (Boston, Little, Brown, 1974).
14. Lesley Browder, *Who's Afraid of Educational Accountability?* (Denver, Cooperative Accountability Project, 1975); Phyllis Hawthorne, *Legislation by the States: Accountability and Assessment in Education* (Denver, Cooperative Accountability Project, 1974).

15. Peter W. Doe v. San Francisco Unified School District, Ca. Ct. of Appeals, Sup. Ct. No. 653312, Aug. 6, 1976. See generally, Stephen Sugarman, "Accountability through the Courts," 82 *School Review* 233 (1974).
16. See generally, Martin Mayer, *The Teachers' Strike: New York 1968* (New York, Harper and Row, 1969); Rhoady McCoy, *American School Administration, Public and Catholic* (New York, McGraw-Hill, 1961); Henry Levin (ed.), *Community Control of Schools* (Washington, D.C., Brookings Institution, 1970).
17. See generally, Walter Garms, James Guthrie, and Lawrence Pierce, *School Finance: The Economics and Politics of Public Schools* (Englewood Cliffs, N.J., Prentice-Hall, 1977).
18. Fantini, *Public Schools of Choice.*
19. Stephen Arons, "Equity, Option, .nd Vouchers," 72 *Teacher's College Record* 337 (1971).
20. Milton Friedman, "The Voucher Idea," *New York Times Magazine,* Sept. 23, 1973, p. 21.
21. Center for the Study of Public Policy, *Education Vouchers, A Report on Financing Elementary Education by Grants to Parents* (Cambridge, Mass., CSPP, 1970); Judith Areen and Christopher Jencks, "Education Vouchers: A Proposal for Diversity and Choice," 72 *Teachers College Record* 327 (1971).
22. Theodore Sizer and Phillip Whitten, "A Proposal for a Poor Children's Bill of Rights," 5 *Psychology Today* 58 (1968).
23. John Coons and Stephen Sugarman, *Family Choice in Education: A Model State System for Vouchers* (Berkeley, Institute of Governmental Studies, 1971).
24. Judith Areen, "Public Aid to Nonpublic Schools: A Breach in the Sacred Wall?" 22 *Case Western Reserve Law Review* 230 (1971). See also, Walter McCann and Judith Areen, "Vouchers and the Citizen—Some Legal Questions," 72 *Teacher's College Record* 389 (1971).
25. David Sonnenfeld, *Family Choice in Schooling: A Case Study,* Working Paper 3 (Eugene, University of Oregon, 1972).
26. Hugh Calkins and Jeffrey Gordon, "The Right to Choose an Integrated Education: Voluntary Regional Integrated Schools—A Partial Remedy for De Facto Segregation," 9 *Harvard Civil Rights-Civil Liberties Law Review* 171 (1974).
27. Stephen Klees, "The Role of Information in the Market for Education Services," Occasional Papers in the Economics and Politics of Education (Palo Alto, Stanford University, 1974).
28. *Education Vouchers.*
29. Coons and Sugarman, *Family Choice in Education.*
30. Martin Carnoy and Henry Levin (eds.), *The Limits of Educational Reform* (New York, D. McKay, 1976); Samuel Bowles and Herbert Gintis, *Schooling in Capitalist America: Educational Reform and the Contradictions of Economic Life* (New York, Basic Books, 1976).

CHAPTER 3

1. Frederick Mosteller and Daniel Moynihan (eds.), *On Equality of Educational Opportunity* (New York, Random House, 1972).

2. See generally, Garms, Guthrie, and Pierce, *School Finance: The Economics and Politics of Public Schools.*
3. Coons, Clune, and Sugarman, *Private Wealth and Public Education*; Charles Benson, *The Economics of Public Education* (Boston, Houghton Mifflin, 1968).
4. San Antonio Independent School District v. Rodriguez, 411 U.S. 1, 59 (1973). (Concurring opinion.)
5. Armin Rosencranz, "The Politics of Choosing Textbooks" (Berkeley, Childhood and Government Project, Working Paper #1, 1976); Dinah Shelton, "The Role of the State in Moral Education: The Experience of California's Moral Guidelines" (paper delivered at Northridge Conference on Moral Education, Oct. 1974).
6. Dinah Shelton, "Legislative Control over Public School Curriculum" (Berkeley, Childhood and Government Project, Working Paper #2, 1976).
7. W. F. Murphy, *Class Size and Teacher Load* (Newton, Mass., New England School Development Council, 1975).
8. See, for example, *The Fleischman Report on the Quality, Cost, and Financing of Elementary and Secondary Education in New York State* (New York, Viking Press, 1973), vol. 1, chap. 4.
9. Nancy St. John, *School Desegregation: Outcomes for Children* (New York, John Wiley, 1975), and Derrick Bell, "Waiting on the Promise of *Brown*," 39 *Law and Contemporary Problems* 341 (1975).
10. Derrick Bell, "Serving Two Masters: Integration Ideals and Client Interests in School Desegregation Litigation," 85 *Yale Law Journal* 470 (1976).
11. John Elson, "State Regulation of Non-Public Schools: The Legal Framework," in Donald Erickson (ed.), *Public Controls for Non-Public Schools* (Chicago, University of Chicago Press, 1969), pp. 103–134.
12. California Education Code §48222 (1977).
13. Jeanne Chall, *Learning to Read: The Great Debate* (New York, McGraw-Hill, 1967).
14. Lau v. Nichols, 414 U.S. 563 (1974); Hannah Geffert, Robert Harper, Salvador Sarmiento, and Daniel Schember, "The Current Status of U.S. Bilingual Education Legislation," *Papers in Applied Linguistics* (Arlington, Va., Center for Applied Linguistics, May 1975); Richard Hiller and Herbert Teitelbaum, "Bilingual Education: The Legal Mandate," 47 *Harvard Educational Review* 138 (1977).
15. Urie Bronfenbrenner, *The Two Worlds of Childhood: USA and USSR* (New York, Russell Sage Foundation, 1970).

CHAPTER 4

1. See generally, Johannes Messner, *Social Ethics: Natural Law in the Western World* (St. Louis, B. Herder, 1965); E. F. Schumacher, *Small Is Beautiful: Economics as if People Mattered* (New York, Harper and Row, 1973); Coons, Clune, and Sugarman, *Private Wealth and Public Education.*
2. Aaron Cicourel and John Kitsuse, *The Educational Decisionmakers* (Indianapolis, Bobbs-Merrill, 1963).
3. Mary Jo Bane, *Here to Stay: American Families in the Twentieth Century* (New York, Basic Books, 1976).

4. Bertrand Russell, *Education and the Good Life* (New York, Boni and Liveright, 1926), p. 9.
5. Diana v. State Board of Education, Consent Decree No. C-70-37, June 18, 1973 (U.S. Dist. Ct. N. D. Cal.).
6. Hobson v. Hansen, 327 F. Supp. 844 (D.D.C. 1971).
7. David Kirp, "Schools as Sorters: The Constitutional and Policy Implications of Student Classification," 121 *University of Pennsylvania Law Review* 705 (1973).
8. Robert Mnookin, "Child Custody Adjudication: Judicial Functions in the Face of Indeterminacy," 39 *Law and Contemporary Problems* 226 (1975); Michael S. Wald, "State Intervention on Behalf of 'Neglected' Children: Standards for Removal of Children from Their Homes, Monitoring the Status of Children in Foster Care, and Termination of Parental Rights," 28 *Stanford Law Review* 625 (1976).
9. Robert Mnookin, "Foster Care: In Whose Best Interest?" 48 *Harvard Educational Review* 599 (1973).
10. Peter Doe v. San Francisco School District.

CHAPTER 5

1. B. F. Skinner, *Beyond Freedom and Dignity* (New York, Knopf, 1971).
2. Herbert Spencer, *Social Statics: The Conditions Essential to Human Happiness* (London, John Chapman, 1851), p. 188.
3. Dietrich Bonhoeffer, *The Cost of Discipleship* (New York, Macmillan, 1963), p. 278.
4. Lawrence Kohlberg, "Moral Development and Identification," *Child Psychology* (Chicago, University of Chicago Press, 1963), and "Stage and Sequence: The Cognitive-Developmental Approach to Socialization," in *Handbook of Socialization Theory and Research* (Chicago, Rand McNally, 1969).
5. Herbert Kohl, *The Open Classroom* (New York, Random House Vintage, 1970).
6. Reprinted in appellee's brief, appendix B. *Oregon School Cases: Complete Record* (Baltimore, Belvedere Press, 1925), p. 368.
7. Albert Keim (ed.), *Compulsory Education and the Amish* (Boston, Beacon Press, 1975).
8. California Education Code §13556.5 (1977).
9. *International Herald Tribune*, interview, July 14, 1974.
10. G. K. Chesterton, *What's Wrong with the World* (New York, Sheed and Ward, 1956), p. 149.
11. Norman Williams, "What the Psychologist Has to Say," in John Wilson, Norman Williams, and Barry Sugarman, *Introduction to Moral Education* (Baltimore, Penguin Books, 1967), p. 307.
12. Lawrence Kohlberg, "Stages of Moral Development as a Basis for Moral Education," in C. M. Beck, B. S. Crittenden, and E. V. Sullivan, *Moral Education: Interdisciplinary Approaches* (Toronto, University of Toronto Press, 1971), p. 83.
13. Robert Heilbroner, *An Inquiry into the Human Prospect* (New York, W. W. Norton, 1974), p. 111.
14. Andrew Greeley, William McCready, and Kathleen McCourt, *Catholic Schools in a Declining Church* (Kansas City, Sheed and Ward, 1976).

CHAPTER 6

1. Michael Novak, *The Rise of the Unmeltable Ethics* (Toronto, Macmillan, 1971).
2. John Coons, "To West, Mostly with Love," and Stephen Sugarman, "New Perspectives on 'Aid' to Private School Users," in E. G. West (ed.), *Nonpublic School Aid* (Lexington, Mass., Lexington Books, 1976). For a summary of the cases, see William Lockhart, Yale Kamisar, and Jesse Choper, *Constitutional Law—Cases, Comments and Questions* 1211 (St. Paul, West, 1975).
3. Lewis A. Coser, *The Functions of Social Conflict* (Glencoe, Free Press, 1956); Georg Simmel, *Conflict*, trans. Kurt H. Wolff (Glencoe, Free Press, 1955).
4. Robert Dahl, *Who Governs: Democracy and Power in an American City* (New Haven, Yale University Press, 1961); David Truman, *The Governmental Process* (New York, Knopf, 1971).
5. Robert Wolff, *The Poverty of Liberalism* (Boston, Beacon Press, 1968); Theodore Lowi, *The End of Liberalism: Ideology, Policy, and the Crisis of Public Authority* (New York, W. W. Norton, 1969); Roberto Unger, *Knowledge and Politics* (Glencoe, Free Press, 1975).
6. For example, Dahl (*Who Governs?*) and Truman (*Govermental Process*).
7. Thomas Jefferson, *Notes on the State of Virginia, Query 17* (Boston, David Carlisle, 1801), p. 232.
8. James Madison, *The Federalist, No. 51* (New York, Random House, 1937), p. 339.
9. Alfred North Whitehead, *Science and the Modern World* (New York, Mentor, New American Library, 1954), p. 166.
10. Lawrence Cremin, *The Transformation of the School* (New York, Random House, 1964); David Tyack, *The One Best System: A History of American Urban Education* (Cambridge, Mass., Harvard University Press, 1974); Bernard Bailyn, *Education in the Forming of American Society* (New York, W. W. Norton, 1960); Marvin Lazerson, "Consensus and Conflict in American Education: Historical Perspectives," in *Parents, Teachers, and Children*, p. 15.
11. George Santayana, *The Sense of Beauty* (New York, Modern Library, 1955), p. 113.
12. Ibid., p. 45.
13. John Stuart Mill, *On Liberty*, pp. 293–294.
14. See, for example, George LaNoue, "The Politics of Education," 73 *Teachers College Record* 304 (1971).
15. Dinah Shelton, "Legislative Control over Curriculum Content," unpublished paper; California Education Code §51227 (1977).
16. See examples in David Kirp and Mark Yudof, *Educational Policy and the Law* (Berkeley, McCutchan, 1974), pp. 125–126, 432–433; Mark Yudof, "Suspension and Expulsion of Black Students from the Public Schools: Academic Capital Punishment and the Constitution," 39 *Law and Contemporary Problems* 374 (1975).
17. Sherbert v. Verner, 374 U.S. 398 (1963); see generally, Robert O'Neil, "Unconstitutional Conditions: Welfare Benefits with Strings Attached," 54 *California Law Review* 443 (1966).

CHAPTER 7

1. Derrick Bell, "Is *Brown* Obsolete? Yes!" 14 *Integrated Education*
   28 (May–June 1976).
2. St. John, *School Desegregation: Outcomes for Children,* pp. 118–120,
   122–123, 136–137.
3. Edgar Cahn, "Jurisprudence," 30 *New York University Law Review*
   150, 157–168 (1955); John Coons, "Recent Trends in Science Fiction:
   Serrano among the People of Number," 6 *Journal of Law and
   Education* 23 (1977).
4. Brown v. Board of Education, 347 U.S. 483 (1954).
5. ". . . enrollment statistics compiled by the Department of Health,
   Education, and Welfare (HEW) for the school year 1974 show
   that two of every three black children in the country attend
   predominately minority schools and two of every five attend
   schools that are intensely segregated (90 to 100 percent minority
   in their enrollment). . . . [I]n the 26 largest cities of the
   United States almost three of every four black pupils are
   assigned to such [intensely segregated] schools. . . . .
   "Census statistics for 1970 showing black people as a proportion
   of the population of the largest cities and their suburbs reveal in
   a striking fashion the racial dividing line between city and suburbs.
   "In Chicago, for example, blacks constituted 33 percent of the
   population of the central city, but only 3 percent of the population
   of the suburbs. The city of Detroit was 44 percent black in 1970,
   while its suburbs were only 4 percent black. Baltimore was 46
   percent black in 1970, and its suburban population was only 3
   percent black.
   "In Boston, one in every six residents is a black citizen, while
   in its suburbs only one person in every 100 is black. In Dallas,
   one person in four is black, and in the suburbs one person in
   every 50 is black. Similar patterns exist in other metropolitan areas."
   Statement of Metropolitan School Desegregation, A Report of the
   United States Commission on Civil Rights (Feb. 1977), pp. 6 and
   15.
   See generally, Reynolds Farley, "Residential Segregation and Its
   Implications for School Integration," 39 *Law and Contemporary
   Problems* 164 (1975); Willis D. Hawley and Ray C. Rist, "On the
   Future Implementations of School Desegregation: Some Consider-
   ations," 39 *Law and Contemporary Problems* 412 (1975).
6. James Coleman, Sara Kelly, and John Moore, "Trends in School
   Segregation, 1968–1973," working paper for the Urban Institute
   (Washington, D.C.), Aug. 15, 1975, p. 36.
7. Dayton Board of Education v. Brinkman, 97 S.Ct. 2766 (1977).
8. Charles Haar and Demetrios Iatrides, *Housing the Poor in Suburbia:
   Public Policy at the Grass Roots* (Cambridge, Mass., Ballinger, 1974).
9. *Your Children and Busing,* A Report of the U.S. Commission on
   Civil Rights (Washington, D.C., Government Printing Office, May
   1972).
10. *Desegregation of the Nation's Public Schools,* A Report of the U.S.
    Commission on Civil Rights (Washington, D.C., Government Print-
    ing Office, Aug. 1976).

11. Milliken v. Bradley, 418 U.S. 717 (1974).
12. Evans v. Buchanan, 393 F.Supp. 428 (D. Del. 1975), affirmed 423 U.S. 963 (1976).
13. Dayton Board of Education v. Brinkman, 97 S.Ct. 2766 (1977), p. 2772; see also School District of Omaha v. United States, 97 S.Ct. 2905 (1977); Brennan v. Armstrong, 97 S.Ct. 2907 (1977).
14. *Public Knowledge and Busing Opposition,* A Report of the U.S. Commission on Civil Rights (Washington, D.C., Government Printing Office, 1973).
15. Green v. County Board of New Kent County, 391 U.S. 430 (1968).
16. Bell, "Is *Brown* Obsolete? Yes!"
17. Data based on official records made available by the Richmond Unified School District, Richmond, California.
18. The data here derive from interviews and district records. See Stanton v. Sequoia Union High School Dist., 408 F. Supp. 502 (N.D. Cal.) 1976.
19. Zeke Wigglesworth, "Alternatives in Public Schools: The Minneapolis Experiment," in Don Davies (ed.), *Schools Where Parents Make a Difference* (Boston, Institute for Responsive Education, 1976), p. 121.
20. John McAdams, "Can Open Enrollment Work?" 37 *Public Interest* 69 (1974).
21. John Coons, "Report to the U.S. Office of Education on Illinois Elementary District 65 (Evanston-Skokie)," 1965; John Coons, "Evanston," in Roscoe Hill and Malcolm Feeley (eds.), *Affirmative School Integration* (Beverly Hills, Sage Publications, 1967).
22. See generally, David Armor, "The Evidence on Busing," 30 *Public Interest* 119 (1972); "Are We Losing Our Enthusiasm for METCO?" *The Boston Phoenix,* Sept. 7, 1976.
23. For the range of litigation, see Michael Wise (ed.), *Desegregation in Education: A Directory of Reported Federal Decisions* (Notre Dame, Center for Civil Rights, 1977).
24. Dayton Board of Education v. Brinkman, 97 S.Ct. 2766 (1977).
25. See Mark Yudof, "Suspension and Expulsion of Black Students from the Public Schools."
26 Wood v. Strickland, 420 U.S. 308 (1975).
27. See generally, *Desegregation of the Nation's Public Schools.*
28. Green v. County Board of New Kent County, 391 U.S. 430 (1968).
29. Milliken v. Bradley, 418 U.S. 717 (1974).
30. See, for example, "Amicus Brief Supporting Integration Plan in *Crawford* v. *Los Angeles Unified School District* (1977)," in *Parents, Teachers and Children,* p. 301.
31. Milliken v. Bradley, 97 S.Ct. 2749 (1977).
32. Swann v. Charlotte-Mecklenburg Board of Education, 402 U.S. 1 (1971).
33. Pasadena City Board of Education v. Spangler, 427 U.S. 424 (1976).
34. See Moose Lodge No. 107 v. Irvis, 407 U.S. 163 (1972).
35. Runyon v. McCrary, 427 U.S. 160 (1976).
36. Internal Revenue Code of 1954 as amended §501(c)(3).
37. Internal Revenue Service, Revenue Ruling 71-447, interpreting §501(c)(3) of Internal Revenue Code.
38. 42 U.S. Code §2000d (1970).

39. Lau v. Nichols, 414 U.S. 563 (1974).
40. Norwood v. Harrison, 413 U.S. 455 (1973).
41. For helpful analogies, see Wisconsin Statutes §121.85 (added by Chapter 220, Laws of 1975); California Senate Bill 1064 introduced by Senator Bill Greene (April 18, 1977); John Coons and Stephen Sugarman, "Choice and Integration: A Model Statute," in *Parents, Teachers and Children*, p. 279.
42. For an analysis of the application of Title VII of the Civil Rights Act of 1964 to the problem of racially imbalanced teaching staffs, see Hazelwood School District v. United States, 97 S.Ct. 2736 (1977).

CHAPTER 8

1. See, for example, California Education Code §48221 (1977); see generally, Kirp, "Schools as Sorters."
2. See, for example, Berkelman v. San Francisco Unified School District, 501 F.2d 1264 (9th Cir. 1974) (challenging sex discrimination in a special academic preparatory school).
3. Greeley, *Catholic Schools in a Declining Church.*
4. For the classic application of the "effects test" to problems of employment discrimination, see Griggs v. Duke Power Co., 401 U.S. 424 (1971).
5. See Coons and Sugarman, *Family Choice in Education,* pp. 80–84.
6. Goss v. Lopez, 419 U.S. 565 (1975).
7. *Voucher Choices: A Family Directory of Minischools* (Alum Rock, Calif., Alum Rock Sequoia Institute, 1975).

CHAPTER 9

1. John Coons and Stephen Sugarman, "Vouchers for Public Schools," 15 *Inequality in Education* 60 (1973).
2. See Friedman, "The Voucher Idea," p. 21.
3. See Irwin Garfinkel and Edward Gramlich, *A Statistical Analysis of the OEO Experiment in Educational Performance Contracting* (Washington, D.C., Brookings Institution, Technical Service Reprint T-002, 1972).
4. See Welford Wilms, *Public and Proprietary Vocational Training: A Study of Effectiveness* (Berkeley, Center for Research and Development in Higher Education, 1974).
5. See generally, Lawrence Sullivan, *Handbook of the Law of Antitrust* (St. Paul, West, 1977).
6. Compare Stephen Arons, "Equity, Option and Vouchers," 72 *Teachers College Record* 337 (1971).
7. *The Danish Sex Education Cases,* European Court of Human Rights (decided Dec. 7, 1976), "Observations of the Danish Government on the Merits," p. 35 (Mar. 26, 1976).
8. See Phillips and Agelasto, "Housing in Central Cities," p. 811.
9. Ibid., p. 812.
10. Albert Hirschmann, *Exit, Voice and Loyalty: Response to Decline in Firms, Organizations and States* (Cambridge, Mass., Harvard University Press, 1970).

CHAPTER 10

1. See Donald Erickson, *Super-Parent, An Analysis of State Educational Controls* (Lansing, Ill., Illinois Advisory Committee on Nonpublic Schools, 1973); Kirp and Yudof, *Educational Policy and the Law*, pp. 40–52.
2. See generally, Robert Thorndike, "Concepts of Culture-Fairness," 8 *Journal of Educational Measurement* 63 (1971); David White and Richard Francis, "Title VII and the Masters of Reality: Eliminating Credentialism in the American Labor Market," 64 *Georgetown Law Journal* 1213 (1976).
3. California Education Code §48412 *et seq.* (1977).
4. Doyle, "The Politics of Choice," p. 240.
5. See generally, Stephen Sugarman, "Family Choice: The Next Step in the Quest for Equal Educational Opportunity?" 38 *Law and Contemporary Problems* 513, 535–36 (1974). For NLRB jurisdictional limits as they apply to schools, see decision in *The Windsor School Inc.,* 82 *Labor Relations References Manual* 1341 (1972).
6. Kirp and Yudof, *Educational Policy and the Law*, pp. 275–277.
7. See, for example, Sheldon Nahmod, "Controversy in the Classroom: The High School Teacher and Freedom of Expression," 39 *George Washington Law Review* 1032, 1054–6 (1971).
8. For an extreme example in which the teaching of the theory of evolution was both a crime and subjected Arkansas teachers to loss of their jobs, see Epperson v. Arkansas, 393 U.S. 97 (1968) (law held unconstitutional).
9. Baird v. State Bar, 401 U.S. 1 (1971); In re Stolar, 401 U.S. 23 (1971); Elfbrandt v. Russel, 384 U.S. 11 (1966).
10. Stephen Goldstein, "The Asserted Constitutional Right of Public School Teachers to Determine What They Teach," 124 *University of Pennsylvania Law Review* 1293 (1976). But see Parducci v. Rutland, 316 F. Supp. 352 (M.D. Ala., 1970).
11. 42 U.S. Code §2000e-1 (supp. 2, 1972).
12. See City of Madison Joint School District No. 8 v. Wisconsin Employment Relations Comm'n, 429 U.S. 167 (1976); Pickering v. Board of Education, 391 U.S. 563 (1968).
13. See generally, Kern Alexander and K. Forbis Jordan, *Legal Aspects of Educational Choice: Compulsory Attendance and Student Assignment* (Topeka, National Organization on Legal Problems in Education, 1973), pp. 26–30.
14. See, for example, California Education Code §48224 (1977).
15. See generally, Kirp and Yudof, *Educational Policy and the Law*, chap. 2.
16. For example, the constitutional attack on corporal punishment failed; see Ingraham v. Wright, 97 S.Ct. 1401 (1977).
17. See Goss v. Lopez, 419 U.S. 565 (1975).
18. See, for example, Application of Auster, 198 Misc. 1055, 100 N.Y.S. 2d 60 (S.Ct., 1950) (Jewish Yeshiva); the story of the fight between New Mexico authorities and the Santa Fe Community School in *New Schools Exchange Newsletter*, April 15, 1973, pp. 36–38; State of Ohio v. Whisner, 47 Ohio St. 2d 181, 351 N.E. 2d 750 (1976) (school for children of "born-again" Christians in Bradford, Ohio); Donald Erickson, "Showdown in an Amish Schoolhouse: A Descrip-

tion and Analysis of the Iowa Controversy," in *Public Controls for Non-Public Schools,* p. 15.

CHAPTER 11

1. Friedman, "The Voucher Idea," p. 21.
2. Coons and Sugarman, *Family Choice in Education,* pp. 9–10.
3. For a fuller discussion, see Coons, Clune, and Sugarman, *Private Wealth and Public Education.*
4. Serrano v. Priest, 18 Cal. 3d 728, 557 P. 2d 929 (1976).
5. San Antonio Independent School District v. Rodriguez, 411 U.S. 1 (1973).
6. Mr. Justice Stewart.
7. See generally, John Callahan and William Wilken (eds.), *School Finance Reform: A Legislators' Handbook* (Washington, D.C., National Conference of State Legislatures, 1976).
8. See, for example, Michigan Compiled Laws Annotated, ##388.1101 *et seq.*; Wisconsin Statutes ##121.07, 121.08 (chap. 90, Laws of 1973, effective July 1, 1973). The Wisconsin provisions were later held to violate provisions of the state constitution. Buse v. Smith, 74 Wis. 2nd 550, 247 N.W. 2d 141 (1976).
9. Sizer and Whitten, "A Proposal for a Poor Children's Bill of Rights," p. 58.
10. Center for the Study of Public Policy, *Education Vouchers* (1970).
11. Coons, Clune, and Sugarman, *Private Wealth and Public Education,* pp. 256–268.
12. See, for example, Christopher Jencks et al., *Inequality* (New York, Basic Books, 1972).
13. For the rules governing schools at which G.I. Bill benefits may be used, see 38 *Code of Federal Regulations* §§21.4200 *et seq.*; for the rules relating to schools whose students are eligible for the federal-guaranteed student loan program, see 45 *Code of Federal Regulations* §§177 *et seq.* The FTC has proposed regulations with respect to the advertising, disclosure, and tuition practices of proprietary vocational and home study schools. See 40 *Federal Register* 21048 (May 15, 1975).
14. John Coons, "Non-Commercial Purpose as a Sherman Act Defense," 56 *Northwestern University Law Review* 705 (1962).
15. See Peter Berger and Richard Neuhaus, *To Empower People: The Role of Mediating Structures in Public Policy* (Washington, D.C., American Enterprise Institute, 1977), p. 23.
16. See Robert Singleton, "California: The Self-Determination in Education Act, 1968,"in *Parents, Teachers and Children,* p. 77.
17. See Sugarman, "Family Choice: The Next Step in the Quest for Equal Educational Opportunity?" p. 546.
18. See generally, Barbara Heyns, *Exposure and the Effects of Schooling* (Washington, D.C., National Institute of Education, 1977).
19. 268 U.S. 510 (1925).

CONCLUSION

1. Based on unpublished paper by Mary Jo Hollender, "Vermont Tuition System" (Dec. 29, 1975).

2. See, for example, California Education Code §56031 (1977).
3. For a sampling of the litigation surrounding these vouchers, see Kruse v. Campbell, 431 F.Supp. 180 (E.D. Va. 1977); McMillan v. Board of Education, 430 F.2d 1145 (2nd Cir. 1970). See generally Kirp and Yudof, *Educational Policy and the Law,* pp. 710–717.
4. See "Parents Seek State Vouchers for 'Outside' Mental Care," San Francisco *Chronicle,* Dec. 9, 1976, p. 39, col. 1.
5. See generally, Sugarman, "Family Choice: The Next Step in the Quest for Equal Educational Opportunity?" pp. 555–563; Joel Levin, "Alum Rock: Vouchers Pay Off," 15 *Inequality in Education* 57 (1973); Alum Rock Union School District, "Transition Model Voucher Proposal," April 12, 1972, for the Office of Economic Opportunity; Rand Corporation, *Technical Analysis Plan, Evaluation of the OEO Elementary Education Voucher Demonstration: Technical Dissertation* (1972); *Education Vouchers: The Experience at Alum Rock* (National Institute of Education, HEW, Dec. 1973); Daniel Weiler, *A Public School Voucher Demonstration: The First Year at Alum Rock* (Santa Monica, Rand Corporation, 1974); David Stern, Richard Delone, and Richard Murnane, "Evolution at Alum Rock" (review), 1 *Review of Education* 309 (1975); Joel Levin, *Final Report on the Implementation of the Second Year of the Alum Rock Voucher Project* (Alum Rock, Calif., Alum Rock Sequoia Institute, undated); Elliott Levinson, *The Alum Rock Voucher Demonstration: Three Years of Implementation* (Santa Monica, Rand Paper Series P-5631, April 1976).
6. California Education Code §69530 *et seq.* (1977).
7. 38 U.S. Code §1620 (1970).
8. See Chapter 11, note 13.
9. Internal Revenue Code §44A.
10. Internal Revenue Code §214.
11. See generally, Josephine Brown, *Public Relief: 1929–1939* (New York, Henry Holt, 1940), and Winifred Bell, *Aid to Dependent Children* (New York, Columbia University Press, 1965).
12. 42 U. S. Code §607 (1970).
13. 42 U.S. Code §608 (1970).
14. See, for example, Robert Taft, *Welfare Alternatives* (Washington, D.C., Government Printing Office, Aug. 1976), pp. 13–14.
15. See Wyman v. James, 400 U.S. 309 (1971). Compare Joel Handler and Ellen Hollingsworth, *The "Deserving" Poor* (Chicago, Markham, 1971).
16. See generally, Andy Schreider, "Proceedings of a Seminar on Alternative Futures for the Medicaid Program" (unpublished paper, Mar. 30, 1977).
17. 42 U.S. Code §602(a)(7) (1970).
18. See Title XX of the Social Security Act of 1935, as amended.
19. See Milton Shapp, *The National Education Trust Fund* (Harrisburg, Governor's Office, 1976); Senate Bill 1570 (Sen. Moynihan, 1977); *National Educational Opportunities Act of 1975,* H.R. 10146 (numbered as originally introduced by Rep. Preyer).
20. Berger and Neuhaus, *To Empower People: The Role of Mediating Structures in Public Policy.*
21. Mancur Olson, *The Logic of Collective Action* (Cambridge, Mass., Harvard University Press, 1965).

BIBLIOGRAPHY

BOOKS

Abbot, Grace, *The Child and the State*, 2 vols. (Chicago, University of Chicago Press, 1938).

Alexander, Kern, and K. Forbis Jordan, *Legal Aspects of Educational Choice: Compulsory Attendance and Student Assignment* (Topeka, National Organization on Legal Problems in Education, 1973).

Aries, Philippe, *Centuries of Childhood* (New York, Random House, 1962).

Bailyn, Bernard, *Education in the Forming of American Society* (New York, W.W. Norton, 1960).

Bane, Mary Jo, *Here to Stay: American Families in the Twentieth Century* (New York, Basic Books, 1976).

Banfield, Edward, *The Unheavenly City* (Boston, Little, Brown, 1970).

———, *The Unheavenly City Revisited* (Boston, Little, Brown, 1974).

Barry, Brian, *Political Argument* (London, Routledge and Kegan Paul, 1965).

Barzun, Jacques, *Teacher in America* (Garden City, Doubleday, 1944).

Bates, Frank, *The Child and the Law*, 2 Vols. (Dobbs Ferry, state? Oceana Publications, 1976).

Baumol, William, *Welfare Economics* (Cambridge, Mass., Harvard University Press, 1952).

Bell, Daniel (ed.), *The Radical Right* (Garden City, Doubleday Anchor Books, 1964).

Bell, Daniel, and Winifred Bell, *Aid to Dependent Children* (New York, Columbia University Press, 1965). Benson, Charles, *The Economics of Public Education* (Boston, Houghton Mifflin, 1968).

Berdyaev, Nicholas, *The Meaning of History* (London, Geoffrey Bles, 1936).

Berger, Peter and Neuhaus, Richard, *To Empower People: The Role of Mediating Structures in Public Policy* (Washington, D.C., American Enterprise Institute, 1977).

Blum, Virgil, *Freedom of Choice in Education* (New York, Macmillan, 1958).

Bonhoeffer, Dietrich, *The Cost of Discipleship* (New York, Macmillan, 1963).

Bowles, Samuel, and Herbert Gintis, *Schooling in Capitalist America: Educational Reform and the Contradictions of Economic Life* (New York, Basic Books, 1976).

Bremner, Robert (ed.), *Children and Youth in America: A Documentary History,* 3 vols. (Cambridge, Mass., Harvard University Press, 1974).

Brogan, D. W., *Politics in America* (Garden City, Doubleday Anchor Books, 1960).

————,*The American Character* (New York, Knopf, 1944).

Bronfenbrenner, Urie, *The Two Worlds of Childhood: USA and USSR* (New York, Russell Sage Foundation, 1970).

Browder, Lesley, *Who's Afraid of Educational Accountability?* (Denver, Cooperative Accountability Project, 1975).

Brown, Josephine, *Public Relief: 1929–1939* (New York, Henry Holt, 1940).

Burgess, Tyrrell, *A Guide to English Schools* (Baltimore, Penguin Books, 1964).

Burleigh, Ann (ed.), *Education in a Free Society* (Indianapolis, Liberty Fund, 1973).

Callahan, John, and William Wilken, (eds.), *School Finance Reform: A Legislators' Handbook* (Washington, D.C., National Conference of State Legislatures, 1976).

Carnoy, Martin, and Henry Levin, (eds.), *The Limits of Educational Reform* (New York, D. McKay, 1976).

Castle, E. B., *A Parents' Guide to Education* (Baltimore, Penguin Books, 1968).

Chall, Jeanne, *Learning to Read: The Great Debate* (New York, Mc-Graw–Hill, 1967).

Chapman, John, and Roland Pennock (eds.), *Equality* (New York, Atherton Press, 1967).

Chesterton, G.K., *What's Wrong with the World* (New York, Sheed & Ward, 1956).

Childs, John, *Education and Morals* (New York, Appleton-Century Crofts, 1950).

Cicourel, Aaron, and John Kitsuse, *The Educational Decisionmakers* (Indianapolis, Bobbs-Merrill, 1963).

Clignet, Remi, *Liberty and Equality in the Educational Process* (New York, John Wiley, 1974).

Conger, John, Jerome Kagan, and Paul Mussen, *Readings in Child Development and Personality* (New York, Harper and Row, 1965).

Coons, John and Sugarman, Stephen, *Family Choice in Education: A Model State System for Vouchers* (Berkeley, Institute of Governmental Studies, 1971).

Coons, John, William Clune III, and Stephen Sugarman, *Private Wealth and Public Education* (Cambridge, Mass., Harvard University Press, 1970).

Coser, Lewis A., *The Functions of Social Conflict* (Glencoe, Free Press, 1956).

Cox, C.B., and A.E. Dyson (eds.), *The Black Papers on Education* (London, David-Poynter, 1971).

Cremin, Lawrence, *The Transformation of the School* (New York, Random House, 1964).

Dahl, Robert, *Who Governs: Democracy and Power in an American City* (New Haven, Yale University Press, 1961).

de Mause, Lloyd (ed.), *The History of Childhood* (New York, Psychohistory Press, 1974).

Demos, John, *A Little Commonwealth* (London, Oxford University Press, 1970).

Deutsch, Karl, *Politics and Government* (Boston, Houghton Mifflin, 1970).

Dewey, John, *Liberalism and Social Action* (New York, Capricorn Books, 1935).

Douglas, J. W. B., *The Home and the School* (Manchester, Philips Park Press, 1964).

Erickson, Donald (ed.), *Public Controls for Non-Public Schools* (Chicago, University of Chicago Press, 1969).

Erickson, Donald, *Super-Parent, An Analysis of State Educational Controls* (Lansing, Ill., Illinois Advisory Committee on Nonpublic Schools, 1973).

Erikson, Erik, *Childhood and Society* (New York, W. W. Norton, 1950).

Fantini, Mario, *Public Schools of Choice* (New York, Simon and Schuster, 1973).

Fesler, James (ed.), *The Fifty States and Their Local Governments* (New York, Knopf, 1967).

Freidenberg, Edgar, *Coming of Age in America* (New York, Random House, 1963).

————, *The Vanishing Adolescent* (New York, Dell, 1959).

Freud, Anna, Joseph Goldstein, and Albert Solnit, *Beyond the Best Interests of the Child* (Glencoe, Free Press, 1973).

Friedman, Milton, *Capitalism and Freedom* (Chicago, University of Chicago Press, 1962).

Furnival, Frederick, *Early English Meals and Manners* (London, Kegan Paul, 1868).

Galbraith, John Kenneth, *The New Industrial State* (New York, Signet Books, 1967).

Garfinkel, Irwin, and Edward Gramlich, *A Statistical Analysis of the OEO Experiment in Educational Performance Contracting* (Washington, D.C., Brookings Institution, Technical Service Reprint T-002, 1972).

Garms, Walter, James Guthrie, and Lawrence Pierce, *School Finance: The Economics and Politics of Public Schools* (Englewood Cliffs, Prentice Hall, 1977).

Gil, David, *Violence against Children* (Cambridge, Mass., Harvard University Press, 1970).

Goffman, Erving, *Asylums* (Garden City, Doubleday Anchor Books, 1961).

Goldstein, Joseph, and J. Katz, *The Family and the Law* (Glencoe, Free Press, 1965).

Goldstein, Stephen, *Law and Public Education: Cases and Materials* (New York, Bobbs-Merrill, 1974).

Goode, William, *World Revolution & Family Patterns* (London, Collier-Macmillan, 1963).

Goodlad, John, Gary Festermacher, Thomas LaBelle, Val Rust, Rodney Skager, and Carl Weinberg, *The Conventional and the Alternative in Education* (Berkeley, McCutchan, 1975).

Goodman, Paul, *Compulsory Miseducation* (New York, Horizon Press, 1964).

——,*Growing Up Absurd* (New York, Random House, 1956).

Goodman, Paul, Paul Adams, and Leila Berg, *Children's Rights* (New York, Praeger, 1971).

Greeley, Andrew, William McCready, and Kathleen McCourt, *Catholic Schools in a Declining Church* (Kansas City, Sheed and Ward, 1976).

Greer, Colin, *The Great School Legend* (New York, Viking Press, 1972).

Gross, Ronald and Beatrice, *Radical School Reform* (New York, Simon and Schuster, 1971).

Grubb, W. Norton, and Stephan Michelson, *States and Schools* (Lexington, Lexington Books, 1974).

Haar, Charles, and Demetrios Iatrides, *Housing the Poor in Suburbia: Public Policy at the Grass Roots* (Cambridge, Mass., Ballinger, 1974).

Habermas, Jurgen, *Knowledge and Human Interest* (Boston, Beacon Press, 1968).

Handler, Joel, and Ellen Hollingsworth, *The "Deserving" Poor* (Chicago, Markham, 1971).

Handlin, Oscar, *The Uprooted* (Boston, Little, Brown, 1952).

Hartman, Robert, and Robert Reischauer, *Reforming School Finance* (Washington, D.C., The Brookings Institution, 1973).

Hawthorne, Phyllis, *Legislation by the States: Accountability and Assessment in Education* (Denver, Cooperative Accountability Project, 1974).

Heilbroner, Robert, *An Inquiry into the Human Prospect* (New York, W.W. Norton, 1974).

Heyns, Barbara, *Exposure and the Effects of Schooling* (Washington, D.C., National Institute of Education, 1977).

Hirschmann, Albert, *Exit, Voice and Loyalty: Response to Decline in Firms, Organizations and States* (Cambridge, Mass., Harvard University Press, 1970).

Hofstadter, Richard, *The American Political Tradition* (New York, Random House Vintage, 1948).

Holt, John, *How Children Fail* (New York, Dell, 1964).

——,*The Underachieving School* (New York, Dell, 1969).

Hutchins, Robert, *Two Faces of Federalism* (Santa Barbara, Center for the Study of Democratic Institutions, 1961).

Illich, Ivan, *Deschooling Society* (New York, Harper and Row, 1971).

Jefferson, Thomas, *Notes on the State of Virginia, Query 17* (Boston, David Carlisle, 1801).

Jencks, Christopher, *Inequality* (New York, Basic Books, 1972).

Keim, Albert (ed.), *Compulsory Education and the Amish* (Boston, Beacon Press, 1975).

Kirp, David, and Mark Yudof, *Educational Policy and the Law* (Berkeley, McCutchan, 1974).

Kirst, Michael, and Frederick Wirt, *The Political and Social Foundation of Education* (Berkeley, McCutchan, 1976).

Kohl, Herbert, *The Open Classroom* (New York, Random House Vintage, 1970).

Kozol, Jonathan, *Free Schools* (Boston, Houghton Mifflin, 1972).

Kraushaar, Otto, *Schools in a Changing City* (Baltimore, Sheridan Foundation, 1976).

Lambert, William, and Leigh Minturn, *Mothers of Six Cultures* (New York, John Wiley, 1964).

Laqueur, Walter, and George Mosse (eds.), *Education and Social Structure* (New York, Harper and Row, 1967).

Levin, Henry (ed.), *Community Control of Schools* (Washington, D.C., The Brookings Institution, 1970).

Levin, Joel, *Final Report on the Implementation of the Second Year of the Alum Rock Voucher Project* (Alum Rock, Calif., Alum Rock Sequoia Institute, undated).

Levinson, Elliott, *The Alum Rock Voucher Demonstration: Three Years of Implementation* (Santa Monica, Rand Paper Series P-5631, April 1976).

Litt, Edgar, *Beyond Pluralism: Ethnic Politics in America* (Glenview, Scott, Foresman, 1970).

Lockhart, William, Yale Kamisar, and Jesse Choper, *Constitutional Law—Cases, Comments and Questions* 1211 (St. Paul, West, 1975).

Lowi, Theodore, *The End of Liberalism: Ideology, Policy, and the Crisis of Public Authority* (New York, W.W. Norton, 1969).

McCoy, Rhoady, *American School Administration, Public and Catholic* (New York, McGraw-Hill, 1961).

McDermott, John (ed.), *Indeterminacy in Education* (Berkeley, McCutchan, 1976).

McGarry, Daniel, and Leo Ward, *Educational Freedom and the Case for Government Aid to Students in Independent Schools* (Milwaukee, Bruce Publishing, 1966).

Madison, James, *The Federalist, No. 51* (New York, Random House, 1937).

Mayer, Martin, *The Teachers Strike: New York 1968* (New York, Harper and Row, 1969).

Messner, Johannes, *Social Ethics: Natural Law in the Western World* (St. Louis, B. Herder, 1965).

Mill, John Stuart, *On Liberty* (Chicago, Great Books Edition, Encyclopedia Britannica, 1952).

Montessori, Maria, *The Secret of Childhood* (Notre Dame, Tides Publishers, 1966).

Mosteller, Frederick, and Daniel Moynihan (eds.), *On Equality of Educational Opportunity* (New York, Random House, 1972).

Moustakas, Clark (ed.), *The Child's Discovery of Himself* (New York, Ballantine Books, 1966).

Murphy, W. F., *Class Size and Teacher Load* (Newton, Mass., New England School Development Council, 1975).

Novak, Michael, *The Rise of the Unmeltable Ethics* (Toronto, Macmillan, 1971).

Olson, Mancur, *The Logic of Collective Action* (Cambridge, Mass., Harvard University Press, 1965).

Paine, Thomas, *Rights of Man* (New York, E. P. Dutton, 1915).

Pellegrini, Angelo, *Americans by Choice* (New York, Macmillan, 1956).

Phelps, Edmund (ed.), *Private Wants & Public Needs* (New York, W. W. Norton, 1965).

Piaget, Jean, *The Construction of Reality in the Child* (New York, Ballantine Books, 1954).

Pincus, John (ed.), *School Finance in Transition* (Cambridge, Mass., Ballinger, 1974).

Rabb, Theodore, and Robert Rotberg (eds.), *The Family in History* (New York, Harper and Row, 1971).

Ravitch, Diane, *The Revisionists Revised,* Proceedings of the National Academy of Education, vol. 4 (1977).

Rawls, John, *A Theory of Justice* (Cambridge, Mass., Harvard University Press, 1971).

Reimer, Everett, *An Essay on Alternatives in Education* (Cuernavaca, CIDOC, 1970).

Rubinstein, David, and Colin Stoneman (eds.), *Education for Democracy* (Baltimore, Penguin Books, 1970).

Russell, Bertrand, *Education and the Good Life* (New York, Boni and Liveright, 1926).

St. John, Nancy, *School Desegregation: Outcomes for Children* (New York, John Wiley, 1975).

Santayana, George, *The Sense of Beauty* (New York, Modern Library, 1955).

Schumacher, E.F., *Small Is Beautiful: Economics as if People Mattered* (New York, Harper and Row, 1973).

Shapp, Milton, *The National Education Trust Fund* (Harrisburg, Governor's Office, 1976).

Simmel, Georg, *Conflict,* trans. Kurt H. Wolff (Glencoe, Free Press, 1955).

Skinner, B.F., *Beyond Freedom and Dignity* (New York, Knopf, 1971).

Skolnick, Arlene and Jerome (eds.), *Family in Transition* (Boston, Little, Brown, 1971).

Smith, Adam, *Wealth of Nations* (Chicago, Great Books Edition, Encyclopedia Britannica, 1952).

Sonnenfeld, David, *Family Choice in Schooling: A Case Study,* Working Paper 3 (Eugene, University of Oregon, 1972).

Spencer, Herbert, *Social Statics: The Conditions Essential to Human Happiness* (London, John Chapman, 1851).

Steiner, Gilbert, *The Children's Cause* (Washington, D.C., The Brookings Institution, 1976).

Sullivan, Lawrence, *Handbook of the Law of Antitrust* (St. Paul, West, 1977).

Taft, Robert, *Welfare Alternatives* (Washington, D.C., Government Printing Office, August 1976).

Talbot, Nathan, *Raising Children in Modern America* (Boston, Little, Brown, 1976).

Truman, David, *The Governmental Process* (New York, Knopf, 1971).

Tyack, David, *The One Best System: A History of American Urban Education* (Cambridge, Mass., Harvard University Press, 1974).

Unger, Roberto, *Knowledge and Politics* (Glencoe, Free Press, 1975).

von Giercke, Otto, *Political Theories of the Middle Ages* (Cambridge, At the University Press, 1913).

Weil, Simone, *The Need for Roots* (New York, G. P. Putnam, 1952).
Weiler, Daniel, *A Public School Voucher Demonstration: The First Year at Alum Rock* (Santa Monica, Rand Corporation, 1974).
Weintraub, Sidney (ed.), *Income Inequality* (Philadelphia, American Academy of Political and Social Science, 1973).
Wilms, Welford, *Public and Proprietary Vocational Training: A Study of Effectiveness* (Berkeley, Center for Research and Development in Higher Education, 1974).
Whitehead, Alfred North, *The Aims of Education* (Glencoe, Free Press, 1929).
——,*Science and the Modern World* (New York, Mentor, New American Library, 1954).
Wilson, Edmund, *To the Finland Station* (Garden City, Doubleday, 1940).
Wise, Michael (ed.), *Desegregation in Education: A Directory of Reported Federal Decisions* (Notre Dame, Center for Civil Rights, 1977).
Wolff, Robert, *The Poverty of Liberalism* (Boston, Beacon Press, 1968).

TABLE OF CASES

Application of Auster, 198 Misc. 1055, 100 N.Y.S. 2d 60 (1950).
Baird v. *State Bar,* 401 U.S. 1 (1971).
Berkelman v. *San Francisco Unified School District,* 501 F.2d 1264 (9th Cir. 1974).
Brennan v. *Armstrong,* 97 S.Ct. 2907 (1977).
Buse v. *Smith,* 74 Wis. 2nd 550, 247 N.W. 2d 141 (1976).
City of Madison Joint School District No. 8 v. *Wisconsin Employment Relations Comm'n,* 429 U.S. 167 (1976).
Dayton Board of Education v. *Brinkman,* 97 S.Ct. 2766 (1977).
Diana v. *State Board of Education,* Consent Decree No. C-70-37, June 18, 1973 (U.S. Dist. Ct. N.D. Cal.).
Elfbrandt v. *Russel,* 384 U.S. 11 (1966).
Epperson v. *Arkansas,* 393 U.S. 97 (1968).
Evans v. *Buchanan,* 393 F.Supp. 428 (D. Del. 1975), aff'd 423 U.S. 963 (1976).
Goss v. *Lopez,* 419 U.S. 565 (1975).
Green v. *County Board of New Kent County,* 391 U.S. 430 (1968).
Griggs v. *Duke Power Co.,* 401 U.S. 424 (1971).
Hobson v. *Hansen,* 327 F.Supp. 844 (D.D.C. 1971).
In re Stolar, 401 U.S. 23 (1971).
Kruse v. *Campbell,* 431 F.Supp. 180 (E.D. Va. 1977).
Lau v. *Nichols,* 414 U.S. 563 (1974).
McMillan v. *Board of Education,* 430 F.2d 1145 (2nd Cir. 1970).
Milliken v. *Bradley,* 418 U.S. 717 (1974).
Milliken v. *Bradley,* 97 S.Ct. 2749 (1977).
Moose Lodge No. 107 v. *Irvis,* 407 U.S. 163 (1972).
Norwood v. *Harrison,* 413 U.S. 455 (1973).
Parducci v. *Rutland,* 316 F.Supp. 352 (M.D. Ala., 1970).
Pasadena City Board of Education v. *Spangler,* 427 U.S. 424 (1976).
Peter W. Doe v. *San Francisco Unified School District,* Ca. Ct. of Appeal, appeal from Sup.Ct. No. 653312, Aug. 6, 1976.
Pickering v. *Board of Education,* 391 U.S. 563 (1968).

Runyon v. *McCrary,* 427 U.S. 160 (1976).
San Antonio Independent School District v. *Rodriguez,* 411 U.S. 1 (1973).
School District of Omaha v. *United States,* 97 S.Ct. 2905 (1977).
Serrano v. *Priest,* 18 Cal. 3d 728, 557 P. 2d 929 (1976).
Sherbert v. *Verner,* 374 U.S. 398 (1963).
Stanton v. *Sequoia Union High School Dist.,* 408 F. Supp. 502 (N.D. Cal. 1976).
State of Ohio v. *Whisner,* 47 Ohio St. 2d 181, 351 N.E. 2d 750 (1976).
Swann v. *Charlotte-Mecklenburg Board of Education,* 402 U.S. 1 (1971).
Wood v. *Strickland,* 420 U.S. 308 (1975).
Wyman v. *James,* 400 U.S. 309 (1971).

ARTICLES

The number preceding a journal title refers to the
volume; the number following the journal title refers
to the beginning page of the article. The year is
in parentheses.

Amicus Brief Supporting Integration Plan in *Crawford* v. *Los Angeles Unified School District* (1977), in *Parents, Teachers and Children* (San Francisco, Institute for Contemporary Studies, 1977).
Areen, Judith, "Public Aid to Nonpublic Schools: A Breach in the Sacred Wall?" 22 *Case Western Reserve Law Review* 230 (1971).
Areen, Judith, and Christopher Jencks, "Education Vouchers: A Proposal for Diversity and Choice," 72 *Teachers College Record* 327 (1971).
Armor, David, "The Evidence on Busing," 30 *Public Interest* 119 (1972).
Arons, Stephen, "Equity, Option, and Vouchers," 72 *Teachers College Record* 337 (1971).
Bell, Derrick, "Is *Brown* Obsolete? Yes!" 14 *Integrated Education* 28 (May–June 1976).
———,"Serving Two Masters: Integration Ideals and Client Interests in School Desegregation Litigation," 85 *Yale Law Journal* 470 (1976).
———,"Waiting on the Promise of *Brown,*" 39 *Law and Contemporary Problems* 341 (1975).
Bennett, Robert, "Allocation of Child Medical Care Decisionmaking Authority: A Suggested Interest Analysis," 62 *Virginia Law Review* 285 (1976).
Berube, Maurice, "The Trouble with Vouchers," 3 *Community* 1 (Nov. 1970).
Cahn, Edgar, "Jurisprudence," 30 *New York University Law Review* 150 (1955).
Calkins, Hugh, and Jeffrey Gordon, "The Right to Choose an Integrated Education: Voluntary Regional Integrated Schools—A Partial Remedy for De Facto Segregation," 9 *Harvard Civil Rights-Civil Liberties Law Review* 171 (1974).
Campbell, Donald, "Reforms as Experiments," 24 *American Psychologist* 409 (1969).
———,"Assessing the Impact of Planned Social Change," in *Social Research and Public Policies* (Hanover, University Press of New England, 1975).

Clark, Burton, "The Benefits of Disorder," *Change* 31 (Oct. 1976).
Cohen, Jack, Charles Corese, and R. Frank Falk, "Further Considerations in the Methodological Analysis of Segregation Indices," 41 *American Sociological Review* 630 (1976).
Coleman, James, "Toward Open Schools," 9 *Public Interest* 20 (Fall 1967).
Coleman, James, Sara Kelly, and John Moore, "Trends in School Segregation 1968–1973," working paper for The Urban Institute (Washington, D.C.), Aug. 15, 1975.
Coons, John, "Evanston," in Roscoe Hill and Malcolm Feeley (eds.), *Affirmative School Integration* (Beverly Hills, Sage Publications, 1967).
——, "Law and the Sovereigns of Childhood," 58 *Kappan* 19 (1976).
——, "Non-Commercial Purpose as a Sherman Act Defense," 56 *Northwestern University Law Review* 705 (1962).
——, "Recent Trends in Science Fiction: *Serrano* among the People of Number," 6 *Journal of Law and Education* 23 (1977).
——, "Report to the U.S. Office of Education on Illinois Elementary District 65 (Evanston-Skokie)," 1965.
——, "To West, Mostly with Love," in E. G. West (ed.), *Nonpublic School Aid* (Lexington, Mass., Lexington Books, 1976).
Coons, John, and Robert Mnookin, "Toward a Theory of Children's Rights," *Harvard Law School Bulletin* 18 (Spring 1977).
Coons, John, and Stephen Sugarman, "Choice and Integration: A Model Statute," in *Parents, Teachers and Children* (San Francisco, Institute for Contemporary Studies, 1977).
——, "Vouchers for Public Schools," 15 *Inequality in Education* 60 (1973).
Doyle, Dennis, "The Politics of Choice: A View from the Bridge," in *Parents, Teachers and Children* (San Francisco, Institute for Contemporary Studies, 1977).
Elson, John, "State Regulation of Non-Public Schools: The Legal Framework," in Donald Erickson (ed.), *Public Controls for Non-Public Schools* (Chicago, University of Chicago Press, 1969).
Erickson, Donald, "Showdown in an Amish Schoolhouse: A Description and Analysis of the Iowa Controversy," in Donald Erickson (ed.), *Public Controls for Non-Public Schools* (Chicago, University of Chicago Press, 1969).
Farley, Reynolds, "Residential Segregation and Its Implications for School Integration," 39 *Law and Contemporary Problems* 164 (1975).
Friedman, Milton, "The Voucher Idea," *New York Times Magazine*, Sept. 23, 1973.
Geffert, Hannah, Robert Harper, Salvador Sarmiento, and Daniel Schember, "The Current Status of U.S. Bilingual Education Legislation," *Papers in Applied Linguistics* (Arlington, Center for Applied Linguistics, May 1975).
Geiser, Robert, "The Rights of Children," 28 *Hastings Law Journal* 1027 (1977).
Getzels, Jacob, "Schools and Values," 12 *The Center Magazine* 28 (1976).
Ginzberg, Eli, "The Economics of the Voucher System," 72 *Teachers College Record* 373 (1971).
Goldstein, Stephen, "The Asserted Constitutional Right of Public School

Teachers to Determine What They Teach," 124 *University of Pennsylvania Law Review* 1293 (1976).

Greenbaum, William, "America in Search of a New Ideal: An Essay in the Rise of Pluralism," 44 *Harvard Educational Review* 411 (1974).

Hain, Elwood, "School Desegregation in Detroit: Domestic Tranquility and Judicial Futility," 23 *Wayne Law Review* 65 (1976).

Hawley, Willis D., and Ray C. Rist, "On the Future Implementations of School Desegregation: Some Considerations," 39 *Law and Contemporary Problems* 412 (1975).

Hiller, Richard, and Herbert Teitelbaum, "Bilingual Education: The Legal Mandate," 47 *Harvard Educational Review* 138 (1977).

Jencks, Christopher, "Is the Public School Obsolete?" 2 *Public Interest* 18 (Winter 1966).

Kirp, David, "Schools as Sorters: The Constitutional and Policy Implications of Student Classification," 121 *University of Pennsylvania Law Review* 705 (1973).

Klees, Stephen, "The Role of Information in the Market for Education Services," Occasional Papers in the Economics and Politics of Education (Palo Alto, Stanford University, 1974).

Kohlberg, Lawrence, "Moral Development and Identification," in *Child Psychology* (Chicago, University of Chicago Press, 1963).

———, "Stage and Sequence: The Cognitive Developmental Approach to Socialization," in *Handbook of Socialization Theory and Research* (Chicago, Rand McNally, 1969).

———, "Stages of Moral Development as a Basis for Moral Education," in C.M. Beck, B.S. Crittenden, and E.V. Sullivan, *Moral Education: Interdisciplinary Approaches* (Toronto, University of Toronto Press, 1971).

LaNoue, George, "The Politics of Education," 73 *Teachers College Record* 304 (1971).

Lazerson, Marvin, "Consensus and Conflict in American Education: Historical Perspectives," in *Parents, Teachers, and Children* (San Francisco, Institute for Contemporary Studies, 1977).

Leichter, Hope (ed.), "The Family: First Instructor and Pervasive Guide" (symposium), 76 *Teachers College Record* 173 (1974).

Levin, Henry, "Educational Vouchers and Educational Equality," Occasional Paper 74-2, School of Education (Palo Alto, Stanford University, Aug. 1974).

———, "The Failure of the Public Schools and the Free Market Remedy," 2 *The Urban Review* 32 (June 1968).

Levin, Joel, "Alum Rock: Vouchers Pay Off," 15 *Inequality in Education* 57 (1973).

McAdams, John, "Can Open Enrollment Work?" 37 *Public Interest* 69 (1974).

McCann, Walter, and Judith Areen, "Vouchers and the Citizen—Some Legal Questions," 72 *Teacher's College Record* 389 (1971).

Mayer, Milton, "Community, Anyone?" 8 *The Center Magazine* 2 (1975).

Mnookin, Robert, "Child Custody Adjudication: Judicial Functions in the Face of Indeterminacy," 39 *Law and Contemporary Problems* 226 (1975).

———, "Foster Care: In Whose Best Interest?" 48 *Harvard Educational Review* 599 (1973).

Nahmod, Sheldon, "Controversy in the Classroom: The High School Teacher and Freedom of Expression," 39 *George Washington Law Review* 1032 (1971).

O'Neil, Robert, "Unconstitutional Conditions: Welfare Benefits with Strings Attached," 54 *California Law Review* 443 (1966).

Phillips, Kenneth, and Michael Agelasto II, "Housing and Central Cities: The Conservation Approach," 4 *Ecology Law Quarterly* 797 (1975).

Rosencranz, Armin, "The Politics of Choosing Textbooks" (Berkeley, Childhood and Government Project, Working Paper #1, 1976).

Schreider, Andy, "Proceedings of a Seminar on Alternative Futures for the Medicaid Program" (unpublished paper, March 30, 1977).

Shanker, Albert, "Parental Choice of School? Some Words of Caution," New York *Times*, July 21, 1974.

Shelton, Dinah, "Legislative Control over Public School Curriculum" (Berkeley, Childhood and Government Project, Working Paper #2, 1976).

———, "The Role of the State in Moral Education: The Experience of California's Moral Guidelines" (paper delivered at Northridge Conference on Moral Education, Oct. 1974).

Singleton, Robert, "California: The Self-Determination in Education Act, 1968," in *Parents, Teachers and Children* (San Francisco, Institute for Contemporary Studies, 1977).

Sizer, Theodore, and Phillip Whitten, "A Proposal for a Poor Children's Bill of Rights," 5 *Psychology Today* 58 (1968).

Sowell, Thomas, "'Affirmative Action' Reconsidered" 42 *Public Interest* 47 (1976).

Stern, David, Richard Delone, and Richard Murnane, "Evolution at Alum Rock" (review), 1 *The Review of Education* 309 (1975).

Sugarman, Stephen, "Accountability through the Courts," 82 *School Review* 233 (1974).

———, "Education Reform at the Margin—Two Ideas," *Kappan*, Nov. 1977.

———, "Family Choice: The Next Step in the Quest for Equal Educational Opportunity?" 38 *Law and Contemporary Problems* 513 (1974).

———, "New Perspectives on 'Aid' to Private School Users," in E. G. West (ed.), *Nonpublic School Aid* (Lexington, Mass., Lexington Books, 1976).

Sugarman, Stephen, and David Kirp, "Rethinking Collective Responsibility for Education," 39 *Law and Contemporary Problems* 144 (1975).

Thomas, D. A. Lloyd, "Competitive Equality of Opportunity," 86 *Mind* 388 (1977).

Thorndike, Robert, "Concepts of Culture-Fairness," 8 *Journal of Educational Measurement* 63 (1971).

Wald, Michael S., "State Intervention on Behalf of 'Neglected' Children: Standards for Removal of Children from Their Homes, Monitoring the Status of Children in Foster Care, and Termination of Parental Rights," 28 *Stanford Law Review* 625 (1976).

Wald, Pat, "Making Sense Out of the Rights of Youth," *Quarterly Focus* (Winter 1975).

White, David, and Richard Francis, "Title VII and the Masters of Reality: Eliminating Credentialism in the American Labor Market," 64 *Georgetown Law Journal* 1213 (1976).

Wigglesworth, Zeke, "Alternatives in Public Schools: The Minneapolis Experiment," in Don Davies (ed.), *Schools Where Parents Make a Difference* (Boston, Institute for Responsive Education, 1976).

Williams, Norman, "What the Psychologist Has to Say," in John Wilson, Norman Williams, and Barry Sugarman, *Introduction to Moral Education* (Baltimore, Penguin Books, 1967).

Yudof, Mark, "Suspension and Expulsion of Black Students from the Public Schools: Academic Capital Punishment and the Constitution," 39 *Law and Contemporary Problems* 374 (1975).

BIBLIOGRAPHIES AND REPORTS

Alum Rock Union School District, "Transition Model Voucher Proposal," April 12, 1972, for the Office of Economic Opportunity.

51 *Child Welfare* 141 (Journal of the Child Welfare League of America, 1977).

The Danish Sex Education Cases, European Court of Human Rights (decided Dec. 7, 1976), "Observations of the Danish Government on the Merits" (Mar. 26, 1976).

Desegregation of the Nation's Public Schools, A Report of the U.S. Commission on Civil Rights (Aug. 1976).

Education Vouchers, A Report on Financing Elementary Education by Grants to Parents, Center for the Study of Public Policy (Cambridge, CSPP, 1970).

The Fleishmann Report on the Quality, Cost and Financing of Elementary and Secondary Education in New York State (New York, Viking Press, 1973).

Handbook of Public Income Transfer Programs, Studies in Public Welfare, Paper #20, A Staff Study Prepared for the Subcommittee on Fiscal Policy of the Joint Economic Committee of Congress (Washington, D.C., Government Printing Office, 1974).

Kanawha County West Virginia: A Textbook Study in Cultural Conflict (Washington, D.C., National Education Association, 1975).

Oregon School Cases: Complete Record (Baltimore, Belvedere Press, 1925).

Parent Involvement in Early Childhood Education, Selected Titles, Bernard van Leer Foundation (The Hague, Bernard van Leer Foundation, 1976).

Public Knowledge and Busing Opposition, A Report of the U.S. Commission on Civil Rights (Washington, D.C., Government Printing Office, 1973).

Racial Isolation in the Public Schools, A Report of the U.S. Commission on Civil Rights (Washington, D.C., Government Printing Office, 1967).

Reading, Language, and Learning, A Special Issue, 47 *Harvard Educational Review* 257 (1977).

Report of the Committee on One-Parent Families, Department of Health and Security (London, Her Majesty's Stationery Office, 1974).

Statement of Metropolitan School Desegregation, A Report of the United States Commission on Civil Rights (Washington, D.C., Government Printing Office, Feb. 1977).

Technical Analysis Plan, Evaluation of the OEO Elementary Education Voucher Demonstration: Technical Dissertation (1972); *Education*

Vouchers: The Experience at Alum Rock (Rand Corporation for National Institute of Education, HEW, Dec. 1973).

Voucher Choices: A Family Directory of Mini-Schools (Alum Rock, Calif., Alum Rock Sequoia Institute, 1975).

Your Children and Busing, A Report of the U.S. Commission on Civil Rights (Washington, D.C., Government Printing Office, May 1972).

Youth: Transition to Adulthood, Report of the Panel on Youth of the President's Science Advisory Committee (Washington, D.C., Office of Science and Technology, June 1973).